THE ASCENT OF
EVEREST

THE
ASCENT
OF
EVEREST

JOHN HUNT

The Mountaineers
Seattle, Washington

Published in the USA in 1993 by The Mountaineers
Founded 1906 . . . to explore, study, preserve and
enjoy the natural beauty of the outdoors. . .'
1011 SW Klickitat Way, Seattle WA 98134
by arrangement with Hodder & Stoughton

Published simultaneously in Canada by Douglas &
McIntyre, 1615 Venables St., Vancouver B.C. V5L 2H1

Published simultaneously in Great Britain by
Hodder and Stoughton, a division of Hodder and Stoughton Ltd,
Editorial Office: 47 Bedford Square, London WC1B 3DP

U.S. Library of Congress Catalog Card Number 92-063272
ISBN (North America) 0-89886-361-9

Photoset by Rowland Phototypesetting Ltd,
Bury St Edmunds, Suffolk

Printed in Great Britain by BPCC Hazell Books
Member of BPCC Ltd, Aylesbury, Bucks.

TO

ALL

WHO HELPED

TO MAKE THIS POSSIBLE

FOREWORD
TO THE ORIGINAL EDITION

By His Royal Highness the Duke of Edinburgh, k.g.

IN this book you will find the full and detailed account of the climbing of the highest mountain in the world. You will find more than that, you will find the reasons for trying to climb it and how much success depended on previous expeditions, careful planning, close-knit team-work and all the hundred and one details which had to be taken into account.

In spite of, rather than because of all these details I am still left with a sense of profound admiration for the achievement of this expedition, both as a team and as individuals. In the human terms of physical effort and endurance alone it will live in history as a shining example to all mankind.

PATRON, BRITISH EVEREST EXPEDITION 1953

FOREWORD
TO THIS EDITION

IN the last chapter of this book I offered some thoughts on the reasons for our success in being the first mountaineers to climb Everest, and on the shape of things to come. Today, forty years on, I would like again to acknowledge the contributions made by a great many people, other than those who were on the mountain that year; to salute the memory of those other alpinists who, during all the earlier attempts, had provided the lessons from which we had benefited; and who, on several occasions, had so nearly succeeded. I wanted the many people who did not go to Everest—on whose help with money, equipment and expert advice we had so greatly depended—to know how much we had valued their help.

The part played by our scientific consultants was especially important. Their knowledge of the physiological problems of human activity and survival at high altitudes powerfully influenced the selection, manufacture and preparation of our equipment, clothing and food; their advice informed the overall planning of the expedition and decisions on the mountain.

But the relative importance to be attached to each one of the reasons for our success will remain a matter of opinion. I do not believe that any particular reason merits greater prominence than the others. Indeed, whether they were human, technological or scientific in character, they are not strictly comparable. It was the harmonious blend of them all which resulted in two men reaching the summit on 29th May, 1953.

As regards the future, my speculations at that time have in part been overtaken by events. I say "in part" because the story of Everest, and the impact of its first ascent, will continue; it is, to use current jargon, an "on-going" story. It was easy to predict that others would follow us to the top. Yet for a number of years, few did so; only three expeditions, from countries other than Britain, climbed Everest in the course of the next twelve years. Then the pace quickened. Today it has become akin to a Gold Rush. The mountain has been climbed by all its ridges and each of its three great precipices, and by a number of routes—other and harder than ours. Hundreds of climbers have stood on the summit; between forty and fifty expeditions climb, or attempt to climb, the mountain every year; at any one time, there may be ten or more parties on their way up the Khumbu Icefall. And as everyone knows, tourists in their thousands have, for many years past, been trekking along the litter-strewn track which leads to our old Base Camp, itself (so they tell me) a débris dump of monumental proportions.

Meanwhile, the numbers of climbers have greatly increased and their activities have spread far and wide. All the higher mountains, and many lesser peaks in the more remote regions have been climbed; many of them by routes of an order of difficulty beyond our imagination in the years just after the war. Eric Shipton, who played so distinguished a part in earlier Everest expeditions, expressed his delight at our own success, but went on to say: "Thank goodness, we can now get on with some real climbing." That sentiment was shared by myself and my companions in 1953, for Everest was not our idea of the kind of climb we were accustomed to enjoying. At that point in time, it symbolized rather more than a mountain.

The tale of exceptional enterprises in other fields of adventure has unfolded far and wide. In 1953 I expressed my belief that there was plenty of scope "among the hills, in the air, upon the sea, in the bowels of the earth or on the ocean bed". I pointed out that "there is always the moon to reach." The word "always" was mistaken. I should have realized the urgency of man's quest to extend his knowledge of his environment and beyond. Intrepid men have traversed both the Poles; men and women have circumnavigated the globe in small sailing craft; the liner *Titanic* has been located and photographed on its ocean bed at 12,000 feet beneath the waters of the North Atlantic. Yuri Gagarin has led the way into outer space; Americans have landed on the moon and unmanned spacecraft have come to rest on one other planet in the solar system; others are cruising even further in the universe.

It is clear that, in all these later great achievements, science and technology have played a major, even total part. Man's inventions would seem to bid fair to take over from man himself. Is this the shape of things to come? Can I still say, with confidence, that there remains much to be achieved? In the realm of science and the development of technology, the answer is undoubtedly "yes". On our planet earth, there is a wealth of detailed knowledge to be gleaned about our environment, especially beneath the oceans; the exploration of space is still in its infancy. Innumerable secrets about the nature of the universe and our own globe remain to be revealed. The saga of discovery will continue.

But what of us humans, and the spirit which moves us? My concluding words in this book were, "There is no height, no depth that the spirit of man, guided by a higher Spirit, cannot attain." I was probably too starry-eyed and emotionally in thrall, immediately after our return from Everest, to make a reasonable judgment when I made this claim. The urge which drives people to explore beyond the frontiers of human experience is more complex than I averred all those years ago; motives are usually mixed. For most, the "reason why" cannot be explained in a single word, or a sentence such as Mallory's much quoted "because it's there". In an age in which we in the developed countries have grown richer, more materialistic, more competitive, it cannot be said that all explorers set forth in the pure spirit of Excelsior; fewer still, I suspect, are guided by a higher Spirit.

But the inspiration for the rest of mankind rests still, I believe, on a higher plane. People everywhere appear to feel uplifted by deeds of daring. There is no gainsaying the personal achievement of Hillary and Tenzing in becoming the first human beings to stand at the highest point on earth. It has been rightly acclaimed the world over and we, the other members of the Everest team, rejoiced at their triumph. The rejoicing which attended the return to earth of Gagarin, of Armstrong and the other pioneering cosmonauts derived from public amazement at the quality of their courage. It mattered not whether they were Russians, or Americans; they were perceived as heroes of the human race. Most people were less interested in the marvellous technology of the vehicles which conveyed them, than (to borrow the title of a well remembered film) in "those marvellous men in their flying machines". Indeed, public admiration appears especially to be bestowed on those who, notwithstanding the availability of aircraft, rockets, snow-cats or any other safer and speedier methods of travel, choose to do it the slow, hard way. I find this reassuring for the future.

Men and women have climbed the highest mountain, crossed the ends of the earth, and reached the moon. What else remains to be done? My answer is that the opportunities for further quests are legion. In this book I suggested that, if justification were needed for the first ascent of Everest, it would be found in the seeking of their own Everests by others. That hope has been fulfilled. The story of Everest in 1953, and other high mountains elsewhere, has proved to be a spur to action for millions of people—particularly for youth. In our country alone groups of young people—from schools, youth organizations, colleges and universities—plan their own expeditions, into the countryside beyond their urban homes, and to countries beyond our shores. The sheer number and diversity of these enterprises are astonishing. On the grand scale, numerous mountaineers, many of them advised and assisted by the Mount Everest Foundation (which was created largely from the telling of this story) have climbed in all the great mountainous regions of the earth. Their achievements have been replicated in journeys across deserts, through tropical forest, through cave systems and in underwater exploration. The Expedition Idea has also been exploited with positive results in diverting youngsters from a life of crime. It has served as a link between people of many nations.

The ultimate regions have been reached. But millions of erstwhile spectators have become players in the vast arena of adventure. While other omens may give cause for concern about the future of mankind, in this evidence, at least, of the abiding spirit of man, I see good reason for hope about the future.

JOHN HUNT
Henley, 1993

CONTENTS

ACKNOWLEDGMENTS
FOR THE FIRST EDITION

ALTHOUGH I have written it, this is really the book of all
members of the 1953 British Expedition to Mount Everest, who
together lived and created the events which go to make up the story.
My thanks are therefore due in the first place to my companions: to
those who read the manuscript and offered helpful advice and corrected the facts; to others who have contributed the appendices; to
Gregory and Lowe, who sorted and helped me to select the photographs from among the thousands in our collection; to Evans, whose
pen sketches bring to life some of my more inadequate descriptions.
Especially am I indebted to Hillary for his stirring chapter on the
final part of the climb.

I owe much also to my wife, whose inspiration and encouragement
has been a priceless help throughout the period covered by the story
and who has guided me in the telling of it. B. R. Goodfellow has read
the manuscript on behalf of the Joint Himalayan Committee and
given me much sound advice in matters of fact and drafting. Others,
too, have helped in this way: Joan Kemp-Welch, Dr Harold Harley
of Knighton, the Reverend Jack Williams of Stowe and Llanvair Wat-
erdine. A. W. Bridge prepared a fine memorandum on the work of
producing the oxygen equipment, which was a useful source of information and will be a memorial of the work involved.

The Indian Air Force have been good enough to allow me to repro-
duce some of their magnificent photographs, taken during a flight
over the mountain shortly after we had left it. It was especially gratify-
ing that the design for the wrapper and the sketch of the Lhotse Face
should have been done by my friend W. Heaton Cooper, who has
captured so brilliantly the lines and character of the mountain. Mr
Holland of the Royal Geographical Society has done a fine job in
drawing the maps.

I am grateful to the Swiss Foundation for Alpine Research for the
spelling of Sherpa names. These have been used throughout this book,
with the exception of Tenzing; in the latter case I have naturally spelt
his name as he himself desired.

The demand to tell the story quickly has been urgent and it was
written within a month. This would never have been possible but for
the quite splendid assistance given me by Miss Elsie Herron, so kindly

made available by my publishers, Hodder and Stoughton; she typed
the manuscript, read and corrected the proofs, managed all correspon-
dence dealing with the book and helped in many other ways in the
writing of it.

I thank them all.

JOHN HUNT

PHOTOGRAPHIC ACKNOWLEDGMENTS FOR THIS EDITION

First black and white photograph and colour doublespread reproduced by permission of Chris Bonington. All other photography from
1953 courtesy of the Royal Geographical Society.

Part I

BACKGROUND

CHAPTER ONE

PERSPECTIVE

T HIS is the story of how, on 29th May, 1953, two men, both endowed with outstanding stamina and skill, inspired by an unflinching resolve, reached the top of Everest and came back unscathed to rejoin their comrades.

Yet this will not be the whole story, for the ascent of Everest was not the work of one day, nor even of those few anxious, unforgettable weeks in which we prepared and climbed last spring. It is, in fact, a tale of sustained and tenacious endeavour by many, over a long period of time. To unfold the whole of this long-drawn-out drama within the compass of this book would either make it so broad a survey as to be dull reading, or else fail to do justice to some of those who took part. Moreover, these earlier feats have already been competently told of in detail and summarized by others. So I will do no more than sketch the past in barest outline.

It is now well over thirty years since an expedition was first sent to explore the mountain with the serious intention of making a sub-sequent attempt to climb it. Since that date, 1921, no less than eleven major expeditions have followed one another, eight of them with the definite mission to get to the top. In the course of three of these expeditions, at least four British climbers, in 1924 and 1933, and last year a Sherpa and a Swiss together, arrived within about 1,000 feet of the peak, only to be forced back at the limit of endurance or by climatic or snow conditions. In addition, there have been several minor expeditions to Everest by small parties, or even by individuals. It is also worth remembering that a number of lives have been lost in attempts to reach the summit.

Before the last war, all attempts on the mountain had been made from the north, following a long and wearisome march from India through Tibet. At that time the frontiers of that remote land were open to us, and the Dalai Lama, its spiritual and temporal ruler, was kindly disposed towards our interest in their mountain group of Chomolungma, strange though this may have appeared to him and his people. It became a ritual for those earlier expeditions to seek and receive the blessing of the abbot of a famous Buddhist monastery,

3

Rongbuk, situated within sight and close range of the mountain on that side. Then the radical change in the political mastery of Tibet in 1951 dimmed for a time our hopes of renewing the attempts to climb Everest from that direction.

At that time very little was known about the southern side of the mountain. As early as 1921, Mallory had looked down upon the Khumbu Icefall during the first reconnaissance of Everest from the northern side. Not being able to see the western and southern flanks of the mountain and impressed by the difficulties of the Icefall, he had entertained little hope of this approach. His impression was later confirmed by members of the 1935 reconnaissance party.

The southern flanks of Everest lie in Nepal, and it was only as recently as 1949 that the rulers of that kingdom opened its frontiers to foreigners; thus it was that, apart from impressions gained by incomplete inspection, it had never been possible to make a survey of that side. It was therefore a momentous event in mountaineering history when this approach could be made. Although previous conclusions had not been encouraging, climbers were not slow to seize this opportunity to inspect this view of Everest close at hand. In mountaineering perhaps more than most other activities, it is a golden rule to press on and on no account be dismayed by unfavourable impressions—to rub your nose, as it were, against the obstacle.

In 1950 a small Anglo-American party which included Charles Houston, the leader of the American expeditions to K2 (28,250 feet) in 1938 and 1953, and Tilman, the leader of the last British expedition to Everest before the war, went to have a look. With little time at their disposal, they just failed to push their inspection far enough and came away understandably dubious, for Everest is cunning in concealing the chinks in its armour. Their report was sufficiently inconclusive, however, to encourage a second and more thorough visit. So it came about that another expedition, initiated by M. P. Ward, W. H. Murray, T. Bourdillon and C. Secord, and led by that renowned veteran of pre-war Everest expeditions, Eric Shipton, was sent out with a small reconnaissance party in the summer of 1951, to examine and test the defences of the mountain from the south. They went with little expectation of success. Yet this, the brilliant Reconnaissance of 1951, not only traced a hypothetical route to the top—it proved to be the most practicable line in the light of later experience—but forced a way up one of the most formidable sections of it.

This discovery of an apparently feasible route created all the greater stir throughout the world of climbers. The Swiss were quick to exploit this welcome knowledge; in two remarkable attempts during last spring and winter, in which they endured exceptional hardships, two of their party, the guide Lambert and the Sherpa Tenzing, reached approximately the same height on the South-East ridge as had Norton eighteen years before on the north face of the mountain.

Meanwhile, we were getting ready to follow the Swiss, should they fail. A training expedition, led by Eric Shipton and including prospective members of an eventual Everest team, went out to the Himalaya in the summer of 1952. Their aims were to prepare themselves for Everest, to test oxygen equipment and to study physiological problems at high altitude. In the course of doing this, they made an attempt to climb one of the major Himalayan peaks, Cho Oyu (26,860 feet), and carried out some exploration of a rugged and hitherto unvisited valley. The oxygen tests had an important influence on the development of our equipment this year and the knowledge gained by the physiological studies undertaken was valuable in drawing up our own programme of preparation. On Cho Oyu Shipton and his party made yet one more important contribution towards success on Everest.

These, the Reconnaissance of 1951, the two Swiss attempts and the Cho Oyu experiments, were the immediate milestones behind the final journey to the top. The knowledge provided by all four expeditions, the difficulties revealed and indeed the sufferings endured were a sobering thought which governed my planning. But they also inspired us to carry the flag of adventure to its ultimate goal.

*　　　*　　　*

These bare facts enable me to place our part in its right perspective, for ours was no new venture; it was, after all, only the climax to a story which had already been lived and written in large part before we set out. When, last year, the Swiss entered the lists against Everest, they recognized that they owed much to earlier British experience; they were particularly indebted to the British party led by Shipton which, the previous year, had been the first to investigate the possibility of a way to the summit from the south. Immediately after their return they placed all their valuable experience and information of this southern route at our disposal. So it was that we who followed them were already, in knowledge, more than half-way on our arduous journey towards the summit, for by their achievements on the mountain our predecessors had acquired a great deal of experience.

We have a very proper sense of pride that no less than nine of the eleven expeditions to Everest have been British sponsored. But it must be remembered too that we then enjoyed a privileged position in India which gave us a certain advantage in obtaining permission to visit Everest between the wars, and we also have to thank climbers of other

5

nations who, in that vast arena of the Himalaya, recognized in the continuing struggle our precious stake in that mountain. It was as if an agreement existed in those years, by which it was tacitly understood that certain of the big peaks were the special concern of climbers of a particular nation.

The mission we undertook was not, in our eyes, in the nature of some competition on a giant scale in which we vied to outdo the efforts of previous expeditions, dramatic and popular as such a concept might be. Indeed, prolonged attempts to climb a difficult mountain are, or should be, essentially different from those of a competitive sport. A possible analogy, however, might be that of a relay race, in which each member of a team of runners hands the baton to the next at the end of his allotted span, until the race is finally run. The Swiss last year received that baton of knowledge from the latest in the long chain of British climbers and they in turn, after running a brilliant lap, passed it on to us. We chanced to be the last runners in this particular race, but we might well not have succeeded in finishing, in which case we would have handed on our knowledge to our French comrades who were preparing to take up the challenge.

But this tussle between men and a mountain reaches beyond the scope of mountain climbing in its physical aspect. It seems to me to symbolize man's struggle to come to terms with the forces of nature; it speaks eloquently of the continuity of this struggle and of the bond between all those who have taken part in it. The opponent was not other parties, but Everest itself.

*   *   *

And this will not be the story of those two men alone who reached the top. In this or any other mountain venture, sound and successful climbing is fundamentally a matter of teamwork. A particular route on our home crags or on a mountain of Alpine dimensions may safely be climbed by no more than two men, unsupported by any others. Yet even they comprise a team; they are linked by a rope which does more than provide mutual security—it symbolizes their unity of purpose. Each man plays his own important part, whether he is in the lead, finding and preparing a passage, or acting as second man on the rope, carrying the gear, perhaps improving the track, safeguarding and advising his leader. The bigger the scale or technical difficulty, or both, the more vital this teamwork and, probably, the larger the team required to accomplish the task. To achieve success on Everest, the biggest mountain and in some respects the toughest problem of all, we needed to be imbued not only with that sense of unity with the past, but also among ourselves.

6

There are exceptions to every rule, and Everest might well have been one such exception. We had agreed that in certain favourable circumstances it might be justifiable and indeed necessary for one single climber to carry on alone over the last short distance to the top. This seems to have been the view held and the policy adopted by earlier expeditions. In 1924 Norton, and again in 1933 Smythe, continued on their own above a certain point when their respective companions on the rope found themselves unable to go on. The opportunity first to reach the top of Everest is one so special, so unique, that it might have been right to break the golden rule I have described. But this does not in any way affect the teamwork essential to the enterprise as a whole.

*   *   *

Shortly after we had returned from Everest, some of us were interviewed by a party of students. One of them turned to me and asked: "What was the point of climbing Everest? Had you any material objective, or was it just some kind of madness?" Some may wonder why it was that we, and those who were before us, went to try to climb Everest, and it may be as well that I should attempt to answer this question at the outset of the story.

To those looking for a material objective, there is no satisfactory answer, for there was indeed no desire for, nor expectation of any material reward. The Himalaya is a rich field for exploration and scientific research, but there are many regions equally profitable and less known than the close surroundings of Everest for those who want to break new ground or whose interests are scientific. In the course of the many efforts to climb that mountain, the area has become relatively well known; during most other expeditions many interests have been pursued aside from climbing. But these other interests have always been secondary to the basic aim of climbing the mountain. Moreover, one of the lessons learned from the past is that science and mountaineering do not readily mix; I was always sure that we must concentrate single-mindedly on the main purpose of getting up.

Nor is the question answered simply by a passion for climbing mountains. To those who do so the sport is, or should be, a source of happiness. We climb mountains because we like it. But I doubt whether any one of our party went to Everest this year expecting to enjoy the climbing as much as in the mountains nearer home. Mountain craft acquired on more accessible peaks tends to suffer in the Himalaya from lack of stern testing; most of us had been to the Himalaya before and we knew that, even on minor expeditions, the technical climbing problems are fewer and less severe, and the actual amount of climbing opportunities in a given time much less than, for example, in the Alps.

Yet to solve a problem which has long resisted the skill and persistence of others is an irresistible magnet in every sphere of human activity. It was this urge to which Mallory alluded when he gave his apparently ingenuous reply to this same question—"Because it's there". It was Mallory, who disappeared with his companion Irvine high on the North-East ridge of Everest in 1924, during his third expedition to the mountain, and since his time many more seeking without success to reach the summit, who by their example spurred us to try where they had failed. The fact that Everest still remained unscaled despite so many onslaughts was certainly sufficient to tame in us any foolish optimism, yet we were encouraged, as others must have been before us, by the possession of a great sum of experience. The possibility of entering the unknown; the simple fact that it was the highest point on the world's surface—these things goaded us on. The problem aroused no invidious comparisons; it was intimate to us as a team and personal to each of us as individuals. There was the challenge, and we would lay aside all else to take it up.

CHAPTER TWO

THE PROBLEM

W HAT is the problem of Everest? What were the weapons with
which the mountain had so long succeeded in holding at bay so
many resolute men? By last autumn, when we were preparing to
tackle it, the nature of the undertaking had already been largely
exposed; indeed, in a sense it was almost solved, with only the last
1,000 feet unclimbed. It was romantic to suppose that some spell had
been cast over the final keep, that a barrier had been reached at about
28,000 feet beyond which even such stout spirits as Norton, Smythe,
Wyn Harris and Wager, Lambert and Tenzing could not pass. It
might appear that the problem was confined to the breaking of this
spell, the forcing of this invisible obstacle, a point in space comparable
with the barrier of sound. Although perhaps true in a physiological
sense, to follow this line of thought would be to give a totally false
impression, just as it would be untrue to say that, with the climbing
of the mountain this year, there is no further problem for future
aspirants to reach the top. Others had gone before us to approximately
the same height on opposite sides of the final peak, but they had not
been turned back by any physical obstacle beyond their technical skill
to surmount. The terrain was passable; in descriptive mountaineering
jargon, "it would go". Some among this select band maintain that
they could have gone farther but for lack of time. I will return to this
point later; it is enough to say for the moment that they had been
defeated by the cumulative effects of altitude, effects which had been
telling both on them and on their supporting comrades from a much
earlier stage.

There are three factors of awe-inspiring magnitude facing those
who seek adventure among the highest peaks. They are this matter
of vertical scale, the climatic conditions and the climbing difficulties.
Let us look at altitude first.

The rarefied air surrounding the upper part of Everest, or any other
of the big peaks, obviously makes movement, even over easy ground,
much more difficult. Lack of oxygen also slows down and blurs the
mental processes. Beyond a certain point life itself is no longer possible. On the other hand, it is now sufficiently proved that the ill-effects

9

of altitude on the climber may at least be retarded by a careful regimen of what we call acclimatization, a gradual getting used to increasing height over a certain period of time. Individual performances on a mountain naturally vary, but it may be said that those among us who are best adapted to climb high mountains, provided they follow this policy of gradualness, can reach an altitude of at least 21,000 feet and remain there without serious detriment—at any rate long enough to make a supreme final effort to reach a higher point, provided it is not too far above.

Trouble begins above that height, which is one main reason why the really high peaks—those of 26,000 feet and over—are in a different category of difficulty from any lesser ones. The policy of gradualness breaks down, for the muscle tissues begin to deteriorate fairly rapidly and the climber's resistance to cold, his fortitude in the face of wind and weather, are weakened. He tends to lose the promptings of appetite and thirst and he is denied the relaxation of normal sleep. In fact, from about 21,000 feet onwards, he really needs greatly to speed up the rate of his progress and employ "rush" tactics. But this he cannot do. On the contrary, he is increasingly handicapped by the height as he climbs and his progress becomes painfully slow; the mental effort, like the physical, is infinitely greater. If this is true of easy ground, it is the more so when difficulties arise, even minor ones which would not deter a moderate performer at a lower height. A slight change of gradient may be a straw which will break the camel's back. Considering that Everest is over 29,000 feet and that some 8,000 feet have to be climbed above this established level of successful acclimatization, one aspect of our problem, which also played an important part in defeating former expeditions, becomes clear. It would be very desirable, in order to minimize the factor of physical deterioration, to climb those 8,000 feet in a day, or at most two; but this is clearly quite out of the question. For so slowly does the climber move by his own unaided efforts, that four or five days would be required to get up, quite apart from the subsequent descent, and by about the fourth day at the latest, he would already be so weakened, mentally as well as physically, that he would be unlikely to have the strength or the determination for the last lap —just when he needs it most. This is what had happened before at about the 28,000-foot level.

But the problem is much more complex than this. These days above 21,000 feet involve the establishment of a number of high camps, and these in turn represent tents, sleeping-bags, mattresses, food, cooking equipment and fuel, as well as climbing gear. All this must be carried up, and because of the need to provide even a modicum of comfort and—more important—protection against the cold, some of this baggage is inevitably fairly heavy. The loads would be far beyond the capacity of those destined to climb to the top, who should be spared as much as possible for their mission; they must be carried up by others in a supporting rôle. Moreover, in order to keep the size and stocks of these high camps to a minimum, the baggage parties must be staggered in time; the loads must be shifted upwards over a period of days. This period in turn is likely to be protracted because the amount any man can carry at high altitude is so small. So climbing Everest takes a long time, not only because of the need to acclimatize slowly up to a certain point, but also because of the slowing down of the final effort by lack of oxygen.

And in the final stages particularly, the saving of time is vital, not only because of physical deterioration but also because of another factor, the most important of all—weather.

*　　*　　*

On all but the smallest mountains, or those on which no serious difficulties are met, the weather obviously plays a big part in mountaineering plans. It imposes a serious handicap on the climber's ability to negotiate difficult ground; it slows his progress and exposes him to cold and wind. He may lose his way and stray on to even more difficult territory, and he may become benighted. The dangers of bad weather on a mountain need no further emphasis, and I mention them only to introduce their more deadly effect on the biggest mountains of all. The periods when weather conditions may be fair enough to permit a serious attempt on the summit of Everest are not only brief and few in any one year; they appear to be rare as assessed over a number of years. Throughout the winter, from November to March, a fierce gale blows fairly constantly from the north-west. It is strong—wind speeds of at least seventy to eighty knots are probable—and it is desperately cold. It scours the northern flanks of the range and deposits snow on the southern faces; and snow thus overlaid on the existing layer is usually unstable and dangerous, for it is apt to peel off in avalanches. During the winter this great westerly wind rules supreme in these high and lonely places. It is scarcely possible to climb a major Himalayan peak at this season, unless it be by some quite exceptionally protected and straightforward route.

In the early summer—it may be late May or the beginning of June, depending on the position of the mountain along the range—a countering element comes up from the south-east in the form of the monsoon. This warm, damp wind from the Bay of Bengal deposits heavy snow on the higher flanks of the mountain barrier; it is particularly intense in the south-east part of the Himalaya, on which it unleashes its force soon after reaching the head of the Bay, and it is in this area that Everest is situated. Monsoon conditions normally continue to prevail in this region until towards the end of September. Some climbing may be done during this period, but the difficulty of climbing all high peaks, particularly in the south-east Himalaya, is greatly increased by the handicaps and dangers of the deep new snow. The chance to get up Everest is probably limited to the gap, or lull, between the departure of the one Fury and the onset of the other; these lulls may occur in May and early October, that is, just before the monsoon sets in, and when it dies away. Nearly all attempts to climb Everest have been made in the pre-monsoon period, although the Swiss last year went back to the mountain in the autumn. While there is no conclusive evidence against it, this second period would seem to offer very small chance of success, for the heavy snow must first be swept off the mountain by the westerly wind, and this wind, when it reaches its full force, is beyond human endurance. Whichever the period, it is short. Indeed, there is no assurance of any lull occurring at all between winter conditions and the oncome of the monsoon. This situation was encountered by each of the Everest expeditions in 1936 and 1938.

*   *   *

These two factors, the altitude and the weather, tend separately and together to defeat the climber. The height weakens, slows him down; it forces him to spend days and nights in the course of his assault on the summit; the weather, besides adding to the demands on his energy and moral fortitude, conspires to deny him the time he needs to complete his mission. Whereas in lower mountains and on easy ground the weather may be no more than a handicap, in the high Himalaya it is decisive, regardless of terrain.

The deduction to be drawn from these two factors was clear enough. We must either so fortify ourselves that we could continue, without detriment, to live and have our being above the limit of natural acclimatization, or, better still, we must solve the problem of speed. It was desirable, in fact, that we should meet both these requirements and thus give to those chosen to attempt the summit and to their supporters some measure of insurance against the vagaries of the weather, for safety in mountain climbing is as much a matter of swiftness as of sureness of foot. Either or both could be achieved only by the administration of oxygen in sufficient quantities to make up for the deficiency in the air, and for the duration of the upward journey above the limit of successful acclimatization. In other words, oxygen may be looked upon as a height-reducer, producing conditions comparable with climbing on more familiar mountains.

This need for oxygen on Everest was no new problem; it had been well known for many years past, although all climbers had not admitted it was essential; some even considered it undesirable on ethical grounds. It had been used on the first expedition ever to make a serious attempt on the summit, by Finch and Bruce in 1922. But the equipment used hitherto had not brought climbers to within range of the summit in much better shape than others who had been climbing without it, owing to the small amount of oxygen provided for a given weight. This question of weight at great heights, unless more than compensated by the oxygen supply, is of capital importance. It would seem that all earlier equipment did comparatively little to reduce the effects of strain, fatigue and deterioration. Our problem was to produce apparatus markedly better in performance than this. The lighter the apparatus, provided always that it would enable the climber to continue for reasonably long periods without replenishing his oxygen supply, the faster we would be able to climb.

*   *   *

I now come to the purely physical obstacles along our route to the top, difficulties requiring a degree of mountain skill and experience to overcome. It is often said by those who do not know the mountain that Everest is, technically speaking, easy. While admitting that there are tougher climbing problems, I must stress that this is emphatically not the case. If I have reserved until last among the difficulties with which we were faced when preparing the expedition this matter of the physical make-up of our peak, it is partly to establish the topography freshly in mind, and partly also because, considerable as they were, the technical difficulties were enhanced and dominated by the two factors of altitude and weather.

But now let us examine the south-facing structure of Everest (see page 15). This illustration alone would probably give an adequate idea but for the matter of scale; we are very apt to judge the size of mountains by the yardstick of our own experience, and for those who are not familiar with the Himalaya, and at close range, it would be easy to fail to grasp their hugeness from a picture, as indeed those do who first see them in actuality.

Everest is one of a group of three great peaks standing astride the Nepal–Tibet frontier. Between them on the western side they embrace a hidden valley which is a wonder of mountain architecture —a high-level glen whose floor slopes gently from about 22,000 feet to 19,000 feet, in a westerly direction. When Mallory saw it during

13

the first reconnaissance of Everest in 1921, he named it the "Western Cwm", doubtless from affection for his Welsh climbing haunts. At its head stands the centre-piece of the trinity, the great rock peak of Lhotse, over 27,000 feet, whose west face falls steeply to the head of this valley, effectively blocking the upper exit. Looking up the Western Cwm, Everest is on the left, its west ridge forming the north enclosing wall. On the opposite side is Nuptse, a ridge rather than a mountain, whose sharp and jagged crest, taking its origin from the southern battlements of Lhotse, runs for over two miles at a constant elevation of over 25,000 feet. Thus contained between Everest and Nuptse, barred by the face of Lhotse, this astonishing freak of nature leads the climber to the very foot of the mountain; it is the focal point of ascent from the south.

But the Cwm has first to be entered, and its threshold is well guarded. Its floor is lined with a layer of ice, probably some hundreds of feet in thickness. This, the origin of the Khumbu glacier, after pursuing a fairly gentle course for at least three miles, spills abruptly down an immense step, over 2,000 feet in height. Then, having dropped to about 18,000 feet, the Khumbu glacier makes a left-handed swing through an angle of ninety degrees and, levelling out, flows gradually to its snout, some eight miles downstream. This step or icefall forms the exit to the Western Cwm; it presents a formidable problem to the mountaineer bent on attaining the Cwm and beyond. An icefall is a frozen cascade of ice, often on a gigantic scale. The Khumbu Icefall is indeed a monster of the species. Moving over the steep underlying bed of rock, the surface of the glacier becomes split and tortured into a maze of chasms, tottering and fallen blocks of ice. It is in a constant state of activity and change, for Himalayan ice movement is generally much more marked than, for example, in our European Alps. Crevasses appear on a hitherto smooth surface over-night. They widen or close with startling suddenness. Great masses of ice, many tons in weight, are at one moment of time poised precari-ously above the void; at the next they crash downwards, obliterating all in their path, bestrewing the slopes with huge boulders of ice. Despite the fact that it had been forced by Shipton's party in 1951 and twice by the Swiss last year, here was clearly a most serious obstacle, whose character could be expected to have changed beyond recognition by the time we reached it in 1953.

Now let us advance in imagination to the head of the Western Cwm, to look briefly at the west face of Lhotse, for this is the barrier which must be surmounted to arrive at the foot of the final pyramid. Our immediate objective is the saddle or depression between Lhotse and Everest, which we have come to know as the South Col. To reach

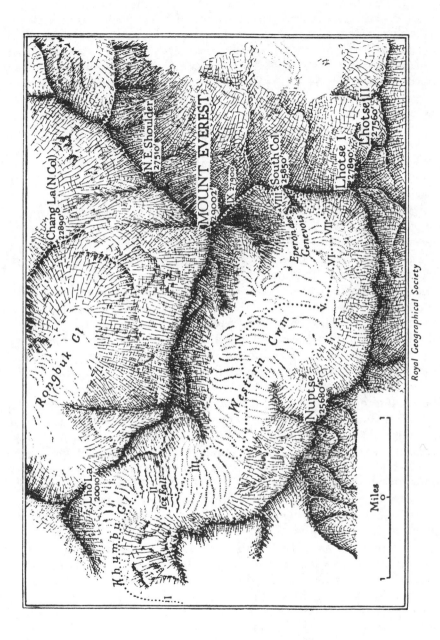

Chang La (N Col)
22890'

N.E. Shoulder
27510'

MOUNT EVEREST
29002'

IX 27900'

South Col
25850'

VIII

Lhotse I
27890'

Lhotse II
27560'

Rongbuk Gl.

Western Cwm

Eperon des Genevois

VII
VI
V
IV

Nuptse
25680'

Lho La
20010'

I
II
Ice Fall
III

Khumbu Gl.

I

Miles
0
1

Royal Geographical Society

it we must climb the steep slopes of ice and snow falling from the Col and Lhotse over a vertical distance of some 4,000 feet. It seemed to us that here lay the crux of the ascent of Everest. The South Col is at a height of 26,000 feet; no less than 3,000 feet remain to be climbed even after attaining this quite exceptional altitude—little below that of Annapurna, which until this year was the highest summit reached by man. Not only would it be a most strenuous and difficult undertaking to reach the Col; it would be necessary for considerable numbers of us to do so, carrying a large quantity of stores and equipment to enable the final assault to be launched with adequate support. It was on this section of the route that the Swiss, magnificent though their effort had been, foundered. Admitted that Tenzing and Lambert went so high above the South Col, they had behind them inadequate backing for their wonderful effort. It was the problem of providing this backing, in terms of equipment, stores and fit climbers in support on the South Col of Everest, which would be our particular concern for the months ahead of us.

Let us pursue our flight of fancy still further and arrive at the South Col, possessed of the knowledge which was ours last autumn in the light of the Swiss spring expedition, and study the upper part of the mountain. To reach the top the climber must set foot on and follow the South-East ridge which runs down from the summit to, or towards the South Col, passing on its way over a minor eminence known as the South Peak, over 28,700 feet in height. As we then understood it, this ridge would present no mountaineering difficulty as far as the South Peak; the riddle on this final section was what lay beyond, between the two summits. It could not be seen from the Col, so the Swiss had been unable to throw light on the problem. From air photographs in our possession we had the impression of a narrow crest of snow or ice, leaning ominously in heavy eaves of snow over the eastern precipice, these cornices being formed by the prevailing westerly wind. Indeed, the utmost point itself appeared, at the time these pictures were taken, to stand at the crest of one such monster cornice, overhanging perhaps by as much as twenty-five feet. Even in those days last autumn, we realized that this was, to say the least of it, a worthy finish to the climb, and we may some of us have nursed an unspoken resentment that Everest should have reserved this last glacis for those who had dared thus far. It was obvious that to tread the 500 yards and 400 vertical feet dividing the South Peak from the peak of Everest would demand a clear and undistracted mind, as well as a reserve of strength, in particular because the return journey as far as the lower summit would tax the climber almost as much as the ascent. How could we ensure for our eventual summit climbers these

16

essential powers? This was indeed the supreme question to whose solution the whole of our planning was ultimately directed.

Here then, in very general terms, were the three big factors comprising the problem of Everest, those of altitude, weather and terrain. It was in a careful study of these, and their effect on successive expeditions through the years, that our preparatory planning and eventually the operational plan itself, had their source. We were greatly inspired by the fact that many of the difficulties arising from these factors had already been mastered by others before us; but we were also aware that we should have to face up to them again in our turn, probably in altered circumstances and possibly in more difficult conditions. Finally, we knew that in order to reach the top we must somehow avoid the situation arrived at hitherto by even the most skilled and determined of our predecessors, when two, or sometimes only one man, had struggled upwards to within 1,000 feet of the goal, with insufficient reserves to reach it—or at any rate to arrive there and return to join their friends.

To enter once more into the realm of romance, we had to pass beyond that enchanted barrier, dispersing beforehand any spell by which the mountain might hold the trespasser hostage for ever in its icy grip.

Part II

PLANNING

CHAPTER THREE

PREPARATIONS: ONE

O RGANIZING a major expedition, whether it be to the Himalaya, the polar regions or darkest Africa, is a formidable business. I have experience only of the first of these undertakings, but I can now sympathize deeply with those who have the cares of planning and preparing missions in other realms of adventure or research. Imagine that you are charged with the task of fulfilling, in company with others, a long and exceptionally arduous task, in some remote and uninhabited corner of the earth's surface, where climatic conditions are extreme. The success of your mission depends primarily on the human factor, on the joint efforts of every man in your team, and failure—moral or physical—by even one or two of these would add immensely to its difficulties. You have the responsibility of seeking and selecting these men, in whom you are looking for a happy combination of qualities which are difficult to reconcile. You will not be able, in most cases at any rate, to test these qualities, at least in conditions comparable with those which will confront you—it is unlikely that you will even be acquainted with most of them beforehand. You have to ensure that the party is suitably clothed and equipped to carry out its job in the especially rigorous conditions, and that it takes with it all the tools it is likely to require for the job, bearing in mind that communications will be so extended, slow and difficult that you must be entirely self-contained for the duration of your mission. Some of this equipment is highly specialized, and difficult questions of design and quantities have to be decided. Provisions have to be calculated for the whole period of your absence from civilization and they must be carefully chosen; a diet must be established suitable to the climate and the nature of the work. All these numerous items of equipment and food must be ordered, many of them only after thorough testing in conditions as nearly as possible approximating to those likely to be met. Arrangements must be made for packing, cataloguing and moving them, as well as the party, to the starting-point in a distant land, and from that point onwards by more primitive transport to the area of operations. Last but by no means least of these manifold headaches, and governing the whole enterprise, is the problem of financing it; it is your job to calculate the costs. To complete this picture, suppose that you are given a bare minimum of time to launch the expedition and that you take it on with the ever-present possibility of its being cancelled when the preparations are well under way. You also realize that it will be necessary for you to make provision for a second expedition to carry on in the event of failure. In such a predicament you would, I fancy, be inclined to think that you were faced with as tough an assignment as any you had ever undertaken or were ever likely to in the future.

This, at any rate, was my impression when on 11th September, 1952, I received a telegram inviting me to take on the leadership of the British Expedition to Mount Everest in the spring of 1953. At that moment I was heavily involved with the final preparations for Allied manoeuvres in Germany and knew that I could not be made available for another month at the earliest. I experienced excitement and apprehension in more or less equal proportions. Let me hasten to reassure you, however, that the situation was not as bad as I feared.

Ever since the first expedition to explore Everest was conceived in 1919, these enterprises have been sponsored, financed and encouraged by a Committee formed jointly by the Alpine Club—the doyen of mountaineering societies—and the Royal Geographical Society, one of whose main functions is to foster exploration. This Committee had been helping to prepare for the forthcoming expedition since 1951. The 1951 Reconnaissance of Everest and the training expedition to Cho Oyu last year were designed to lead up to a full-scale attempt to climb the mountain in 1953, in the event of the Swiss failing to do so. There was, therefore, a degree of continuity in the matter of over-all direction. One of the principal tasks of the Joint Himalayan Committee, in addition to those of conceiving the idea of an Everest expedition, seeking political sanction, deciding matters of policy in preparations, is to finance it. Only those who have had this care can fully appreciate the work and anxiety of raising very substantial funds for an enterprise of this nature, coloured as it inevitably is in the mind of the public by a succession of failures, with no financial security other than the pockets of the Committee members themselves. I cannot adequately express my personal debt to its members, especially to B. R. Goodfellow, its Honorary Secretary, and L. P. Kirwan, Director of the Royal Geographical Society, for their support. A number of organizations and individuals contributed to the finances of the expedition, and in particular *The Times* newspaper, which had given valuable backing to earlier expeditions also. The Medical Research Council had set up a High-Altitude Committee, as it had before earlier expeditions, to advise on equipment and diet; a physiologist from this body, Dr L. G. C. Pugh, had accompanied Shipton to the Himalaya in 1952 and had prepared a report from which a number of useful lessons could be learned. Eric Shipton himself had already started to lay down the foundations for planning and was available to give advice from his immense fund of Himalayan experience. An organizing secretary had been appointed and was busy with tentative contacts concerning equipment. In fact, on my return to London from Germany to start work on Everest, a good deal of preliminary work was in progress (see Appendix II, Preparations for the Everest Expedition, 1953: Organization).

But it was evident that a very great deal more remained to be done in a very short time and that more willing and experienced helpers must be enlisted before a full and adequate machinery could be set in motion to launch us. These helpers should, as far as possible, be the eventual members of the expedition themselves. They would have a very personal interest in the preparations, since they would later be taking part in the venture. One of the most urgent needs, then, was to choose the party. Here again some groundwork had already been done. There were the members of the 1951 Reconnaissance and of the Cho Oyu Expedition, with their special advantages of recent experience in the area of Everest: other private expeditions had visited the Himalaya from this country since the war: the various mountaineering clubs had been invited to make recommendations from among their members and long lists of candidates were available; many of these had Alpine experience and a few had made climbs of outstanding merit in the Alps in the past few years. In addition, numerous offers to join the expedition were coming in from all over the country, some of them with slender qualifications, but all fired by the pure spirit of adventure. Indeed, there was an embarrassingly large field from which to choose.

With the need to spread the load very much in mind, I set 1st November as the target date for submitting my proposals to the Committee, whose responsibility it was to issue the formal invitations. In the three weeks after my arrival, I was much occupied with sorting the many names, preparing lists of increasing brevity, interviewing candidates and hearing personal recommendations from others who knew them. It was in many ways the hardest part of the whole affair, for so very much depended on the choosing of the best possible team; I was sure that would be the biggest factor of all for success. At the same time, it was very hard to turn down so many promising and ardent candidates. I remembered my own feelings sixteen years before, when I had been chosen for Everest and later rejected by a Medical Board. In whittling down the short list to its final

23

proportions, I was looking for four qualifications. They were those of age: temperament: experience: physique; and I wanted a team every member of which would be a potential "summiter".

As regards age, I was looking for men within a bracket of between twenty-five and forty. It had been my previous experience, and that of others, that for those below twenty-five the bigger mountains of the Himalaya—25,000 feet or over—tend to be too ambitious an undertaking, demanding as they do quite exceptional powers of endurance and unusual patience. Patience, if it needs to be acquired at all, normally comes with increasing years. The upper bracket was less easy to arrive at—there have been some remarkable exceptions—but it seemed to me wiser to assume that I should be lucky to find mountaineers over forty who had maintained their stamina by constant climbing practice.

Age was an easy yardstick; temperament was much harder to assess. It was all the more difficult because I was looking for two qualities which do not easily coincide in any one mortal. There was the need to be sure that each one of the party really wanted to get to the top. This desire must be individual as well as collective, for such are the exigencies of Everest that any one of us might be called upon to make this attempt; I was looking for the "Excelsior" spirit in every member of the team. In contrast with this, Everest also demands a quite unusual degree of selflessness and patience. The final climb to the top must, by common consent among us, be an entirely impersonal choice, and for those not chosen for it there might be thankless, even frustrating jobs during the most critical phase of the expedition. This was certainly asking a good deal of prospective members of the team; temperaments are put to great and prolonged strain during big expeditions. But one man can endanger the unity and spirit of a whole party, and unity on Everest would be all-important.

As regards experience, it was desirable that those who were to join us should have done a number of major climbs in the Alps, combining problems of snow, ice and rock—what the French call "Grandes Courses"—and the longer the period of this experience the better, for one is unlikely to learn all the conditions of weather and snow in one, or even two Alpine seasons. In this country, our opportunities for climbing are mainly restricted to rock. It is true that good snow and ice climbing is to be had in some of our mountain districts in winter, particularly in the Highlands, but generally speaking there is a tendency for our young mountaineers to carry to the Alps a native preference for rock climbing. Outstanding ability as a rock climber is not an essential attribute for the Himalaya, at any rate at the present stage of the game. Unfortunately the opportunities to climb the big snow and ice peaks in the Alps do not fall to many of our home climbers, and this qualification considerably narrowed the field of candidates. An additional and most desirable label to those who remained eligible was that of Himalayan experience; and this because of the essentially different climbing conditions, as much as the testing it gave to their ability to climb at high altitudes. Those falling into this category were naturally few; it led me to wish then, as I hope now, that more of our young people might have the chance to share our experience in the bigger ranges.

Physique was a subject on which Himalayan climbers held strong and varying views. Some claimed that the potential climbers of Everest must be small and stocky; others pointed out that in practice many tall men have gone high on that and other mountains. As a generality, it is obvious that the larger the human frame the more energy required to propel it, and this may possibly be a disadvantage at high altitude. To me it seemed that, where actual proof was lacking, the important thing was the proportions of the climber—his general physical make-up, regardless of his height. You can be disadvantageously heavily built even if you are short, and energy is presumably given in proportion to your frame. Beyond taking note of the fact that the bigger men would probably consume more oxygen, therefore, I was influenced by the build of candidates rather than their height. As it turned out, a majority of us were about six feet, some of us taller.

Finally, I was insistent on meeting candidates personally where I did not know them beforehand. Because of this, some from overseas who were not in this country and whose qualifications were outstandingly good had to be turned down. Other matters apart, it was so important to our enterprise that everyone should "fit in" and of this I could not be sure without forming my personal impressions. The only exceptions made to this principle were two New Zealand mountaineers who had been with Shipton in 1952 and who were known to others whose place in the team was assured. One of them, Hillary, had also taken part in the 1951 Reconnaissance. So strong were their claims that I accepted a reflected view of these candidates, given by those whose judgment I respected.

One of the first questions to be decided was whether this expedition should be international in composition, for there were candidates from other nations eligible for consideration. There were several requests from other countries to participate in the expedition, and these were all seriously considered by the Joint Committee.

The principle had already been accepted that, if the party was to be selected from among British mountaineers, this should embrace climbers from Commonwealth countries other than Britain—in New

Zealand and Kenya, in particular, there were very strong aspirants. There was much to be said in favour of an international party, especially as the competitive aspect of the struggle for Everest was being played upon outside climbing circles. But it was clear to me that we should not extend our selection beyond the Commonwealth and this viewpoint was accepted by the Committee. On an expedition of this exceptional nature, the stresses and strains set up between individuals are bound to be considerable, and I could not afford to make even more difficult the achievement of our all-important unity by making it at the same time an experiment in international goodwill. Although it was never our view that Everest was the subject of invidious comparison between climbers of different nations, we were aware that many people thought otherwise and this, despite ourselves, might have added to these stresses. In any case, here was an adventure in which British climbers had a long-standing and intimate interest; there was much to be said for the view that a British team should take up the challenge where it had last been laid down by Tilman and his men in 1938.

Among the many letters of recommendation concerning the composition of the party was one suggesting that the Himalayan Committee should negotiate with Czechoslovakia for the "transfer" and naturalization as a British subject of Zatopek, the famous Czech runner. In the view of the writer, this would make certain beyond any doubt that one of the party reached the top of the mountain.

By 1st November the party was decided and the names were submitted to the Himalayan Committee on the 7th. It consisted of ten climbers, an Expedition Doctor, and a number of reserves. The arguments for a fairly large party have already been given in the previous chapter, and the number of ten had been arrived at as a result of preliminary planning, some account of which will be given later in this chapter.

This was the final choice:

Charles Evans, F.R.C.S., aged 33, short and sturdy, sandy-haired, was at that time a surgeon in the Walton Hospital, Liverpool. At intervals between his professional appointments he had found time to take part in three expeditions to the Himalaya in the preceding three years—with Tilman on the Annapurna range in 1950, in the mountains of Kulu in 1951, and last year with Shipton on Cho Oyu. He had also good experience in the Alps and on the crags in this country.

Tom Bourdillon, aged 28, had accompanied Shipton on both the Reconnaissance and the Cho Oyu Expeditions. During the latter he had experimented with the use of oxygen. An outstanding rock climber before he went to the Himalaya, he had undertaken climbs in the French Alps of a far higher order of difficulty than British climbers had been thought capable of at that time. His achievements have inspired our young mountaineers to follow his example, thus establishing the fact that their standard of performance is comparable with that of the best Continental alpinists. Bourdillon is a physicist working on the development of rocket motors in the Ministry of Supply. He is huge and hefty, built like a second-row rugby forward.

Alfred Gregory, Director of a Travel Agency in Blackpool, also took part in the Cho Oyu Expedition. Apart from myself, he was, at the age of 39, the oldest member of the climbing party; also the smallest, thin, wiry and very tough. With a background of long and varied experience in the Alps and our own hills, he had done well on Cho Oyu, where he had proved his ability to acclimatize to altitude.

Edmund Hillary, aged 33, had, like Bourdillon, been a member of both the "curtain-opener" expeditions, joining the first of them after he had taken part in a very successful New Zealand expedition in the Central Himalaya. Although his climbing experience dates from immediately after the war, he had quickly risen to the foremost rank among mountaineers in his own country. His testing in the Himalaya had shown that he would be a very strong contender, not only for Everest, but for an eventual summit party. When I met Shipton last autumn I well remember his prophesying this—and how right he was. Quite exceptionally strong and abounding in a restless energy, possessed of a thrusting mind which swept aside all unproved obstacles, Ed Hillary's personality had made its imprint on my mind, through his Cho Oyu and Reconnaissance friends and through his letters to me, long before we met. He is lanky in build; by profession a bee-keeper near Auckland.

His countryman, George Lowe, was yet another of Shipton's strong team on Cho Oyu. His New Zealand alpine experience dates from before that of Hillary, to whom he introduced some of the high-standard climbs on those mountains. His ice technique, acquired like Hillary's from the exceptional opportunities offered by New Zealand mountains, is of a very high standard. He is tall, well-built. Aged 28, he was teaching in a Primary school in Hastings, N.Z.

Charles Wylie's services had already been obtained from the War Office early in September. He was working as organizing secretary during the interim period before my arrival and he was to continue in that capacity, as my invaluable assistant, throughout the preparatory period. Charles is a serving officer of the Brigade of Gurkhas; he had spent most of the war in a Japanese prison camp. That he had weathered this so well was doubtless due to his selflessness and sympathy for others, his faith and his cheerful disposition. We have to be grateful to him that the expedition's equipment was so meticulously prepared and documented, that every minor detail was thought of and provided for. He, like Gregory, had good Alpine and home experience of climbing, and he had climbed in Garhwal shortly after the war. His age was 32.

Michael Westmacott was 27. He had no previous Himalayan experience, although he had served in the East at the end of the war as a Sapper officer. An ex-President of the Oxford University Mountaineering Club, he is a mountaineer of the first rank and had recently done some particularly fine routes in the Alps. He is employed on statistical investigation at Rothamsted Experimental Station.

George Band, tall, bespectacled and studious, was the youngest of us; in fact, his age of 23 at the time of his selection was below what I had always considered the minimum age for an Everest climber. His record of Alpine achievement was, however, so exceptionally good, and he possessed other qualities which I should have expected to find only in an older man. He had just taken his degree at Cambridge and was the ex-President of the Mountaineering Club of that University.

Wilfrid Noyce is a schoolmaster and author, built on the same model as Lowe. Aged 34, he was, at the outbreak of war in 1939, one of our foremost young mountaineers, with a very fine record of difficult routes in the Alps and on our own crags to his credit. During a part of the war he was employed in training air crews in mountain craft in Kashmir. For a brief period he assisted me in running a similar course for soldiers. He had climbed in Garhwal, and had made the ascent of one high peak in Sikkim, Pauhunri, 23,400 feet.

Lastly, there was myself. I had been climbing intermittently since 1925, when I climbed my first high Alpine peak at the age of 15. I had fitted in ten Alpine summer seasons, as well as a great deal of ski-ing. I had also done much rock climbing in this country. Owing to the fortune of being stationed in India between the wars, I had taken part in three Himalayan expeditions. Like Noyce, I had trained troops in mountain and snow warfare, and there had been a good deal of incidental climbing in other parts of the world, made possible by military postings. I was 42.

Michael Ward, aged 27, was our Doctor. He is a very fine climber too; he it was who had suggested the Reconnaissance of the south side of Everest two years before, in which he had taken part. Subject to the paramount responsibility of caring for the health of our large caravan, he would be a most useful climbing reserve in case of need.

This party was admittedly a large one. Its size followed logically

28

from our planning, which I will outline shortly. This climbing party was further enlarged by the attachment to the expedition of two others, sponsored respectively by the Medical Research Council and Countryman Films Ltd. The first was Griffith Pugh, a physiologist employed in the Division of Human Physiology of the M.R.C., who had a long experience of what may be termed mountain physiology. He had worked in this capacity at the Middle East School of Mountain and Snow Warfare in Lebanon during the war; more recently he had done some valuable work during the Cho Oyu Expedition. He had some mountaineering experience prior to Cho Oyu, and is a fine skier. Tom Stobart came with us to take a film of the expedition. Highly qualified for work of this nature, he had been to the Himalaya and had accompanied other expeditions to the Antarctic, Africa and North Queensland.

There was considerable discussion in the Joint Committee regarding the two latter additions; the matter was one of policy and quite independent of individual selections. It was obvious that the larger the party the more difficult the task of the leader in creating and conserving its all-important unity of purpose. Moreover, this difficulty is apt to be increased by adding members whose objectives are different from those of the rest of the team. But there was no denying the contribution made by a study of physiology to the problem of Everest in the past, and there remained much still to be brought to light in this sphere. At the very least it could be said that the inclusion of a physiologist was justified as an insurance against failure; there might well have been a need to make further attempts. As regards Stobart, there was already evidence to show that our return to Everest was now attracting a wider public interest than ever before, and the Committee felt that the taking of a film would perhaps be the best way of telling the story to the greatest number of people on our return. There was also, of course, the vital need to make the expedition pay for itself; a film contract would help considerably in this way. In the event, both Pugh and Stobart fitted admirably into the party and helped in more ways than one towards success.

This made a total of thirteen. Reference to this unlucky figure was carefully avoided and I was relieved when, a few months later, I was able to invite Tenzing to join the climbing party. In this and other ways he was to bring us good fortune. His entrance on the stage of Everest comes later.

In addition to the names of those to be included in the expedition, I proposed to the Committee that we should invite a few others who figured in the final short list to consider themselves as reserves. So keen were these and many other mountaineers to assist the expedition that I would be able to call on them to help in our preparations. Moreover, should any member of the party not be able to accompany the expedition when the time came, his replacement would be at hand and already well in the picture. These reserves were J. H. Emlyn Jones, John Jackson, Anthony Rawlinson, Hamish Nicol and, at a later stage, Jack Tucker. It was inspiring to see how these men, whose most cherished dream, far from being realized, was thus held tantalizingly just beyond their grasp, threw themselves into the tasks of preparation which they were invited to undertake.

Before submitting my recommendations, I was very fortunate in being able to avail myself of the generous offer of Lord Horder to examine all the candidates for general fitness. Some earlier expeditions had required the party to pass a rigorous test designed to show whether each man would be able to climb successfully at high altitudes. From personal experience in this test, I was convinced that it was apt to be misleading. The only real proof of adaptability to altitude is on a mountain. Lord Horder's advice on the physique and also on the psychology of those whom he examined was of the greatest value.

* * *

While the selection of the party was going on, it was equally urgent to give a start to the planning and subsequent preparations.

I hope that the problem with which we should be confronted will be familiar after reading the preceding chapter. From a study of it, we had arrived at certain conclusions regarding our own plans for the following year, which may be summarized as follows:

Firstly, the need to allow time for a period of training before we started work on Everest itself. During this period we would be able to become increasingly accustomed to the altitude attainable early in the year, we would get used to our equipment, and it would be an admirable way to work together and get to know one another "on the rope".

Secondly, since we must expect any period of good weather before the monsoon to be short, it was important to be in position and ready in every respect to make an attempt on the summit from the moment when, from experience in previous years, the weather seemed most likely to offer an opportunity. This appeared liable to occur from the middle of May onwards.

Thirdly, it was important to avoid spending more time on the mountain than was necessary to climb it. Earlier parties had suffered not only from the increasing lethargy or deterioration which takes effect high on the mountain, but from the strain and tedium of the task lower down, combined with the cramped and rigorous conditions in which it had to be carried on. We must, in other words, avoid starting operations on Everest unnecessarily soon, consistent with the absolute need to be ready and in position. It would clearly call for a careful calculation of the time problem, judgment and good luck.

Fourthly, we must be able to make the most of the chances offered us by good conditions of snow, wind and weather. We must have enough climbers, equipment and provisions available in the right place and at the right time, and be able to make two or if necessary three attempts, each attempt backed by material and men. From this it followed that the party must be large and that we must take with us all our predictable needs for three full-scale assaults. As a rider to this, our study of the problem had underlined the importance of being so prepared and equipped as to enable us to make the assaults relatively quickly. For this, thorough training and light equipment were important.

Fifthly, we would rely on oxygen to the extent of our ability to carry supplies of it. We would use it for climbing and, in order to prevent or retard deterioration while at the highest camps, we would also use it at night during the Assault, sleeping in oxygen masks.

Lastly, we took into account the limits likely to be placed on the "lift" into the Western Cwm and above of large quantities of stores, drawbacks which made it difficult to provide the desired support. These limits appeared to be set by the dangers of the Icefall, which made it desirable to reduce the journeys through it as far as possible; by the weight of loads which our porters, the Sherpas, could be expected to carry at various altitudes; by the numbers of them sufficiently skilled, as well as willing to make the vital "carry" to the South Col; and finally by the time granted us by the weather to complete the "lift" of the baggage.

Important conclusions had also been reached regarding diet, both as a result of the training expedition of 1952 and the Swiss experiences on Everest in the same year. I have not dealt with these in this chapter as they are the subject of Appendix VI.

From these conclusions or principles emerged a theoretical plan of assault. It may well seem absurd to have drawn up plans in London against the distant moment when a final attempt could be made on the top of Everest. Yet only by making some such plan and entering into considerable detail, only by making certain assumptions based on an unfavourable combination of circumstances, could we work back to the size of the party, the quantities of food, equipment and, in particular, oxygen required to achieve success. We must, in fact, even in October 1952, endeavour to foresee the maximum needs, tempered by the many limiting circumstances and obstacles, in order to climb Everest in May/June 1953. The "plan" was entirely tentative and theoretical; it in no way committed us to any rigid tactics to be employed on the mountain. These could and would be decided only much later, on the scene of operations. Rather than a plan, a basis was laid down from which more detailed planning could take its source, e.g. finally deciding on the climbing party; planning and developing the oxygen supplies and apparatus; ordering the rations, the tents, the mountaineering gear and a multitude of other items. A first edition of this document, "Basis for Planning", was issued to those immediately concerned with our preparations about mid-October; a revised and improved version was distributed early in November, by which time the members of the party had been chosen and could begin to undertake their allotted tasks with its guidance. This paper is of interest in order to compare our forecast of needs and events with those which actually occurred. It is included as Appendix III to this book.

From it I was able to decide, firstly, on the number of climbers and porters required. On the basis of an eventual three assaults, each consisting of two climbers, with others in supporting rôles lower on the mountain, a total of ten seemed the best number. After a detailed calculation of the weight of stores to be carried into the Western Cwm, and of those to be lifted subsequently up the face of Lhotse to the South Col, we arrived at a figure of thirty-four Sherpas. Of these, fourteen would work in the Icefall carrying loads to the lip of the Cwm; another fourteen would shift the loads up the Cwm to a camp we named Advance Base, from which, according to the Swiss experience, it seemed appropriate to initiate the Assault programme. The remaining six were, at that stage of our thinking, intended to accompany each assault, in pairs, from Advance Base to the Col and onwards up the final ridge.

The history of Himalayan expeditions is also one of the weakening of attempts on the summit by sickness. With so large a party whose combined strength would be required to achieve our aim, I was determined that there should be no ambiguity in the responsibilities of a doctor who might also be a climber. In asking Michael Ward to join us, therefore, I made it quite clear that his heavy responsibility would be our health and care, although it was obvious that he would be a most useful reserve for the climbing party should the need arise. Michael unhesitatingly accepted this position.

The ascent was seen as falling into two phases: the period when we would be shifting our stores from a Base Camp, to be located probably near the foot of the Khumbu Icefall, upwards to the head of the Cwm and later to the South Col; and the period of the Assault. The first phase, which we referred to as the "Build-up", was calculated to require up to three weeks. The problem of getting the essential loads into position on the Col presented so many difficulties and imponderable situations that we did not attempt a serious guess at the time required. The Assault period, supposing that only the third party would be successful, assuming certain unfavourable circumstances of fortune and weather, but taking an optimistic forecast of the speed of movement of one of the three parties taking part, was estimated to last over a total period of seven days from Advance Base, until all parties had returned there safely.

In this planning document there was also an estimate of the number of camps to be established, their fluctuating population during the periods of Build-up and Assault and consequently the numbers and types of tents required at each during each period. Most important of all, in view of the amount of preparatory work to be done, were the assumptions made and decisions taken regarding the employment of oxygen. The tactical use of oxygen is dealt with in some detail in Appendix V. I will only mention here that, so urgent to those concerned with its development were firm decisions on this subject, that I was required to outline the theoretical plan at a meeting of the High-Altitude Committee on 14th October, only six days after arriving from Germany.

The need for allowing adequate time for training and acclimatization has already been stressed. Bearing in mind that the best chance of climbing the mountain would probably occur only after the middle of May, and the time required before that period to get our stores into position, it appeared that we should have available for training most of the month of April. The expedition timetable was drawn up so that all our preparations in this country would be completed by mid-February. Travelling to India mainly by sea, we should eventually arrive in the vicinity of Everest towards the end of March; we should then have at our disposal a period of at least three weeks to train before we started work on Everest. For the sake of interest and variety, and because it would be too early in the year to get beyond at most 20,000 feet, this period would be spent in valleys south of the Everest group, where lower peaks and passes abound.

During this period of planning I was seeking advice from several of our earlier Everest climbers, and before finally producing the "Basis for Planning", I sent it to some of them for their criticisms. Among much good advice, I was to remember particularly Norton's words: "The whole history of Himalayan climbing seems to me to emphasize [the fact] that attempts have always been made from too low an

33

assault camp . . . the finalists [have been] defeated by attempting too long a climb on the last day . . . put your assault camp on, or very close under the Southern Summit. Assuming that considerable step cutting will be necessary beyond the Southern Summit I shall never have any great hope of success unless a final camp is so placed." These words, reinforced by Longstaff's recommendation to me to make this final camp my very personal responsibility, remained very much in my thoughts until the day when it had been achieved.

Once this planning basis had been laid down, and with the party selected, the machinery of mounting the expedition, which was already well run-in, could be turned on to full speed ahead. Of these preparations I shall have to tell in the next chapter.

CHAPTER FOUR

PREPARATIONS: TWO

W E now entered upon a period of intense and exciting activity.
A carefully co-ordinated timetable had been drawn up, designed
to ensure that no item of preparatory work should be overlooked and
that each event should be dovetailed into its neighbours; everything
led up to the great moment when our baggage would be stowed
aboard a ship at the beginning of our journey to India. I was able to
gather the party for the first time on 17th November and from then
onwards we met together at intervals of about one month until the
date of departure. It was at once obvious that here was a variety of
talent to take care of all the impedimenta which it was proposed to
employ in our struggle with the mountain; responsibility for obtaining
and finally for assembling the multifarious items of equipment and
stores was smoothly decentralized among the party and our reserves.
With the burden thus distributed on so many enthusiastic and capable
shoulders, I experienced an immense feeling of relief; the tempo of
our preparations would now gather momentum.

Charles Wylie, who had handled all the detailed work regarding
equipment, now became responsible for over-all co-ordination of the
various branches. Anthony Rawlinson, assisted by Wilfrid Noyce,
took over mountaineering equipment; the latter would be in charge
of this item on the mountain. Emlyn Jones, assisted by Ralph Jones,
a promising young climber who had volunteered his services for this
work of preparation, undertook the responsibility for clothing, later
to hand this over to Charles Evans at the time we left this country.
To Michael Westmacott, whose experience as a Sapper was useful,
was handed over the work already started on structural equipment;
he also agreed to look after the problem of tents. George Band, who
had recently completed his National Service in the Royal Corps of
Signals, was an obvious choice for the wireless equipment. He was
also persuaded into nursing, with Griffith Pugh, a most unpopular
"baby"—food. George was to look after weather forecasts to be supplied to us from the Indian Meteorological Service at Alipore. We
were in touch with All-India Radio and the B.B.C. in order that these
forecasts might be broadcast to us daily, starting on 1st May. Tom

Bourdillon already had his hands more than full with the oxygen equipment, which included an experimental Closed-Circuit apparatus that was being developed by the Electro-Medical Research Unit at Stoke Mandeville. I cabled Ed Hillary to ask his help, even at that great distance, with the ordering of sleeping-bags, and at the same time invited him to take on the cooking equipment when the expedition started out on its journey. Meanwhile, this latter and most important item was to be looked after by a Himalayan mountaineer of renown, C. R. Cooke, while my wife undertook to furnish all the kitchen materials. Travel arrangements and the ordering of photographic equipment were Alfred Gregory's task. Charles Wylie, in addition to his secretarial and co-ordinating rôle, was to make all arrangements regarding our Sherpa porters; he would be our Transport Officer during the expedition. Michael Ward was naturally left to obtain the medical stores and equipment. A long and involved list of miscellaneous items fell to the thankless lot of Emlyn Jones, Ralph Jones and my wife. But if you should have the impression that, after unloading all these responsibilities on to others, I was now without a job, I must firmly disillusion you; there was, indeed, an enormous amount to do.

In thus outlining the distribution of our preparatory work, I must explain that a good deal had already been done, before mid-November, under most of these headings. Rations and oxygen were already well in hand. Since my return to London Griffith Pugh had been busy with the problems of diet.

As regards oxygen, the situation at the beginning of October was far from satisfactory. So especially important to our success was this item considered to be that the Joint Himalayan Committee, at a meeting held on 9th October, had agreed with my plea that they should be responsible for its sufficient and timely provision. Peter Lloyd, a member of the Committee, who had taken part in the Everest Expedition of 1938, had undertaken to control the work of development and provision of the Open-Circuit apparatus on which it had been decided to rely for the main part, and to be answerable to the Committee for this task. He was well qualified to do so, both professionally and because he had been in charge of oxygen equipment on Tilman's expedition, when he had used oxygen successfully up to the highest point reached that year. By mid-October Lloyd had the oxygen problem in hand, co-ordinating the activities of the firms contributing particular items of equipment for the oxygen sets and for charging the cylinders, and acting as liaison with the advisory High-Altitude Committee under the chairmanship of Professor Sir Bryan Matthews, the eminent Cambridge physiologist. As Lloyd's executive in this all-important work, I had secured the part-time services of Alfred Bridge, an old climbing companion of myself and some other members of the party. To those of us who knew this fine old-stager, the addition of Bridge to our helpers was a great event in the history of the expedition. His enthusiasm, his immense energy and fixity of purpose—even more, his power of inspiring others to join in any enterprise in which he is engaged—are quite exceptional. I knew that Alf Bridge would never rest until our oxygen consignment was on its way. From the time he joined the active ranks of our supporters, we had no need to worry about the oxygen. Under the wise and able direction of Peter Lloyd; with the help of Mr Mensforth of Normalair; of Sir Robert Davis of Siebe Gorman; of Dr John Cotes of the Pneumoconiosis Research Unit, Cardiff, who was responsible for the production of our oxygen masks; with the sound and experienced advice of Bryan Matthews and his Committee, we were to be well equipped with this essential commodity.

Apart from the more familiar gear—thousands of feet of rope and line, pitons, snap links, ice-hammers and axes, the mountaineering equipment included certain unusual items which it seemed wise to add after studying the difficulties encountered by the Swiss in the Icefall and on the Lhotse Face. We knew that, apart from crevasses of alpine dimensions, there were likely to be a few vast chasms and that these were apt to occur at the sudden change of gradient where the surface ice of the Western Cwm dips over into the Khumbu Icefall. The Swiss had bridged one immense gap at this point with ropes, for no logs long enough could be obtained from the valley. They had used one set of ropes for the climbers and porters to cross by what is known as the "tyrolean" technique, and another to hoist the loads. To deal with similar obstacles, we took a light metal 30-foot sectional ladder, composed of five 6-foot lengths. It would be simple to carry and fit together and could be moved, if need be, from one crevasse to another. By doing so we would be employing methods used in the earliest days of Alpine mountaineering. We were also presented by the Yorkshire Ramblers with a 30-foot rope ladder to deal with any vertical ice pitches.

When discussing the problem of gaps with friends in London, it was suggested that we might contrive some sort of catapult, carrying a rope and armed with a grapnel which would become firmly embedded in the ice on the far bank of the obstacle. This proposal formed the subject of an interesting demonstration in the somewhat confined space of the garden at the Royal Geographical Society. The gadget produced was extremely simple—two toggles for use as hand grips, at either end of a length of rubber rope, consisting of multiple strands of elastic. The grapnel was a wicked-looking affair, a kind of large wooden bullet armed with a number of hooked barbs. To this was attached a long nylon line. While watching the expert laying out yard upon yard of this line, I expressed concern regarding the range of this weapon, for he had paid out some 150 yards, in contrast to the 80 yards' length of the garden. Reassured on this point, Charles Wylie and I took station at about a 6-foot interval, each holding a grip, while the demonstrator stretched the elastic behind us and attached to it the warhead. Just when Charles and I were about to be pulled backwards off our feet, the missile was released. It shot high into the air with the nylon cord in its wake and was going very strongly over the wall into Exhibition Road, where it would most probably have speared a taxi or some unsuspecting pedestrian. Most fortunately, we were spared such a calamity by a tree, which intervened to arrest its flight some fifty feet up. On the whole, we thought, it was unlikely that the famous Icefall or the Cwm would reserve for us any surprises meriting this kind of treatment.

We did, however, allow ourselves to be carried away by the prospect of dangerous snow, notably on the Face of Lhotse, into taking with us a 2-inch mortar, borrowed from the Army in the guise of an avalanche gun. This little weapon is great fun to fire and produces a bang out of all proportion to its size; the explosion would be sufficient, we considered, to dislodge any lurking avalanche for miles around. It is possible that Charles Wylie and I were biased in this matter by our own professional allegiance, but we knew that a similar technique is used in the Alps for the purpose. However it may be, the stir which our proposal caused in political circles when permission was sought almost decided us to leave the mortar out of the inventory. When, at a later stage, two .22 rifles were added in order to provide fresh game for our larder, we were under grave suspicion as to our real motives in visiting Nepal.

Other aids to getting up the mountain were carefully considered and eventually rejected. Realizing the critical nature of the Lhotse Face and the difficulty of carrying to the South Col the quantities of stores which we estimated at that time would be required, we were much attracted by the idea of taking with us a light sledge and winch, by which loads could be hoisted at least some way up the great slope. The difficulties of feeding and operating a suitable engine to work the winch, the alternative labour of winching by hand and the uncertainty of finding suitable terrain up which to run the sledge, caused us to drop this idea. Another original but less practical suggestion was turned down with some regret. This would-be inventor envisaged the construction of a spring-loaded harpoon, which would combine this primary function with that of an ice-axe; it would fire a grapnel from the South Col of Everest to the summit, over 3,000 feet up, invisible and perhaps a mile distant. Not only would we thus have a stout handline by which we could easily haul ourselves to the top, but the cord was to be painted with luminous paint so that we could continue on our way if overtaken by darkness. Carrying this fertile line of thought still further, our correspondent pointed out that we should have ample warning of the dangerous gusts of wind, which would cause the cord to vibrate, thus giving us time to brace ourselves against the risk of being swept off the summit ridge.

Clothing, tents and bedding were the objects of our very particular concern. The effects of cold, enhanced as they are by wind and altitude, are not confined to the physical injury of frostbite, serious as this is. Cold and wind exhaust the climber and make inroads on his morale; as such they are dangerous and subtle enemies. The design of clothing to combat this danger had made great strides since those early days when our Everest climbers even succeeded in climbing on the upper reaches of the North Face clad in tweeds, felt hats and ordinary Alpine boots, but there was plenty of evidence to show that subsequent parties, even in recent times, have been unduly handicapped as well as injured by insufficiently specialized clothing. The problem is the more difficult of solution because it is imperative to reduce weights to a minimum. We paid a visit to the Polar Research Institute at Cambridge, where we received many ideas and much good advice; we enlisted the services of many British and foreign firms.

In the end, our garments conformed to a familiar pattern; the real improvements were in design and material. Our outer suits were of cotton-nylon windproof material, and both smock and trousers were lined with nylon. The combined weight of an average-sized suit of this type was little over 3¾ lb. The smock had a hood with a visor to provide protection against wind and snow. To wear inside the windproofs at high altitude, the climbers would have a two-piece suit of down, the jacket with a hood, like the outer blouse. This down clothing reduces the number of woollen garments needed, but each of us was provided with two featherweight jerseys and one heavy pullover.

One of the main clothing difficulties in the Himalaya had been that of footwear. The conventionally constructed mountaineering boot is apt to allow the cold to strike through both soles and uppers, and because of the tendency of snow to melt, even at great heights, moisture is absorbed either from the feet, or the snow or both, and then freezes the boot to the hardness of rock. With the graphic story of Annapurna fresh in our minds, I decided that we must be equipped

39

with two types of boot, both specially constructed to give exceptional protection against cold. The one must be sufficiently light and close-fitting to enable difficult climbing to be done lower on the mountain, including the Icefall, and it must be durable; the other must give real insulation against extreme cold during the Assault, but would be required only for the upper part of the mountain.

The first type of boot, weighing on an average about 3 lb. 12 oz., was essentially similar in design to the normal mountaineering boot but had a double leather upper with a fur lining between the layers. The leather was specially treated to prevent freezing. The more specialized boot for high-altitude climbing had uppers insulated with almost one inch of "Tropal" (an unwoven web of kapok fibres) contained between a very thin layer of glacé kid and an inner waterproof lining. The sole, instead of being made of the normal heavy treaded rubber, was made from a microcellular rubber, much lighter in addition to having better insulating properties. The weight of an average pair of these boots was about 4 lb. 4 oz.

There was no less need to protect the hands. Here the problem was increased by the need to do intricate manual jobs, such as loading and operating a camera, fixing crampons and, to a lesser extent, wielding an ice-axe. After careful thought, an outer gauntlet of windproof cotton was chosen, enclosing either a down or a woollen mitt; both were provided. Next to the skin would be a loose-fitting silk glove; apart from its value in providing additional warmth to the hands inside the mitts, it had been found that, provided the silk glove is retained, these outer layers can be safely discarded for brief spells when it is necessary to perform some intricate task with the hands.

Apart from finding a material which would be truly wind-resistant, and if possible warm as well as light, we considered carefully the design of our tents. In general, it would be convenient to camp on a two-man basis at high altitude, each tent unit being thus light and mobile, as well as capable of being pitched on a restricted space. There would be occasions, however, when a larger tent would be more economical as well as being warmer and more congenial; we knew, too, that our Sherpas were gregarious and found no discomfort in sleeping on the sardine-tin principle.

Our standard tents were the conventional two-man ridge design with a sleeve entrance at both ends, enabling each one to be joined to its neighbour so as to provide internal communication between tents. Apart from minor improvements in the matter of fittings, the only novelty about these tents was the cloth used. This, a cotton-nylon weave, proofed with Mystolen, had been shown both by laboratory and field tests to be exceptionally tough and wind-resistant, as well as light. These standard "Meade" tents weighed about 15 lb.

In addition, it was decided to take two large dome-shaped tents, each capable of holding twelve men, to ensure extra comfort at the main camps. Although they were comparatively heavy—one weighed 110 lb. and the other 85 lb.—we hoped to erect one of them at our Advance Base. At the opposite end of the scale, and bearing in mind the critical matter of weight of the equipment to be lifted from the Western Cwm upwards, we decided on three small Assault tents, one of which was intended for a final camp high up on the South-East ridge. One of the three was a smaller version of the conventional "Meade"; the second, of a new design, was ordered from the United States; the third, designed by Mr Campbell Secord, was lozenge or blister-shaped. The weights of these miniature tents averaged 8 lb. Unless we were to increase very materially the cost and weight of our baggage, tents would always be in short supply on the mountain, and a complicated scheme for their movement at each phase was worked out in London as a part of our planning.

Our sleeping-bags were manufactured variously in Canada, New Zealand and in this country to designs decided on as a result of trials carried out in the Alps. Each climber would have an inner and an outer bag of down, the fabric of which was nylon. The total weight was about 9 lb. Our air mattresses were expected to be an improvement on earlier models. In order to solve the problem of preventing the cold striking up between the air-filled inner tubes, and also to ensure greater comfort, two layers of tubes were superimposed one above the other, the upper tubes lying in the grooves between the lower ones. By inflating the lower tubes fully, but leaving the upper layer only partly air-filled, a very comfortable surface resulted.

Wireless sets were taken for two purposes: inter-communication between camps on the mountain and reception of weather bulletins. A number of very small and light equipments were presented to the expedition to fill the former need.

Cooking-stoves were another item to which we attached special importance. One most significant physiological need at high altitude is to drink considerable quantities of liquid. For a number of reasons, this is very difficult to achieve in a high camp. The snow has first to be melted; the process is a very long one, partly because the heat generated by the average cooker is reduced and so much of it is wasted. A special aluminium shield invented by my friend C. R. Cooke was attached to our Primus and Butane gas stoves, with the object of retaining the heat in a jacket around the cooking vessels.

The question of diet was a most controversial one. Since there is an Appendix dealing fully with the subject, I will only mention briefly here that we were guided in our provisioning by Service experience. We accepted as our basic diet two types of composite ration, one of them in current use by the Army—the so-called "Compo" ration, made up in fourteen-man-day packs, for use at periods other than the Assault. Its contents were adapted specially to meet the diet scale recommended by Pugh. The Assault ration, a small 3-lb. one-man-day pack, was made up to suit our particular needs at high altitude, for use at and above Advance Base.

Oxygen equipment is the subject of Appendix V. The two essential requirements were that it should be light and that it should have a good endurance; that is, the need to reload with fresh supplies of oxygen should, ideally, be obviated, or, at least, reduced to a minimum. Basically, as I have said, we were relying on a fully proven system based on the "Open-Circuit" principle; that is, an apparatus by which oxygen is administered to the climber from a bottle carried on the back through the medium of a mask which also allows air to enter. It is then breathed out into the surrounding air. Under this system, there is thus no conservation of the oxygen. Once breathed, it is lost. The fact that we had decided to rely to so great an extent on oxygen and to develop an apparatus on the Open-Circuit principle for this purpose was partly a recognition of the advocacy of Professor George Finch, who had been insistent on the need and the system ever since he had himself used it on the mountain in 1922.

The experimental equipment constructed by Dr R. B. Bourdillon and his son Tom, which we also intended to take, was based on the "Closed-Circuit" principle. Under this system, the climber receives one hundred per cent oxygen from the bottle; no air enters, or should be allowed to enter, the mask. A proportion of the oxygen breathed is conserved and re-breathed, thus increasing considerably the "life" of the storage bottles and reducing the problem of their stock-piling. If this system, still in an experimental stage in regard to work at high altitudes, should prove successful, it might greatly simplify our task.

Despite all efforts to limit it, the weight of our oxygen equipment was a matter of the greatest concern. Although we realized that the improvement in performance for a given weight of our apparatus over any previous equipment used on Everest was considerable, the fact remained that it was both bulky and heavy. This was in no way the fault of our advisers, or the producing and assembling firms. The simple truth is that the task was taken in hand far too late to enable any radically modified design to be studied and constructed. Nothing could have been more splendid than the devotion with which all concerned worked against time to meet our requirements. Our worries about this were evidently understood by others, less directly concerned but no less anxious to find a solution. A number of suggestions poured in, unfortunately many of them long after we had perforce decided on the oxygen policy and details of design.

A most attractive, if impracticable idea was put forward to arm ourselves with a bigger and better mortar, and with it to fire our oxygen bottles like bombs, from the Western Cwm up to the South Col. As we were to discover later, the surface of the Col makes hard landing and it seems likely that, however constructed, the bottles would not merely have bounced but burst, quite aside from the fun of indulging in a high-level game of hunt-the-bottle over a wide area. We were also alarmed by the unhappy prospect of seeing our early efforts falling short and rolling, with gathering momentum, down thousands of feet back to the firing-point. It was also tempting to follow up another suggestion, that of laying a pipeline all the way up the Lhotse Face and onwards along the South-East ridge, through which a supply of oxygen would be passed from our supplies in the Cwm. The pipe would be furnished with taps at which the weary climbers could pause and "take a swig" at intervals on their journey. On consideration, we decided that it would be preferable to carry the bottles, ungainly and heavy though they were. Again, we were adjured to lessen the burden of our apparatus by attaching to ourselves a hydrogen balloon, nicely charged so as just not to lay us open to the accusation of cheating by making an aerial ascent of the mountain. This vision of the summit pair tiptoeing upwards, their feet barely brushing the snow, was only dispelled when we learned the monstrous dimensions of the balloon required to provide the "lift".

If yet another notion had been adopted, we might have put ourselves into pressurized suits and, operating the pressurizing machinery by an attachment to the foot or allowing the wind to turn a small propeller worn elegantly on our fronts, have tackled the manifest climbing diffi- culties of the Lhotse Face looking very like advertisements for "Michelin" tyres. This again had to be turned down. In more serious vein was the project for dropping the bulk of our gear, including oxygen, into the Western Cwm by air; the question of an air lift to the South Col was even mooted. A study of this suggestion was made by the Air Ministry and it was shown that the technical problems would be very great. So uncertain, in fact, would a successful drop be that it would, in any case, be necessary to duplicate all the stores with which this experi- ment was to be made, unless we were either to accept the risks of having them landed in Tibet or of diverting our energies to rescue and salvage work on the wreckage of the aircraft.

*   *   *

Party Meetings; Meetings of Committees and sub-Committees; discussions with numerous experts; visits to the Continent to consult fellow Himalayan comrades and to inspect equipment; broadcasts; articles for *The Times*; a bulky daily mail bag; tests of equipment and, not least, social obligations—these things kept us continually active between November and February. During the first part of this period we were working in an atmosphere of increasing suspense and anxiety regarding the outcome of the gallant attempt then being made by the Swiss, who were trying to crown with success their magnificent earlier effort in the spring. Our worry was not so much lest they should climb the mountain, although it was natural to hope that, now we were so far ahead in our preparations, the prospect would not be removed from before our eyes. Our real concern was the deadline for ordering the equipment and stores; a date had been fixed when we must do so, in order to leave a bare minimum of time for the various items to be produced and to reach the packers; these latter in turn would have an enormous amount to do before the sailing date. 10th December was the deadline. This situation involved a considerable financial risk to the Committee, causing understandable anxiety to R. W. Lloyd, its conscientious Treasurer.

At the beginning of December, I took a party consisting of Wylie, Gregory and Pugh to test certain items of our equipment and diet in Switzerland. At the time of leaving there was still no definite news of the Swiss result, although a number of unconfirmed reports credited them variously with triumph and near success. We would be returning to this country on 8th December, and we left well knowing that all our effort thus far might be in vain. But this in no way lessened the enjoyment of this rehearsal for Everest. We spent a day in Paris in order to discuss and order equipment from Gaston Rébuffat, a friend and climbing companion of mine and one of our most enthusiastic Continental helpers. Gaston is one of the foremost guides in the Alps and was a member of the Annapurna Expedition.

We chose as our testing-ground the Jungfraujoch, an 11,500-foot saddle at the head of the Aletsch glacier in the Bernese Oberland. Situated between two of that well-known trinity of peaks, the Eiger, Mönch and Jungfrau, we reckoned that in mid-winter this Col might bear comparison with that other Col, similarly related to three yet greater giants, on the real stage of our mission. And so it proved to be. We found just the conditions needed to try out our equipment.

It was blowing a blizzard when, after the long, enclosed train journey in the very bowels of the Eiger, we emerged on to the terrace above the station, which in summer is crowded with tourists. We had to fight our way in the teeth of the gale, fortunately over a distance

44

of only a few yards, to the crest of the Joch in order to set up our little camp of experimental tents; the conditions were so bad that it was no easy job to erect them. A scene of wild confusion reigned around us, with snow being torn off the surrounding slopes and the enclosing peaks. Mönch and Jungfrau were shrouded in ominous cloud. That first night the temperature dropped to −20° C., which we expected would probably be as low as any we should have to endure on Everest. We were testing a variety of clothing, boots, tents, bedding, food and cooking-stoves; some of these items in embarrassing quantities for the short time at our disposal. For instance, we each had no fewer than eight different designs of high-altitude boot. We had first to discard a few of these out of hand, and then to wear one type of boot on each foot during each day. As for clothing, while the models and materials were also varied, we had fewer suits available; we had, therefore, to exchange windproofs each day and compare notes at the end of the period. In the same way we changed from one tent and sleeping-bag to another.

Of the four days spent on the Jungfraujoch, two were brilliantly fine and two were stormy. On one glorious day, two of us were able to climb the Mönch, from the summit of which we had all the Alps spread before us, unobscured by a single cloud. On the other, a larger party made an excursion on skis across the Ewigschneefeld to a point on the ridge below the Gross Fiescherhorn. We had mutually agreed from the start that we were not putting our own fortitude to the test; there would be plenty of enforced opportunities for that later on. When the conditions became unbearable, therefore, we retreated from our bleak little camp into the shelter of the Jungfraujoch Hotel, comforting ourselves over beer or coffee with the reflection that only thus could we draw sound conclusions on how our gear was standing up to the rigorous conditions outside. The experience of this winter journey to Switzerland enabled us to order on the spot down clothing and to arrange for special crampons to be made in Grindelwald to fit the high-altitude boots which we had finally decided on.

The evening before we left the Jungfraujoch I received a telegram bearing the news that the Swiss Expedition had at last abandoned its attempt, after holding out in the face of appalling conditions for several weeks. While we were glad to know at last that we should now be going to Everest and thankful that the prolonged uncertainty, which was about to cause a crisis in our own preparations, was ended, we could not but feel admiration and sympathy for the fine Swiss mountaineers, and especially for those who had had the determination and courage to go twice to Everest in one year. When, much later on Everest, I had to face up to the ever-present possibility of our having

45

to continue our effort in the autumn of this year, I had to admit that it was a most unwelcome prospect. I was then able fully to appreciate the spirit of Chevalley, Lambert and Tenzing for what they had done.

On return to London, then, our first action was to give the "all clear" on the equipment orders. Letters and telegrams had been prepared before we left England so as to simplify this procedure. In addition, a most important meeting was called of representatives from those firms whose equipment we had been testing and on which we were now in a position to comment. Allowing for the Christmas holidays, this left about one month for all our orders to reach the packers, the final date for this being 15th January, 1953.

About mid-January, too, we held a Meet of the party and reserves at the Climbers' Club Hut, Helyg, in North Wales. This was an excellent opportunity to get to know one another better, and the weather smiled upon the occasion. Tom Bourdillon also wanted us to try various types of carrying frame for the Open-Circuit oxygen apparatus. He himself had already carried out a number of field trials with his Closed-Circuit apparatus and on this occasion he and George Band toiled up the Nant Gwynant side of Snowdon wearing it on a warm day. According to George, this demanded considerable strength of mind, so I tried it myself during a short distance uphill near the hut. I nearly exploded with heat and discomfort, but Tom was at pains to explain that his pet engine thrives only in extreme cold. It was admittedly an exceptionally sunny day for January.

Altogether, the occasion was a very happy one. I felt then, as indeed I was to find later, that we should have little difficulty in settling down as a really effective team when we came to grips with Everest. I also knew that we had in our reserves men who would most worthily fill any gaps which might occur.

Meanwhile, the centre of activity was gradually shifting to the warehouses of Messrs. Andrew Lusk at Wapping Wall, where packing for the expedition was in the capable hands of Stuart Bain. Equipment was steadily coming in from the beginning of the New Year, and by the date it was all due to have arrived very few items were outstanding. In all these cases the reasons had been fully explained, and I cannot praise too highly the wonderful co-operation which we received from every supplying firm. The assistance given by those who helped us on our way almost amounted to fervour.

I had invited Charles Evans, Ralph Jones and Wilfrid Noyce to become for a time a working party to deal with the problem of packing, and before all the stores were gathered in, they had a carefully prepared plan ready, designed to avoid any premature unpacking or re-sorting of our gear. The packing cases were made up in coolie loads of about 60 lb. and marked according to the point on our journey to the mountain at which they should be opened. It proved of the utmost value, both to have this excellent arrangement and because at least two members of the party had an intimate knowledge of the whereabouts of every item among our small mountain of cases. Among many jobs which were done well to contribute to our success, the packing of the equipment stands very high; it was of a quite exceptional standard. Nor must I forget the wonderful work done by my wife, Mrs Goodfellow and Mrs Mowbray-Green in sewing many hundreds of name tapes on to our garments, thus avoiding a possible cause of contention among us on the mountain.

Shortly after returning from the oxygen frame tests in Wales, we went to Farnborough to experience an oxygen test in the decompression chamber at the Royal Aircraft Establishment. I was at that time suffering from a severe cold and was considered unfit to take part, but I had an interesting time as a spectator, peering through a porthole and watching the very odd behaviour of some of my companions when, at an atmospheric pressure in the chamber equivalent to about 29,000 feet, their oxygen masks were removed one after another. Griff Pugh was a horrifying sight; so short of oxygen that his tongue was hanging out, he stubbornly insisted to Dr John Cotes, the designer of our masks, who was in charge of the test, that he did not require to have the mask replaced on his face. Altogether it was a revealing experience showing, as it was intended to, how insidious is the onset of anoxia, or the ill-effects of oxygen lack.

The oxygen was to travel separately, after our departure. Despite all efforts to get it ready in time, so late had this equipment been taken in hand that only a part of our needs, that urgently required for the training period, could be ready by about 20th February. We have to thank the Royal Air Force for agreeing to lift this to India in a replacement aircraft and the Indian Air Force for taking it on from Delhi to Kathmandu. The weight of this first consignment was 2,000 lb. A second consignment, weighing 3,000 lb. and consisting of the supplies calculated to be necessary to meet the theoretical Assault plan, would be sent a month later by the same method. I had asked Major Jimmy Roberts, an officer of the Gurkhas and a Himalayan climber of great experience, to meet this consignment at Kathmandu and escort it to Thyangboche. It would be essential for him to arrive there by 15th April in order to conform with the over-all plan. The dispatching arrangements were left in the safe hands of Alf Bridge.

I was naturally anxious to meet the Swiss team as soon as possible after their return from Nepal. A meeting was arranged in Zürich on 25th January, and Charles Evans came with me on a twenty-four-hour visit to that city. We were most kindly received by Dr Feuz of the Foundation for Alpine Research and there met Dr Chevalley, leader of their autumn expedition, Raymond Lambert, who had climbed so high with Tenzing in the spring of the previous year, and other members of their expedition. We were shown all their equipment and received a very frank and generous "hand over" of their knowledge and experience. There was one point which might be of great importance to us and required instant action. Lambert was able to point out on photographs the approximate positions where charged oxygen cylinders had been left high on the mountain. Should we be lucky enough to find these, and provided we could tap them, this would be a very useful bonus over and above our own supplies. With the help of the Swiss, contact was quickly established between the German firm of Dräger of Lübeck, which supplied their sets, and our own assembly firm of Normalair. Eric Mensforth, the head of that firm, who had taken throughout a close and practical interest in the assembly of our Assault oxygen equipment, intervened directly, and following a visit by Peter Fitt to Lübeck, adaptors were produced with remarkable speed and efficiency. Some months later, we were to be very grateful to all concerned in this fine job of work.

With the approach of the sailing date for the main party, the period of intensive preparatory work by ourselves and many selfless helpers at last drew to a close. There is no better testimonial to this work than the Inventory and Packing Lists, both of them monumental documents which sum up these labours, not the least of them secretarial. It is appropriate here to mention the splendid assistance given us by our Secretaries, Ann Debenham and Elizabeth Johnson, also the voluntary help of Bill Packard and Norman Hardy. Jack Tucker, too, one of the reserves, replaced Charles Wylie for a short period.

But there remained one more thing to be done. When the Swiss Expedition just failed in the spring, they had decided to send out another expedition with the least possible delay, to make another attempt in the autumn. This decision was made only in June, and the second party arrived at the foot of the mountain too late. By the time they had established themselves at the upper end of the Western Cwm, the winter winds were already buffeting the mountain; from that moment there was little hope of success. They held out in terrible conditions of discomfort and mental strain, but never succeeded in getting within striking distance of the summit. We, like the Swiss, had received the sanction of the Nepalese Government to visit the area of Everest during the whole year. Should we fail in the spring the Joint Himalayan Committee decided that the attempt should be continued after the monsoon. It was realized that, in order to be ready to take advantage of any post-monsoon lull, an autumn attempt must be prepared during the absence of the expedition in Nepal, and regardless of its fortunes. Moreover, funds had to be set aside for this.

Just before leaving for India, therefore, I indulged in some more crystal-gazing, looking this time into our eventual needs in men and material to reinforce our present expedition which, after a period of rest, would return to the attack. Assumptions were made regarding the numbers of fresh climbers and amounts of the main items of equipment as well as food, which must be sent out, and the dates to which we would work in such an event. All the preparatory labour to bring this about was taken on by Emlyn Jones, who thus replaced Charles Wylie as Organizing Secretary and would himself be a member of the reinforcement party. Emlyn had not spared himself in our interest since the day when I had to tell him that he would not be in the team, but that he was at the top of the list of reserves. His generosity and selflessness in thus continuing to work for Everest, wishing us success yet ensuring against a temporary setback, are beyond praise.

One of the last and most thrilling events just before leaving was a visit to Buckingham Palace by myself in company with R. W. Lloyd of the Joint Committee. We were commanded to give an account of the expedition's plans and prospects to H.R.H. The Duke of Edinburgh, who had graciously consented to become our Patron. It was vastly encouraging that we should be watched with interest by one who places such value on the spirit of enterprise and high endeavour.

Part III

APPROACH

CHAPTER FIVE

TO NEPAL

ARRANGEMENTS were made for the party to travel to India in the S.S. *Stratheden* on 12th February, less two members who were to leave later by air but arrive well in advance, making preliminary arrangements for our passage through India, entry into Nepal and carrying out other initial tasks.

We did not send the bulk of the party by sea merely to save money, although the resources of our treasury at that time were meagre enough. Some of us were very tired after the intensive preparations for Everest and other work during the previous months; we were in need of mental and physical rest. There is no better way of ensuring this than by the enforced relaxation of a sea voyage. An air journey, invaluable as it is in many ways, would give us virtually no rest between leaving our desks or other labours in England and becoming involved in the many new problems awaiting us in India and Nepal. Most important of all, to my mind, was the further chance which life in a ship would provide for us to settle down as a team in ideal conditions, accompanied by no discomfort, urgency or stress.

Excluded from the main party were Tom Bourdillon, whose work on the Closed-Circuit oxygen would not be completed in time, and Griffith Pugh, for whom separate arrangements had been made by the Medical Research Council. A few days before sailing I succumbed to an antrum infection and had to go to hospital for an operation. I had regretfully to agree to cancel my sea passage and travel at the end of the month by air, happily in company with Tom Bourdillon. The fact that I was able to accompany the expedition despite this last-minute hitch and to take an active part on the mountain was due to the skill of Mr Hargrove, M.B.B., F.R.C.S., and the care I received from the staff of the Quarry Hill Nursing Home at Shrewsbury.

As the time approached for our departure, we became aware that there was a growing public interest in the expedition. Some of us appeared in Sound Broadcast and Television programmes; there were lectures, Press interviews and articles to write for *The Times*. This interest reached a peak at Tilbury, where the six members travelling by sea were under fire by the B.B.C. and Press correspondents for one and a half hours. I was not sorry to escape this ordeal. The brunt of it was borne, in my absence, by Charles Wylie, who acquitted himself very well.

With the main party safely launched, Charles Evans and Alfred Gregory (Greg for short) departed by air on 20th February as Advance Party; Tom Bourdillon and I took flight eight days later, and Griffith Pugh was the last to leave, on 1st March. The expedition was on its way. Meanwhile, Hillary and Lowe were also approaching the rendezvous in Nepal from the opposite end of the world. Lowe, travelling by sea, was due to arrive in Bombay in time to prepare for and receive the main party from this country; Hillary, whose bees were in a busy state at that time of year, flew *via* Calcutta to Kathmandu at the beginning of March. Our various journeys by air, sea, rail and, ultimately, on foot, converged on Kathmandu, the capital city of the Kingdom of Nepal. Throughout, we were most kindly cared for and our travel problems were smoothed by the P. & O. Steam Navigation Company and the British Overseas Airways Corporation. In India we were looked after largely at the initiative of the Himalayan Club. Being a member of this Club, I had presumed on their kindness so far as virtually to place all problems connected with our passage through India and our arrival in Nepal in their capable hands. At each stage of our Indian journey, members of the Club, the United Kingdom High Commission in India and officials of Burma Shell went out of their way to steer us through and offer us hospitality; we are very grateful to them all.

On 3rd March, Tom Bourdillon and I flew over the Terai—the densely wooded foothills of Nepal—into the open Valley beyond. As we skimmed low over the final ridge, the high Himalaya could be seen spread out over a great distance, mile upon mile of remote mountains making a crenellated backcloth of dazzling whiteness behind the browns and greens of the intervening ridges. We could see countless peaks between the bastions of Annapurna, the highest mountain yet climbed, and Everest, so soon to be assailed by ourselves.

During the following few days, those of us who travelled by air gathered in this fascinating city of Kathmandu, to be joined at the end of the first week of March by the main party. They were met and most kindly entertained by Professor George Finch of the National Physical Laboratory of India, one of the outstanding mountaineers at the time when British climbers were making a first acquaintance with Everest. The latter part of their journey had been more tedious than ours, for it involved long, dusty stages from Bombay in a succession of trains, degenerating into a ride on a lorry perched on top of our mountainous baggage, and finally an eighteen-mile march over the ridges which bar entry into the Valley of Nepal. The temperature in India was exceptionally hot for that season—little below 100°F. in the shade—and in the heat and dust they had the anxiety of watching over the transference of 473 packages, weighing seven and a half tons, from ship to train, from large trains to smaller trains, from the miniature Nepal railway to lorries and, finally, from road head in southern Nepal to the conveyor trays of an overhead ropeway on the last stage, over the high ridges to Kathmandu.

Despite all efforts to speed it up, our luggage reached the far terminal of the ropeway only on 8th March, one day before we had planned to start our march. Even after agreeing to a twenty-four-hour postponement, it remained doubtful whether we should be able to get away on time. Great assistance was given us by a contingent of Indian Sappers engaged in constructing a new road over the ridges into the Valley; the Nepalese Army most kindly made space for us to install a baggage dépôt in their lines at the town of Bhadgaon, eight miles east of Kathmandu, whither we arranged to ferry the loads as they descended from the ropeway. This would save us a whole day's march from the city and help to compensate for the inevitable loss of time on the programme.

Meanwhile, our party was being looked after in delightfully informal comfort by our Ambassador to Nepal, Christopher Summerhayes, and his staff. For the third year in succession, Mr Summerhayes was thus helping British climbers on their long journey which was to end at the top of Everest. By negotiating diplomatic approval for these missions; by housing us and caring for our needs in transit; by forwarding our mail in both directions; by these and many other services he, his First Secretary, Colonel Proud, and all others at the British Embassy in Kathmandu, have played a very valuable part in the final triumph. At the start of a big expedition the conditions and circumstances of the final send-off leave their stamp on the memory, just as the prospect of a warm, friendly and comforting welcome on return provides a happy train of thought at more cheerless moments on a high mountain. We could not have had a better send-off, or welcome on return.

Charles Wylie had flown from the ship at Bombay with Tom Stobart, to take up his arduous duties as Transport Officer. They had had the good fortune to travel as far as Calcutta with B. R. Goodfellow, who had done so much for the expedition in London. On his way through Calcutta, where he was very kindly looked after by Mr Charles Crawford, President of the Himalayan Club, Charles Wylie met Dr Mull of Alipore Observatory on behalf of George Band, to discuss our requirements for weather forecasts.

We had requested the Himalayan Club to select for us twenty of the best Sherpas for work at high altitude and to arrange for their arrival at Kathmandu early in March. The Sherpas are hill-men whose home is in the district of Sola Khumbu in Eastern Nepal. Originally of Tibetan stock, to whose language theirs is closely akin, they are small, sturdy men with all the sterling qualities of born mountaineers. Many of them have migrated to Darjeeling in the Indian State of Bengal where, with the encouragement of the Himalayan Club, they have made porterage for foreign expeditions to the Himalaya a livelihood. First employed by the British expedition to Everest in 1921, they have taken part in every subsequent expedition to that mountain. Cheerful, loyal and courageous, possessed of exceptional hardihood, a few of them have now reached a good standard of proficiency as snow and ice climbers, and this has been recognized by the award of a "Tiger" badge by the Himalayan Club. They are wonderful companions on a mountain.

These were to be the men intended for carrying our loads to the head of the Western Cwm, thence to the South Col; a select band of six from this number were to be earmarked for the Assault parties. They duly arrived on 4th March, and with them was our Sirdar, the already renowned Tenzing. His Himalayan climbing experience, and particularly his association with Everest, were quite exceptional. As a young porter he had first taken part in the Reconnaissance expedition to Everest in 1935, and since then he had joined the ranks of nearly every expedition to Everest. When he became one of our climbing party, he was thirty-nine, and it was his sixth visit to the mountain. In addition, he had participated in several other major Himalayan ventures, notably the French expedition to Nanda Devi in 1951, when he climbed the East Peak of that great mountain. By virtue of his wonderful exploit in 1952 with the Swiss guide Lambert, reaching a point on the South-East ridge of Everest only about 1,000 feet from the top, Tenzing established himself not only as the foremost climber of his race but as a mountaineer of world standing.

It was a meeting we had looked forward to with keen anticipation. After his gruelling experiences in 1952, especially his journey with Lambert in the late autumn to the South Col, Tenzing's health had been affected and there had been considerable doubt as to whether he would be fit enough to join us. Such is Tenzing's enthusiasm and spirit, however, that he had written to me while still convalescing to offer his services, if only as far as the top of the Icefall. By the time we met in the Embassy garden, he appeared to be fully restored, if still a little fine-drawn; at any rate, it was obvious that there was no doubt at all in his mind as to his own fitness and the part he hoped to play. We were soon firm friends. Tenzing's simplicity and gaiety quite charmed us, and we were quickly impressed by his authority in the rôle of Sirdar.

The Sherpas from Darjeeling included some well-bespoken and likely-looking characters. Although gregarious in their habits, the Sherpas are decidedly individualistic in appearance, particularly in their choice of dress. They made a colourful sight that morning as they paraded for our inspection. Most of them wore an assortment of garments which they had obtained on previous expeditions—green berets, blue ski-ing caps, balaclavas, bright-coloured sweaters and outsize boots.

Some of these Sherpas were already known to us and had been specially asked for. Thondup, the cook, had been with the 1951 New Zealand Expedition, and last year on Cho Oyu. Older than the others and not an experienced climber, he was nevertheless a key man from the viewpoint of health and morale. Kirken, his assistant, was also known to some members of the expedition. He was a tough-looking customer with the face of a boxer and a huge smile. There were the two brothers, Da Tensing and Annullu. They had both made a very favourable impression on the Cho Oyu party. Da Tensing, nine years the senior, must be about forty years old; wizened and pigtailed, his figure upright and slim, he has the dignity, courtesy and charm of the elders of his attractive race. He had brought with him his son Mingma, in the hope that a job could be found which would enable him to do an apprenticeship in expedition work. Annullu, jaunty, cheerful and robust, had recently dispensed with the characteristic Sherpa pigtail and surprised his friends in last year's expedition by his metamorphosis from a "jungly type" to a spruce and "Europeanized" character. Neither had long climbing experience, but both were reputed to be promising performers. Then there was the solemn, enigmatic Ang Namgyal, whose record book showed him to be a "Tiger" of great merit; and his near namesake, Da Namgyal, who had done illustrious service with the Swiss, in their historic and exhausting journey to the South Col in the spring of 1952. Taking part again in the autumn expedition, he had been injured in an accident on the Lhotse Face, when another Sherpa of the first rank, Mingma Dorji, had been killed by falling ice. Pasang Phutar II was a big, jocular fellow with obvious spirit and liking for the job. Little Gompu was smiling and cherubic, like an overgrown schoolboy—he was in fact only seventeen. A nephew of our Sirdar Tenzing, his parents were a monk and a nun and he had but recently left his studies in the Monastery of Rongbuk, on the northern side of Everest. With his plump figure, he looked a most improbable starter for high work on the mountain, but Tenzing was understandably enthusiastic about his protégé. These and several others came forward, grinning shyly, to be introduced to us in the Embassy garden. We should have to add others when we reached Sola Khumbu, for we were still several men short of the required total, even for the High Altitude team. Annullu had, meanwhile, been sent out to Namche Bazar by the Darjeeling Secretary of the Himalayan Club, Mrs Jill Henderson, who had so ably made the arrangements for the Sherpa team. He was only just back after choosing fourteen local men who were, according to the London plan, needed to lift our loads up the Icefall.

It is of great importance to the success of any Himalayan expedition that a very close understanding should be built up between the climbers and their Sherpas. Here the question of language is difficult, for the Sherpa tongue is scarcely spoken outside Sola Khumbu. Most of the Sherpas, however, have some knowledge of Nepali, which is more widely known, particularly by those who have been associated with the Gurkhas. Those Sherpas living in Darjeeling have a smattering of Hindi, the official language of India. We were fortunate in this respect, for Charles Wylie speaks Nepali fluently; Charles Evans, Michael Westmacott, Wilfrid Noyce and myself knew Hindi from our previous association with India. Several of the others had made great efforts to learn some Nepali from Charles Wylie, who held classes on the *Stratheden*.

Accompanying the Sherpas were a number of Sherpanis: their wives and sweethearts, who hoped to be engaged as coolies on our journey to their native land of Khumbu. I was delighted to agree with this arrangement, for not only would they add colour and gaiety to our company, but they carry loads as stoutly as their menfolk.

9th March was a day of tremendous activity at Bhadgaon, with the baggage party, consisting of Charles Evans and Wilfrid Noyce, sorting and arranging the packages, opening those containing our requirements in clothing and equipment for the march and directing the work of others who had come to help.

Charles Wylie was now faced with the difficult task of engaging a small army of coolies to carry the baggage on the seventeen-day journey to Thyangboche, a monastery which we had chosen from a study of the map as our first Base Camp, and from which we could carry out our initial programme of training. Coincident with the dumping of the loads on the parade ground at Bhadgaon, Charles mustered some three hundred and fifty local men to shoulder their burdens. All had to be recorded in a pay book, receive their tallies and an advance of pay.

The loads proved to be so numerous—considerably in excess of the estimate—that I decided to move off in two caravans at an interval of twenty-four hours. The track along which we should be moving allows only for single-line foot traffic as it enters more rugged country, and only by shortening our "tail" could we avoid a very protracted departure from one stage and arrival at the next. This was a pity, for I was no less anxious now than I had been when leaving England, that we should remain together as a team during this part of the journey, when there would be much to discuss, and while there might yet be a need to rub off the awkward corners. Moreover, the later programme would frequently require us to divide into small groups, from the time we started our training programme, and we were now for the first time assembled as a complete party. In order to minimize the handicap to our unity of moving out in two parts, therefore, it was arranged that all except three should travel in the first caravan.

We had followed an earlier Everest precedent in obtaining from the Brigade of Gurkhas the voluntary services of five N.C.O.s to assist Charles Wylie in his task of organizing the large force of coolies during the march-out. These men had joined us at Kathmandu and accompanied the second caravan.

Finance loomed large among our preoccupations. With so vast a baggage train, and foreseeing numerous other expenses while away from civilization, I, as Treasurer to the expedition, had to draw very considerable funds to take with us on our journey. We were given to understand that the local people decline to accept the flimsy local paper currency, except in the Valley of Nepal itself, so we had to take half our treasure in Nepali coin. We had considerable trouble in finding suitable boxes in which to pack so heavy and bulky a load, which needed no fewer than twelve coolies to carry it.

In addition to these hectic activities, there were also social occasions. We were most kindly entertained by the King of Nepal and by the Indian Ambassador; a charming reception was organized at the British Embassy in our honour. I paid a number of courtesy visits to leading Nepali officials, among them General Kaiser, at that time Chief Counsellor in the King's Advisory Council. As we left his residence, His Excellency handed me three small Nepali flags and requested me to carry one of them to the summit. It was a delicate gesture of confidence on his part and I am most happy to say that we were able to fulfil his wish.

Busy as we were, we could not but be conscious of our enchanting surroundings. The Valley of Nepal is a broad, fertile plateau at over 4,000 feet, encompassed by high wooded hills, beyond whose northern fringe the snow mountains peep tantalizingly. We managed to spare one day for a walk up a neighbouring viewpoint, Sheopuri, in the hope of having an extensive view towards the bigger mountains. It was cloudy, but the rhododendrons, glorious in scarlet blossom with a few of paler hues, were an ample recompense for our journey. We were attracted by the neat Newar houses with their thatched roofs and mud-plastered walls, tidily washed in ochre and white. Below us in the plain, peasants were labouring in their fields in preparation for the grain crop. We realized then that we were going to enjoy our long march to Thyangboche through these broad and friendly hills.

10th March was the date for the departure of the first caravan. I intended to stay in order to ensure that the second party got away without any last-minute hitches, after which I would go forward covering two stages in one day and catch up the leaders. All of us went out to Bhadgaon to see them off; it was a memorable occasion, and there was an upsurge of excitement in the air, as many hundreds of men hurried hither and thither, chattering as they tied and adjusted their burdens. Moving among them were Charles Wylie and Tenzing, the latter attended by a few of our Sherpas. There was an atmosphere of complete order despite the large-scale movement which was about to begin; Charles and Tenzing had done a magnificent job in getting us away to this encouragingly well-organized start. Everyone was in high spirits and the weather, after a spell of gloom, now reflected the general mood.

Pressmen and other onlookers had come to see us off and there was much clicking of cameras as the long stream of coolies started off into the town on their way eastwards. Some of them carried loads which, although they conformed to the standard weight of 60 lb., had a forbidding appearance. One of these was our metal ladder, each length of which measured six feet. An even more formidable monster was a shining aluminium trunk of coffin-like dimensions, in which Griffith Pugh's modest needs were housed. This object was treated with respect by the coolies and caused the rest of us some merriment. It is greatly to Griff's credit that he insisted, despite protests and jests on all sides, on having it transported all the way to our Base Camp at the foot of the Icefall.

Later that morning, I returned to the Embassy with Colonel Proud, the First Secretary, and three members of the party who were to travel with the second caravan. I heaved yet another of many sighs of relief; at last we were on the final stage of our approach to the mountain—planning and preparation had given place to action.

CHAPTER SIX

TO KHUMBU

IT is tempting to linger over our journey through the lovely land of Nepal, to allow my pen to dawdle even as we sauntered lazily along in those clear and beautiful days last spring. If I take you at a brisker pace through this enchanted land, it is only because I must tell the story of Everest within a limited span of time and words. In London I had fretted mentally at the prospect of having to spend nearly three weeks before we should be able to get to grips with the more serious part of the programme. Now, with seventeen days' journey ahead of us, the feeling of urgency was dispelled by the simple beauty of the countryside, by the removal, for a time, of worry and the exasperation of paperwork; it was the most restful period I had known for many months. Our programme was carefully timed and we knew that there was no advantage in forcing the pace, even had this been practicable with so long a train of coolies; we could appreciate the scenery to the full, indulge in our particular interests, be it birds, flowers or insects, and enjoy the company of one another. I think we were the more conscious of the happy present, in view of the more rugged prospect ahead of us; at least, this was so in my case.

Our track led us eastwards, thus cutting across the natural lines of drainage from the Himalayan watershed. We were moving athwart the grain of the land—down into deep valleys, across foaming torrents or broader, swift-flowing rivers and up the far hillsides. This was big country, with long views across broad expanses of mountainside, vast, fertile and dotted with friendly cottages; the land had a warm and hospitable look. Along the track we passed plenty of local folk, the girls colourful with their big ear-rings, glass bangles and red bead necklaces, the men close-cropped, drably and very scantily attired to suit the climate. On the dividing ridges we entered the lovely rhododendron belt, gnarled trees whose blossoms graduated with increasing height from scarlet to pink and, above 10,000 feet, to white and yellow. The forests were besprinkled with white magnolia flowers, heavily scented, fallen from the trees. Mauve primulas bedecked the path and Himalayan bird life was a constant source of wonder. How can I describe such gems of feathered beauty as the sunbirds, the verditer flycatchers, redheaded and greenbacked tits and scarlet mini-vets? But the very names conjure up exotic and fanciful colour. Stobart and Gregory were always busy capturing these scenes. Daily they would be seen at vantage-points along the track, recording some strik-ing view or taking an action picture of the caravan on the move.

We found the people and their simple livelihoods a daily interest: the laborious hand-tilling of the soil along narrow strips of terrace carved into the hillsides; potatoes growing on ridges at 9,000 feet; hill reclamation work such as is being done in my own country on the Welsh border. It was odd to see hayricks planted in the branches of trees. As we passed from one district to the next, the nature of the dwellings changed—in one region were roofs with wooden slats weighted by boulders, as is done in many parts of the Alps, in other places we found them to be thatched or tiled with large flat stones. We would bathe and wash our clothes in the torrents, clear and, in that early season, without taint from glacial silt.

On one of these occasions we nearly lost Charles Evans. He, Ed Hillary and I had gone to bathe in the Likhu Khola one morning, and Charles had stripped and plunged boldly into the current of a big pool. To our horror, Ed and I saw him disappear, sucked under by the drag of the torrent. He soon bobbed up but, worse still, was thrown violently against a submerged rock and again pulled beneath the seething waters. It all happened in a flash, but just as we were reacting sufficiently to move to his rescue, his sandy head reappeared and he, apparently unhurt, managed to strike out towards the far bank—and safety. It was a near thing and an anxious moment for us all.

As we went farther east, the views of the bigger peaks became more magnificent, less unreal. I remember how, on the fifth day's march, we had climbed steadily up to a pass at about 8,000 feet, there to be confronted with a stupendous view to the north. The great group of Gauri Sankar peaks, the highest among them, Menlungtse, over 23,500 feet, were startlingly close and fascinating in their abruptness. We spent a happy half-hour speculating on the most improbable routes, unburdened by any prospect of attempting them. Again, a few days farther on, standing upon yet another ridge, we sighted Everest, distant but unmistakable in the north-east, standing above a high intervening range of snow peaks, its summit picked out by a banner of cloud. The thrill was personal to each of us, but our joint excitement enhanced it; several of us climbed a tree to get a better view.

We followed a leisurely routine. We would rise at 5.30 a.m. with the aid of a cup of tea. The whole caravan would be on the move soon after 6 a.m. Our kitchen staff would go ahead, with Thondup in the lead, to select a suitable place for breakfast. Thondup had the great attribute of knowing how to choose his staff. It included one or two of our best Sherpanis, in particular one stout, strong and cheerful girl whom we nicknamed "Auntie". Arriving at some delectable stream after two to three hours, we would make a prolonged halt, and while the cook made his fire and prepared porridge, eggs and bacon, we would swim and rest, some reading or writing, others watching birds, catching butterflies and insects. Camp would be reached in the early afternoon, allowing plenty of time to settle in, write diaries and dispatches and discuss future plans.

These walks between stages and our leisure hours in camp worked wonders in our mutual relationship. Favourable first impressions warmed into firm friendships; we quickly learned to appreciate one another, comparing our very varied backgrounds and interests, discussing common or contrasting experiences—usually in the sphere of climbing mountains. I began to be preoccupied again with plans and spent hours with Ed Hillary and Charles Evans—our particular job among the allocation of tasks being planning—talking over alternative methods of Assault and calculating their implications in terms of loads. At other times I was able to relax and observe my companions as we lay in our big Dome tent.

There was usually a small group—it might be Michael Westmacott, George Band and Tom Bourdillon, exchanging views on some ultra-severe rock climb, usually it would be in North Wales. Tom Stobart would be recounting some thrilling if slightly improbable experience with wild game in Africa, or giving a vivid description of the Far South. George Lowe might be speaking in serious mood about one of his many experiences and interests, not least among them the apparently unequal struggle between the unfortunate teachers in his country and their unruly and enterprising pupils; or he might equally be competing with the sparkling wit of the other George, to make us ache with laughter in his guise of expedition clown. In contrast to the remainder, Greg would be quietly reading, or talking abstruse photographic technicalities with Stobart; Wilf Noyce, no less unobtrusive, would undoubtedly be scribbling page upon page of closely written manuscript in one of his several large notebooks. Some day I hope that we shall be able to read the product of all he wrote in that tent, or behind some bush while breakfast was brewing. Then there were the incidents of the day to compare between us; the butterflies which Mike Westmacott and I had caught—or missed; the grasshoppers which we had seen but for whose corpses there was no longer room in George Band's collecting-box, and the birds we had observed. Of course, at frequent intervals, there arose the ever-fascinating, if

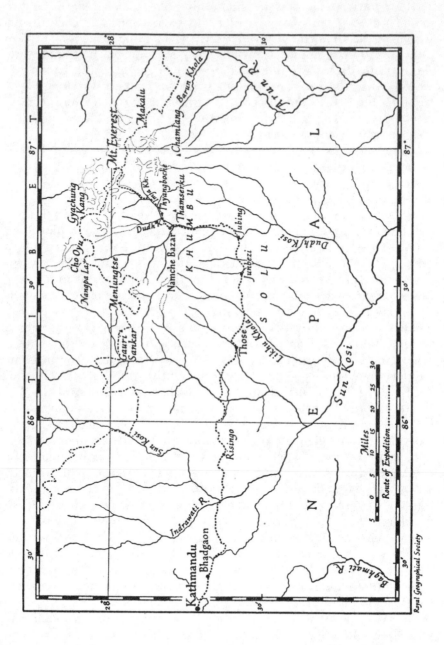

controversial, topic of food. This would arouse even Greg from his corner and provide Ed Hillary with his favourite topic—it was all "tucker" to him. And into any of these groups we might hear a quiet intervention from Charles Evans, rounding off a jest, adding information to some discussion from his wide range of knowledge, always sound and sensible. They were a grand crowd.

At the same time as getting to know each other, we also made friends with our Sherpas. An arrangement which seems to give mutual pleasure in Himalayan travel is that each man is cared for by a faithful follower, who brings him his tea in the morning, lays out his sleeping-bag at night, helps to carry his personal belongings and generally spoils his Sahib. (This Hindi word, denoting superior status, was used between us on the expedition, when necessary, simply to distinguish between members of the party and the Sherpas.) My own retainer was Pemba, a quiet and hefty lad with more than usually pronounced Mongolian features, his thick tresses wound in a massive "bun" and worn on the side of his head. Pemba was by repute one of the stoutest-hearted of our Sherpa team and was a most likeable chap; we very soon understood each other well enough although he had no Hindi and I no Sherpa "Bat"—his only language.

One of the matters which had been impressed on me by our advisers at home was the importance of getting used to the wearing of oxygen masks; John Cotes, their designer, in particular, had insisted that only by constant practice over long periods would we gain enough confidence to use them successfully at high altitude. Others doubted if we would ever tolerate them. Accordingly we observed a daily routine of putting on our masks for some part of the route. Two of us slept in them one night. Those of us who had not worn the masks before were pleasantly surprised to find how little they affected our breathing, and how little discomfort they caused. There is no doubt that their subsequent acceptability to everyone during operational use on the mountain was due to this and to the practice we put in from this early stage.

About half-way along the route, Ed Hillary, Tenzing and I remained behind for a day to see the second party. It was good to find them, like ourselves, in fine form and to discuss future intentions. They had had a few excitements: the visit of a panther to their camp one night; a fight with "kukris"—local knives—between a Sherpa and a coolie, which provided Mike Ward with the first of many calls on his professional assistance. This latter instance was only one of the many problems with which Charles Wylie, aided by his Gurkha N.C.O.s, had to deal, for this second batch of coolies was less reliable than the first. And there had been sacrifices to science which I was

65

glad to have avoided. Griff Pugh had subjected the party to a fearful ordeal known as a "maximum work test", consisting of rushing uphill at best possible speed until the lungs were bursting and then expiring air into an enormous bag until it swelled out like a balloon. It was satisfactory to learn that Griff, an interesting figure wearing pyjamas and sunglasses, his vivid shock of red hair topped by a deer-stalker's hat, had not spared himself the tortures which he inflicted on his guinea-pigs. We hurried forward to catch up the others lest we should be tested in our turn.

On the ninth day of our march we crossed a pass at 9,000 feet and entered the district of Sola Khumbu. This country is the home of our Sherpas and we were at once aware of the changing character both of the landscape and of the inhabitants. The mountainsides became more precipitous and rugged, cultivation was patchy and cottages more scattered; the scenery became first more Alpine and then more truly Himalayan. Equally marked was the changed appearance of the people. We recognized the pronounced Mongolian features, broad and bland, the heavier, more decorative clothing. This was Sherpa-land.

So far we had been moving steadily eastwards; now, shortly after crossing a last ridge, the highest of all—nearly 12,000 feet—we found our track leading us down, down to the deep gorge of the Dudh Kosi, its turbulent waters still a transparent blue-green, draining the area of Everest itself. This was the turning-point of our journey, for after crossing the river by an unstable temporary structure of bamboos, boulders and turf, we swung northwards up the east flank of the gorge, heading straight towards our final destination. We still had many thousands of feet to gain in height, for we had descended to about 5,000 feet, and the route, winding in and out of deep ravines and avoiding numerous impassable bluffs, was still a series of big ups and downs.

We crossed and finally recrossed the torrent, too swift to permit safe bathing, and alternately climbed and descended the steep and forest-clad mountainside. Always we were walking through a colourful foreground of rhododendron and magnolia trees, interspersed with giant firs; early spring flowers and fragrant flowering shrubs bordered the path. The views, whether down the plunging slopes to the distant river, barely audible as it pursued its rocky way thousands of feet below, or skywards to the jagged crest of the enclosing ridges above which peeped the icy pinnacles of Everest's near neighbours, were alike breathtaking. In such stark grandeur it was sometimes a relief to reach some small terrace on which stood a few Sherpa dwellings, low buildings of stone and stout timber, roofed with wooden slats, surrounded by patches of intensive and skilful cultivation. The fields were still bare, but they would soon be sprouting with potatoes, barley and maize.

As we advanced up the valley, we could see the huge buttress of open, grassy hillsides at which the Dudh Kosi is joined by a notable tributary, the Bhote Kosi. This latter stream, carrying the waters of melted ice from the southern flanks of Nuptse and Lhotse and a wide arena of lesser peaks to the north, was the one we were to follow, but first we must climb the buttress dividing the two rivers to reach Namche Bazar, the chief village of Khumbu. Behind Namche rises a huge column of grey granite, over 19,000 feet. This is Khumbila; we eyed it with our minds on the rock peaks of Savoy and Bergell.

We went up the broad path to Namche on 25th March. Many people were on the move, gay and bright-coloured folk, some of them carrying large bundles of thin parchment manufactured from the wood of indigenous shrubs. It was a grand, clear morning, and we climbed for a time aside from the track in order to see the view up the Imja Khola. Suddenly, there was what we had been waiting to see—Everest, now real in its nearness, its solid pyramid soaring above the long snow-fringed arête joining Lhotse and Nuptse. The first thing we noticed was that the upper rocks of our peak were black, almost denuded of snow. In our early mood of optimism, we drew over-hasty conclusions about the state of the mountain as it might be several weeks later. On calmer reflection, however, it could only be that the fierce winter wind was still in command high on the mountain, and was shielding it from the power of any human onslaught. However this might be, it was a cheering sight to find ourselves, almost unexpectedly, so close to the great peak.

Just before entering the village, we were greeted by a small deputation, relatives of our men, waiting by the path with a barrel of milky-coloured *chang*, a beer brewed from rice, and a large teapot of Tibetan tea, its spout and handle decorated with coloured paper. This delightful welcome, mainly for the Sherpas but also for ourselves, is typical of these friendly people.

At Namche we were surprised to find a small wireless station manned by Indian Government officials. Characteristic of the kindness of the Indian Ambassador in Kathmandu were his instructions to Mr Tiwari, who was in charge of this post, that he should assist us by handling urgent messages. We had reason to be most grateful for this concession on several occasions during our stay.

The final day of the march was also the climax to the mounting pleasure—indeed, the thrills—which we had been experiencing since the day we left the Valley of Nepal. Again, a little party of friends

and relations awaited us, this time from the neighbouring village of Khumjung. Moreover, a pony, dejected-looking but none the less an acceptable conveyance, had been sent from the Monastery to carry me up the final slopes. I am no horseman, but this ride up the well-worn track was sheer joy in the clear, sparkling air. My senses were intoxicated by the fantastic surroundings; Thyangboche must be one of the most beautiful places in the world. The height is well over 12,000 feet. The Monastery buildings stand upon a knoll at the end of a big spur, which is flung out across the direct axis of the Imja river. Surrounded by satellite dwellings, all quaintly constructed and oddly mediaeval in appearance, it provides a grandstand beyond comparison for the finest mountain scenery that I have ever seen, whether in the Himalaya or elsewhere. Beyond a foreground of dark firs, lichen-draped birch and rhododendrons, now dwarfed by altitude to bush size, tower immense ice peaks in every quarter. The Everest group bars the head of the valley, the 25,000-foot wall of Nuptse falling in sheer precipice some 7,000 feet from the summit ridge to the glaciers flowing at its base.

Stupendous as this scene is, the eye is even more drawn to a giant fang which stands half-right, in the middle distance, leaning awkwardly towards the valley. This mountain, Ama Dablam, rises to 22,700 feet and appears utterly inaccessible, outrivalling the most sensational aspects of the Matterhorn and bearing comparison with the Mustagh Tower in the far Karakoram.

68

Directly above the Monastery spur, to the south-east, are twin peaks of delicately fluted ice, some of their spires sharp as needles and almost transparent against the blue sky. These are Kangtega and Thamserku, another pair of 22,000-footers. To the north-west, a mountain of perfect, arrow-like symmetry rose at the head of the Dudh Kosi, while south-westwards was another barrier of ice and rock, stretching for several miles at over 20,000 feet: Kwangde.

We stood, spellbound by this wonderful scene, upon an open grassy alp on which yaks were grazing peacefully—an ideal spot for our first Base Camp. Life was very good.

CHAPTER SEVEN

REHEARSALS

O UR Base Camp at Thyangboche was a colourful and active scene during the three days following our arrival there. The period between the end of the march-out and the beginning of "acclimatization" was intended to be restful, but we had very little leisure; there was so much to arrange and plan, and it was important on no account to encroach on the many other activities leading up to the target date of readiness to climb the mountain—15th May. The programme was in fact a very full one. Let me give you a glimpse of this scene from the diary for 28th March.

Sandwiched between the arrival yesterday of the second caravan and the departure tomorrow of the first of our three training parties, it is a particularly busy day. The coolies have been paid off and are now on their way back to their villages. Their loads are neatly stacked, some according to commodities, others depending on the colour stripe which denotes at what stage they are to be opened. Two very prominent piles are the food boxes stacked in a long rectangular wall, and those containing the oxygen which have been roped off in a separate enclosure. Tenzing has encircled the whole area of the camp with climbing rope so as to leave us undisturbed by the many curious onlookers, some of them local folk from the Monastery buildings, others travellers with loads, passing along the near-by track.

For the first time, we have pitched all our tents, about twenty of them of various shapes, sizes and colours: three miniature ones intended for a final camp; orange ones for Advance Base and above; yellow ones of similar pattern to be used as far as the entrance to the Western Cwm; a distinctive Swiss tent which is Tenzing's temporary home, and two bigger dome-shaped tents, one used by the Sherpas and the other by ourselves. Beside some of them, pink, brown and olive sleeping-bags are spread out to air. In one far corner of the compound, Thondup has set up his cookhouse, its walls made of packing-cases and roofed over with a tarpaulin. Among his many minions are the Sherpanis, who are busy, some cleaning cooking-pots or mending garments, others combing and plaiting each other's long black tresses.

We ourselves have finished a leisurely breakfast as the sun was melting the frost off the grass (for we are at nearly 13,000 feet, and it is still cold at night), seated on packing-cases around a table improvised from Tom Bourdillon's oxygen boxes. Surprisingly, most of us are still more or less clean-shaven. This is due to Tom Bourdillon's foresight in providing some clipper-type razors, for too much hair on the face would cause leakages in our oxygen masks.

Now the day's work is in progress in earnest and there are a number of little groups engaged on different jobs. To some, Tom Bourdillon, with Mike Ward to help him, is giving a lesson in the Open-Circuit oxygen, and his pupils are assembling their sets prior to doing their first trial a few hundred feet up the hillside behind the camp. Ed Hillary is the centre of another party, mostly composed of Sherpas, as he demonstrates Cooke's specially adapted Primus stoves, aided by Tenzing as interpreter. George Band is unpacking the portable wireless sets; he is to teach us their use in the afternoon.

At the opposite end of the camp from the cookhouse, our sectional ladder has been put together by Michael Westmacott, who has suspended it between two large boulders. There is an alarming sag in the middle, but it seems to be bearing the weight of his Sherpa assistants as they crawl along it, gingerly at first, then with increasing confidence. In another place there are neat piles of mountain kit, laid out by Charles Evans and Wilfrid Noyce—clothing and equipment which we are to receive at the appropriate time. Some seem already to have received their issue, for here is one dressed in a pale green eiderdown jacket, another in a plum-coloured sweater; a few are even walking on the turf with crampons strapped experimentally to their new mountain boots. Moving from one group to the next is Tom Stobart with his ciné camera, followed by Sherap, a comic and toothless old man who is a lama or priest. He is now also an expert in setting up Tom's tripod and has even some ambition to shoot film himself.

All this, and more, is going on and much else remains to be done. I have the cares of making up the accounts and checking the cash; I have a dispatch to write for *The Times* and plans to consider for some later phase. Charles Wylie and Tenzing have numerous problems on their hands: the allotment of Sherpas to each training party and the engagement of others, to complete our High Altitude team and to work in the Icefall; mail runners to organize in conjunction with Greg, who is in charge of our postal arrangements, as well as co-ordination of photography. George Band has to distribute rations to the acclimatization parties. A sheep has been purchased and the Sherpas, as good

Buddhists, will not kill it, so George Lowe has offered his experience as a butcher.

The arrival of an expedition invariably attracts the halt and the maimed, and Mike Ward has many "cases" to examine. There are teeth to be pulled, sore eyes, ulcers, fevers and obscure stomach pains to be cured. Nor must I overlook Griff Pugh, who is setting up shop in his physiological tent and is anxious to weigh us on the big scales used for assessing our loads, puncture us with needles and drive us down the hill to a starting-point for his "maximum work test".

That afternoon we paid our first official visit to the Monastery at the invitation of the monks. There was a simple ceremony to perform on arrival, the laying of scarves on the thrones of the present Abbot— he, a young boy, was away in Tibet—and of his deceased predecessor. Coached in this formality by Tenzing, I also presented to the acting Abbot our expedition flag. We were briefly shown round the sanctuary, after which a meal was served in an upper room. Seated with Charles Wylie and Tenzing beside our host, a rotund figure robed in faded red, I questioned him about the Yeti—better known to us as the "Abominable Snowman". The old dignitary at once warmed to this subject. Peering out of the window on to the meadow where our tents were pitched, he gave a most graphic description of how a Yeti had appeared from the surrounding thickets a few years back in winter, when the snow lay on the ground. This beast, loping along sometimes on his hind legs and sometimes on all fours, stood about five feet high and was covered with grey hair, a description which we have heard from other eyewitnesses. Oblivious of his guests, the Abbot was reliving a sight imprinted on his memory as he stared across at the scene of this event. The Yeti had stopped to scratch—the old monk gave a good imitation, but went on longer than he need have done to make his point—had picked up snow, played with it and made a few grunts—again he gave us a convincing rendering. The inhabitants of the Monastery had meanwhile worked themselves into a great state of excitement, and instructions were given to drive off the unwelcome visitor. Conch shells were blown and the long traditional horns sounded. The Yeti had ambled away into the bush.

We listened, fascinated by this tale, and continued to be interested, if slightly less convinced, when we heard other and more circumstantial stories—of how, for instance, a whole tribe of Yetis, after making themselves unpopular in Tibet by mimicking the habits of their human cousins, had been massacred by them; this resulted in a decree by the then Government of that country that Yetis would in future be protected by law. This story is curious in view of the Buddhist scruples against taking life. In truth this slaughter of the Yetis was a dastardly deed; the creatures must have allowed their well-known sense of humour to run away with them and have carried their practical joking a little too far.

It is interesting to note here that, under the beneficent influence of the monks, the whole valley of the Imja is a sanctuary for wild life. We were able to observe the results of this around our camp, where kasturi or musk deer, monal pheasants and ram chikor—giant Himalayan partridges—wandered unconcernedly not far from the tents.

Before leaving, I was requested to contribute some thousands of rupees towards the repair of the Monastery roof. As I had sat up most of the previous night vainly trying to square the remaining contents of our cash box with the latest budget, I had to temporize, but it seemed an opportunity to counter this with a request from our side. We had been intrigued by the painted devil masks in the sanctuary, and I asked that on our return we might be allowed to witness a ceremonial Lama dance. This was agreed to and the Abbot announced his intention of blessing our party before we left for Everest.

We now had a period of about three weeks—until 20th April—in which to train and otherwise prepare ourselves for Everest. It will be remembered that the main purpose of this period was to get used gradually to increasing height—to acclimatize—and that we also planned to practise with both types of oxygen apparatus and get accustomed to other equipment. The programme was to be carried out in two halves, each of about eight days, with a break in which we would reassemble at Thyangboche, rest and reorganize before going out again. We divided ourselves into three parties, which would be looked after respectively by Ed Hillary, Charles Evans and myself; the composition would, for obvious reasons, be changed in the second half. Different areas were chosen for each party. Everyone was looking forward keenly to this "running-in" process, for we expected to fit in some serious climbing on the lower peaks and passes in the vicinity: moreover, small parties tend to be more intimate and friendly than large ones.

Charles's group was the first to leave, on 29th March. It was made up of himself, Tom Bourdillon, George Band and Michael Westmacott. They were to use both the Closed- and Open-Circuit apparatus and had, therefore, a particularly full programme. The rest of us were to start off on the following day, and all were to return to Base by 6th April.

Just before the departure of the first party, Tom Bourdillon made a most unwelcome discovery in the oxygen department. No less than fifteen of our forty-eight training bottles were "flat", having leaked at

73

some stage in transport. It was all too evident that here was a crisis which would inevitably affect, and might well prejudice, our plans. The training oxygen bottles—standard wire-bound R.A.F. cylinders —were to be used during the forthcoming rehearsal period and also in the Assault; we must either curtail the oxygen training or modify our Assault planning. There was an even more sinister possibility, namely that other bottles of a similar pattern, included in the second consignment, had suffered from the same defect. I had just received a wireless message that Jimmy Roberts was in Kathmandu and that the consignment of Assault sets had been flown up from India according to plan; he was due to start for Thyangboche almost immediately. Tom drafted an urgent message designed to find out about the state of Roberts's cargo, and this was dispatched by runner with all haste to the wireless station at Namche Bazar.

It was only a week later, when I was on my way back from the first acclimatization period, that our anxiety was removed. Roberts had already left Kathmandu and was, in fact, about to start on the second stage of his journey when the message arrived at the British Embassy. Colonel Proud had dashed out to stop him. A halt was made for a whole day while the sixty-odd crates were laboriously opened and their contents examined. The result of this frantic emergency action was reassuring; it was just as well, for there could scarcely have been any hope of getting replacements from England by 15th May.

The weather was perfect at the time we left Base Camp and everyone was in high spirits at the thought that we were moving off at last, approaching and equipped for the high mountains. Our respective areas were widely separated, for there was no lack of suitable terrain. Charles Evans had already gone up to explore a suspected hidden valley beneath the southern precipice of Ama Dablam; Ed intended to take his men up the unknown glen of Chola Khola in the north-west and, if he could discover negotiable passes, to make a complete girdle of the elegant Taweche peaks. He had with him Wilfrid Noyce, Michael Ward and Charles Wylie. As luck would have it, Ed himself developed a temperature and sore throat at the last moment and had to remain in camp for two more days, handing over his responsibilities to Wilfrid.

My party, consisting of Gregory, Lowe and Tenzing, was bound for the Imja basin, straight up the valley in the direction of the Nuptse–Lhotse wall. Our original hope was to find a suitable training-ground on the northern side of Ama Dablam, but later we changed direction and instead turned left at the head of the valley to follow the near bank of a glacier flowing beneath the tremendous barrier of Nuptse. That evening we camped in the little walled meadow of a farmstead in the village of Dingboche, at a height of just under 15,000 feet. We were now directly under the north-west face of Ama Dablam, so sheer that only ice adhered to the smooth rock precipice; we noticed that the ice slopes on the upper part of the face were inclined at an angle unimaginable in the Alps. The rock on this, and other peaks around us, was composed largely of a beautiful white granite, so pale indeed that it was not easy to distinguish between ice and rock. Equally awe-inspiring was the peak of Taweche across the way, which is built in the same fantastic style as Ama Dablam; from Thyangboche we had only been able to see a part of its South-West ridge, bulging with outsize cornices.

Dingboche is inhabited only in summer, when peasants come up the valley to cultivate these rich alluvial fields, growing excellent potatoes and barley—the latter to be roasted and ground into a fine flour known as *tsampa*, which is the staple food of the Sherpas. A regular event each year is the blessing given by some guest Lama to the fortune of the harvest, and a special house is maintained for him, situated high up on the mountainside. This ceremony was due on the day following our stay there.

There followed five very happy and full days, during which, from our camp at 17,000 feet beside the Nuptse glacier, Greg, George, Tenzing and I, with five High Altitude porters, carried through our appointed programme of oxygen practice, acclimatization to altitude, trials of the High Altitude rations and incidental exploration. Apart from one evening of snowfall, the weather was fine and clear. An unforgettable memory is that great façade of Nuptse which frowned upon us in dominating nearness during every moment of our stay. As I write, I can see every detail of that precipice, the astonishing whiteness of its granite rock with the occasional overlay of ice, topped by the broad band of darker sedimentary rock above which was the narrow crest of snow, like a massive section of Christmas cake half-eaten.

We chose a suitable peak up which we picked out an "oxygen run" and made individual ascents which were carefully timed. This was most enlightening and encouraging. It must be remembered that we had come straight up to an unaccustomed height and that a comparatively small climb in any direction would take us into the neighbourhood of 19,000 feet; at this early stage, therefore, the motive power or altitude-reducing properties of oxygen could be expected to show their value. We reckoned our "run" was about 1,700 feet in height, and we found that our average time for the course was fifty minutes, or little less than 2,000 feet an hour. This timing is good at a lower level, but without oxygen would have been far beyond our capacity at that height and at that stage of our acclimatization. A pleasing discovery about the use of oxygen was that it gave a feeling of well-being. Even encumbered by a mask, it was possible to take an interest in the climbing and enjoy the scenery.

We also climbed an attractive little peak of about 19,400 feet, which stood on the opposite side of the glacier from our camp site. At Tenzing's suggestion we named it Chukhung Peak, after the pasturage of that name in the valley below. Dwarfed by the tremendous precipices of Nuptse, it was none the less a fine ice climb on its northern side. We camped at the head of a little glacier, at slightly under 19,000 feet, and made two attempts on a rickety ridge of rotten ice before eventually climbing it up its steep north face—a lot of step cutting was involved, which provided a good test of our fitness. It was on this occasion that I had my first chance of climbing with Tenzing; it showed me not only what a capable mountaineer he is, but also that he was, even at that time, fitter than any of us. It augured well for the future.

The best indications of our state of health were the maintenance of body weight in spite of the fairly strenuous programme which we had just completed—I had actually put on five pounds—and our gargantuan appetites. Reading through diaries before writing this chapter, I have been struck by the gloating references to menus, especially one eaten on return to Base Camp for the rest period: "a lovely and terrific cake with raisins in it" . . . "a magnificent curry followed by rice pudding and tinned fruit out of the luxury box." By contrast with these, but indirectly making the same point, another writer is plaintive about our necessarily meagre High Altitude diet: "It was hardly a fair test, as we are all as hungry as hunters at 18,000 feet, whereas the rations were designed for over 23,000 feet, when one doesn't feel like eating at all. Breakfast at present is porridge and Grape-nuts and milk and tea, and supper is pemmican and soup and cocoa or coffee." Nor had we found any difficulty in following Griff Pugh's advice to drink an average of six or seven pints of liquid each day.

Although we were eating and drinking well during this first period of fitness training, sleeping came less easily, a sure sign that we were unaccustomed to height. Our laboured, uneven breathing caused us to wake suddenly, gasping and with a choking sensation—it is known as "Cheyne Stokes" breathing. We had been supplied with a variety of sleeping pills by Michael Ward. They were distinguished by their different colouring, red, green and yellow. In most cases, these certainly sent us to sleep, but it was some time before we settled on our own particular preference. I remember one of my companions tripping badly over his words at breakfast one morning, as though he had been at the bottle even at that early hour.

Our party went back by the way it had come and returned to our First Base Camp on the afternoon of 5th April. It was interesting in the following break to compare the experiences of other parties with our own. Charles Evans's party had dispelled the belief in a hidden valley, but they had made up for this by reaching three passes—one of them, which they named Mera Col, about 19,600 feet in height. Tom Bourdillon had made a lone ascent of a 19,000-foot rock peak. Charles's party was now partly trained in both types of oxygen apparatus, and he himself had been collecting photographic and theodolite data for an eventual map of this fascinating country. I had the impression then, which was strengthened later, that the two newcomers to the Himalaya, George Band and Michael Westmacott, had found the altitude telling on them more than the rest of us. However this may be, they were then, and remained throughout, ready to shoulder every task and enjoy each opportunity which came their way.

Ed Hillary, recovered from his indisposition, had hurried on to join his party soon after they had set themselves up in the Chola Khola. In some respects they had enjoyed the most completely successful period of all, for not only had they completed a circular tour around the Taweches, crossing a high pass in doing so, but they had made no less than two first ascents, one of their peaks being an elegant mountain which proved to be a welcome test of their skill and experience of ice work. Known locally as Kang Cho, its height is over 20,000 feet. All had enjoyed experiences in the use of oxygen similar to ours.

Sitting round a huge camp fire that evening, I experienced a great feeling of contentment about our progress thus far. Our objectives had been achieved exactly as we had planned them, for we had all succeeded in climbing to the maximum height attainable in that early season and had done so without distress. It is in fact unlikely that peaks of 20,000 feet have ever been climbed at this time of year. There was unmistakable confidence in the oxygen equipment, both in its design and its effects. Moreover, it was no less obvious that everybody was enjoying himself in the same way as if it were an Alpine climbing holiday; this was important, for there would be plenty of tedium later on. Morale was evidently high. Most satisfactory of all was to observe how our friendship and confidence in each other had increased. We had been together on the rope and had had reason to respect each other's prowess. We had lived for a few days in the conditions of a high camp and found the company not only tolerable but pleasant. Around the blazings logs that night, with the stars winking and the air frosty, there was an atmosphere of relaxation and simple happiness which gave me assurance of our combined strength when the testing time should come.

*   *   *

Although it gave us a welcome physical respite, our second stay at Thyangboche seemed to be even busier than the first. For the majority, this would be the last time we should be returning to this place until our main task was over. About a fortnight would elapse before the whole party would gather together again. This meeting would be at the new Base Camp, to be sited as high as practicable up the Khumbu glacier. So we had to take a longer view of detailed plans, both for each group on its next journey and for the expedition as a whole.

Problems of rationing and equipment loomed larger than before. I had reshuffled our names so as to bring about completely new combinations as far as possible; the new parties were also constituted with a view to the particular tasks next to be performed. Earlier planning had given too little importance to the Khumbu Icefall. Our discussions left me in no doubt that more time must be given to a thorough reconnaissance of this and to the preparation of a route up it, if we were not to lose precious days later and risk being late to seize a possible weather opportunity in mid-May. One party was therefore composed for this task in the second acclimatization period. It consisted of Ed Hillary, whose previous knowledge of the Icefall would be invaluable; George Lowe, by virtue of his outstanding ice-craft; George Band and Michael Westmacott, the latter especially because of his responsibility for the structural equipment, which was expected to be required on this section of the route. He would be able to send messages back to Thyangboche for any local materials, such as tree trunks, which might be needed for bridging, and which must be procured before we left the tree level.

Then there was the need to instruct an élite band of Sherpas in the use of oxygen. This had not been attempted before, but it formed an important part of the plan that six or more of these men should be able to climb above the South Col with the summit parties. Oxygen would immeasurably increase the chances of their doing so, and Charles Wylie, after hearing reports on those who had been with each party in the first period, was able to select the seven best Sherpas. In order to combine this task of instruction with that of closing our present Base, linking up with the oxygen convoy now approaching under Jimmy Roberts, "signing on" our Low Altitude Sherpas and bringing all our remaining gear up to the new site, I requested the

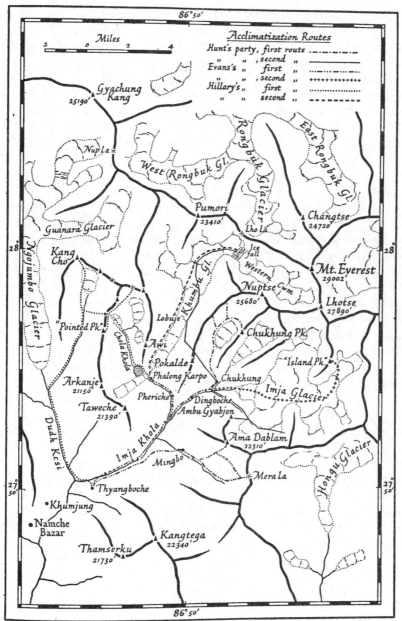

two Charleses, Greg and Tenzing to cut short their training period and return to Thyangboche in time to fulfil this last task.

My own party, this time consisting of Michael Ward, Tom Bourdillon and Wilfrid Noyce, was to join the Icefall team at the end of this period, which was due to be completed by 17th April. After three days' rest we would continue the work in the Icefall from the point reached by the others.

One of our Sherpas added to our worries at this time by fomenting trouble among the others. Complaints were made about food, clothing and tents. This man had proved so unsatisfactory from the beginning that we had already reached the point of deciding to get rid of him. This affair clinched his fate as far as Tenzing and I were concerned, and he left promptly the next morning. His behaviour throughout was in marked contrast with that of the rest, and the grievances which he aired, where they were not deliberate fabrications, were in each case easy to rectify, but he had threatened to upset the happy relationship which existed within the whole party. With his departure, our men were quickly their smiling selves once more.

On 9th April we again found ourselves at Dingboche, this time in company with Charles Evans's party. There was now a complete break in the blissful continuity of clear days; we awoke next morning to find about four inches of snow on the ground, with clouds threatening that more would follow. In these conditions, Charles decided to stay at the village and carry out his indoctrination of the Sherpas in the mysteries of oxygen from that place. I watched the beginning of this; Tenzing and Wylie were the teachers. There had been some doubts about the prospects of giving the Sherpas confidence in this strange auxiliary to uphill movement, if indeed we could teach them to understand the mechanism. But it proved a great success in both respects. Climbing in pairs at intervals throughout that day, all were delighted, Ang Temba even going so far as to voice the view that using oxygen made it like going downhill.

My party decided to carry on up the valley despite the weather conditions; our destination was some point still to be selected on the bank of the Imja glacier, behind and on the north-east side of Ama Dablam. We had a trying time ploughing up in the wet, new snow, and eventually camped at about 16,500 feet, beneath the north ridge of this astonishing mountain. It was cold and bleak, and snow soon began to fall again. After a poor second day, the weather improved and we were able to climb a fine-looking rock needle which, although overshadowed by its huge neighbour Ama Dablam, dominates in its turn the pasturage of Chukhung, where it is known locally as Ambu Gyabjen. Its height must be about 19,500 feet.

The West Ridge of Mount Everest, running toward the camera, divides the pre- and post-war approaches to the attempts to climb the mountain. To the left are the West Rongbuk glacier, the North Col and the North Face, attempted by the British expeditions of the 'twenties and 'thirties. To the right is the South Col at the head of the Lhotse Face and the Western Cwm, destined to become the classic route for future expeditions.

Sorting out some of our eight tons of equipment and provisions at First Base Camp, Thyangboche, with Kwangde beyond.

Negotiating a bridge over the ever-shifting crevasses of the Khumbu Icefall, notorious gateway to Everest from the south, through which all supplies for the higher camps had to be carried. After we established Advance Base Camp, Westmacott kept this dangerous route open through the Icefall for thirteen days until we descended after climbing the mountain.

The team, with our high-altitude Sherpas at Advance Base. Standing left to right: Stobart, Dawa Tenzing, Evans, Wylie, Hillary, Hunt, Tenzing, Lowe, Ward, Bourdillon, Band, Pugh, Gregory, Noyce. Seated from left: 1st Topkie, 2nd Thondup, 5th Ang Namgyal, 7th Ang Tensing (Balu), 9th Dawa Thondup, 12th Pemba, 13th (in front) Pasang Dawa, 16th Phu Dorji, 18th Ang Temba and 21st Ang Nima. (Missing from this photograph are Annullu, Da Namgyal, Gompu and Westmacott.)

Noyce and a party of Sherpas rest while ferrying loads up to Camp IV which became our Advance Base. Beyond is a foreshortened view of the Lhotse Face, rising to the South Col 5,000 feet above.

The Lhotse Face from the air: the South Col is on the left skyline with the Geneva Spur below it. Lhotse is to the right and the Nuptse Ridge runs across the foreground. Note the Lhotse glacier descending steeply towards the head of the Western Cwm.

Camp VII, high on the Lhotse Face, with the Geneva Spur behind.

Bourdillon and Evans working on the oxygen equipment.

Above, the skeleton of the tent Lambert and Tenzing left on the South-East Ridge during the 1952 Swiss expedition which came so near to climbing Everest. *Below left,* Bourdillon and Evans arrive at the South Col after their return from the South Peak on 26th May: *right,* Da Namgyal, with Makalu beyond, at the dump of stores he and Hunt carried that day to 27,400 feet.

The South Peak and the South-East Ridge from the South Col, showing the Snow Shoulder half-way down the ridge and the 1,300-foot couloir by which it was reached left of the dark rocks to the right of the picture.

Hillary and Tenzing in the couloir with the Lhotse Face below.

A summit view down the North ridge, showing the North Col, Changtse, and below right, the Rongbuk glacier, historic route in to Everest for all expeditions before the second world war.

I was particularly keen to have further experience of the Closed-Circuit apparatus, which was still experimental in the sense that I wanted further trials to be continued before deciding on our tactical use of oxygen in the Assault. I found it easy to wear and control, and there was no questioning the amount of boost it gave. But its weight —normally about 35 lb.—effectively kept down the speed, and in these comparatively warm conditions, the heat it generated made it uncomfortable and detracted from the pleasure and ease of climbing. While Tom and I were thus engaged, Mike and Wilfrid were trying out the Open-Circuit equipment over a longer period than had been attempted hitherto; keeping on their sets for over five hours, they reported that they had found the test by no means unpleasant.

After three days, during which we also trained the Sherpas in ice work among the séracs of a wide arena of glaciers flowing from a fine ridge on the opposite side of the combe in which we were camping, the party descended to the valley. Crossing it, we climbed the hillsides to the north-west, making for a col which was known to be used in the summer by yak-herds travelling between the Imja and the Khumbu pastures. By this we reached the left bank of the Khumbu glacier on 14th April. From the Pass, whose height is about 18,000 feet, Bourdillon, Noyce and Ward went on to climb a 20,000-foot snow peak whose name we discovered later to be Pokalde. I was having great difficulty with breathing that day and for that reason had not accompanied them. This trouble was later diagnosed by Ward to be incipient pleurisy. Thanks to his prompt and skilful care, I had fully recovered from this a few days later.

Next day we followed the east bank of the glacier upwards until we could cross the ice-stream to the far side so as to reach a track leading to the head of the valley.

It was a glorious walk and an exciting prospect lay before us. At long last we had turned the corner and were heading directly towards Everest. The exacting months of planning and preparation, the long approach journeys from England and New Zealand, and now the training period—these were all behind us. The big adventure was about to begin. Moreover, we could see before us mountains closely associated in our minds with the great mountain; there was Pumori, a sharp, graceful cone of ice and snow, and beyond it the Lingtren peaks, both climbed during an earlier reconnaissance of Everest in 1935. As we dodged amid the wilderness of colossal granite boulders bestrewing the glacier, we sighted another peak made famous by pre-war expeditions: Changtse, or the North Peak of Everest, standing above the North Col, where on no less than seven occasions British parties had established a camp in their reconnaissances or attempts

81

to climb Everest from that side. We saw it through a saddle, the Lho La, which we knew to be the point at which the Khumbu glacier makes its sensational swing after plunging out of the Western Cwm; the foot of this gap must therefore be about the place intended for our Base Camp.

An air of expectancy remained with us all that day. By the early afternoon, we had reached a shallow glacial lake between the moraine and the mountainside beneath the southern rampart of Pumori, where the Swiss had made their Base Camp last spring; stone circles forming low walls or "sangars" had evidently served as windbreaks for their tents. This, Lake Camp, was to be our resting-place until we moved up to join Ed's party for work in the Icefall.

CHAPTER EIGHT

ICEFALL

H ILLARY'S party for the second acclimatization period was
much larger than Charles Evans's or mine. He had with him
Pugh and Stobart with their considerable specialized baggage, in
addition to the equipment—metal and rope ladders; hoisting gear;
quantities of rope—required to prepare a route up the Icefall as far
as the Western Cwm. Moreover, he would have to be self-contained
in rations until the last party came up from Thyangboche on 22nd
April. He must also have food for my party when we joined him. To
carry his loads he had thirty-nine coolies in addition to five Sherpas,
making his party fifty in all.

Soon after leaving us, he ran into the spell of bad weather which
had overtaken us at Dingboche; for him, this was serious in view of
his numbers and the urgency to get started on work in the Icefall.
What was more, snow had not been expected before he reached his
destination, and we had not thought it necessary to provide his coolies
with special equipment, such as boots and goggles. Ploughing on in
their felt boots through the heavy snow, his caravan arrived in a very
wretched condition at the end of the second day; cold, wet and with
many cases of snow-blindness. There was nothing for it but to make
the best of the conditions that night. They were short of tents and
though a surprising number of the party, which included a good many
women, squeezed into the available shelters, others had to sleep out
in the snow in the shelter of boulders. But these Khumbu folk are
tough and proud of it. All but a few, and those the worst affected by
snow-blindness, were cheerfully ready to start next morning. After
sending down the bad cases, Ed Hillary and his party improvised
protection for the eyes from cardboard, black tape and small pieces of
coloured celluloid. Thus provided, this gallant band of laden carriers
pressed on to their destination, none the worse for their appalling
hardships and making no complaints.

Passing the Lake Camp they continued up-glacier, following a line
of cairns built by the Swiss last year, along a broad stony avenue in
the centre of the ice, hemmed in by a strange forest of miniature ice
peaks on either hand. These pinnacles, some of them rising nearly

100 feet in height, result from intense solar heat, which also produces other curious effects. Boulders great and small would be seen raised high in the air, perched delicately on the very point of an ice needle, marking an earlier level of the glacial surface. It was an odd, unreal landscape, not without a certain beauty. But we were now launched into an unfriendly, dead world, its attractions those of a lunar landscape, for after leaving the moraine above the Lake Camp no grass grows, nothing lives. Its structure is also strange. No one making his way up the Khumbu glacier could divine the presence of the Icefall. He would even be inclined to doubt the evidence of a map. The ice-stream seems to spring from a valley head, enclosed by Lingtren and Nuptse, between which is a promising-looking pass, the Lho La. Thus contained by an apparently unbroken high ridge, it would seem that the only way to the foot of Everest must be over the outlet of the Lho La and on towards the North Col, in Tibet. The North Peak, framed by this col, beckoned us there. Many times we were to make this journey between these glacier camps and our Base, and always I would try in vain to pick out the shoulder of Nuptse's west ridge, beyond which lay the hidden breach. It was simply invisible from below, a freak of mountain architecture.

Close under the Lho La, but at a safe distance from the tell-tale fan of pulverized ice and rock avalanche débris at its foot, they found the remnants of the Swiss Camp I. There they discovered a welcome stock of juniper scrub for firewood, sufficient at least to avoid burning paraffin for cooking during their stay. The site was not an ideal one, but it had the important advantage of being close to the foot of the great Icefall; they had only to climb a minor ice-hill behind the tents in order to enjoy a full view of their problem. Camp was established on 12th April. The Icefall reconnaissance party were ready to set about their important task.

In an earlier chapter, I described this staircase leading to the first floor of the great mansion that is Everest from a glaciological angle, that of an ice-stream falling steeply over an underlying glacis of rock. Now I want to show it from another viewpoint—the scene as we saw it. After its long, level journey from the ramparts of Lhotse, invisible from here, the summit ridge of Nuptse descends in a sudden swoop towards the upper Khumbu glen; in fact, towards the point where we are standing, just above the Base Camp. But it never reaches the valley floor, for it has been sliced away by some cataclysm at over 2,000 feet above. Nothing remains but sheer precipice, overhung with thick slices of blue ice more than 100 feet in depth, which peel off in massive slabs at intervals during each day. The flank of this buttress forms, as we are viewing it, the right-hand containing wall of the Icefall. The other is the west ridge of Everest, no less imposing, which descends in broad, smooth slabs to the Lho La, now seen over our left shoulder. Squeezed between the shoulders of Everest and Nuptse, the ice resembles a gigantic cascade, pouring in leaping waves and eddies over submerged boulders towards us. Almost, you might expect to hear the roar of that immense volume of foaming water which, after flowing peacefully to the brink of the cliff above, is now plunging down with terrifying power. But it has been gripped by the intense cold, frozen into immobility, a silent thing, its force restrained. But not quite. For this labyrinth of broken ice is moving, its surface changing, if not at the pace of water, at least at a speed which makes it a perilous problem to surmount.

Viewed with the more accustomed eye of the climber, the problem falls naturally into two parts. There is a steep lower section, on which there has obviously been some fairly recent and major change in the ice, for over a considerable area it has been shattered into a maze of monstrous ice boulders. At the top of this huge step, at least 1,000 feet high, there is a shelf where the general angle lies back briefly before rising again to the lip of the Western Cwm. This upper section is very foreshortened and partly hidden by the lower step, but it gives, even from here, the impression of being less broken up, the lines of cleavage more clear-cut and on a bigger scale. At both sides of the Icefall are troughs, which in themselves might give passable routes, but so menaced are both by the ice avalanches from the enclosing ridges that to use them would be suicidal; a way must be found roughly up the middle, through the area where the ice is most disfigured and chaotic.

The Icefall party set to work under considerable difficulties. Immediately on arrival, George Lowe fell sick; their strength was further weakened a few days later, when Michael Westmacott was stricken by the same affliction, a sudden bout of diarrhoea, with which most of us were to become acquainted during the following weeks.

Although never reduced below an effective strength of three at any one time, this threw an additional strain on the party, and their already arduous work was made more difficult by the weather.

We were now in the season of daily afternoon snowfall; each morning it was necessary to remake the track prepared so laboriously the day before. For the first two days they were engaged in a struggle to reach that half-way terrace on which the Swiss Camp II had stood. Casting to right and left, making numerous false starts and spending many hours each day in the exhausting labour of hacking away masses of ice, cutting staircases of steps safe for the laden Sherpas, they eventually won through on 16th April and set up two tents at 19,400 feet. This marked the first important step in our progress up the mountain. Camp II, so hard won, possessed in those early days a glamour which it was quickly to lose, owing to familiarity, the dirt from many parties in transit and the increasing heat.

Ed Hillary and the two Georges spent the night there and next day went on to reconnoitre a route up to the edge of the Western Cwm. On that day, 17th April, I left our resting-place at Lake Camp to learn their news and, finding at Base Camp that they were up the Icefall, asked Ang Namgyal to join me in a journey to Camp II. I did not realize at that time that this silent, poker-faced little man had been going up and down this rickety and dangerous route for the past three days; he got ready without a word. Tom Stobart came along with us for some part of the way and pointed out several of the landmarks.

I propose to describe this first trip in some detail. It should be remembered that the route, at that time, was not yet ready for use as a highway by laden men. For over half an hour we threaded our way along a series of twisting, narrow ice channels between pinnacles, heading generally towards the foot of the Icefall, but making many detours to avoid obstacles. We had brought flags, red, yellow and black, from England to mark the route in the Icefall and the Cwm, and the reconnaissance party had already planted them as far as Camp II. At last the ice steepened and it became necessary to put on crampons and rope up. This place was named "the Island". Some distance above us, a staircase had been cut up the steep edge of a large crevasse, down which a fixed rope was hanging. Nicknamed "Mike's Horror" after Westmacott, who had led and prepared it, this pitch, now straightforward, told of a fine feat of icemanship. There followed a number of strides over crevasses, two of them too wide to step or jump across. They had been temporarily bridged by sections of our metal ladder. The crossing of one gap, spanned by two 6-foot sections, demanded a crawling technique, for it was awkward to step

upright on the narrow rungs with our spiked boots. Then a steep rise
—we were nearing the area of greatest ruin—led to the biggest chasm
we had yet encountered. A huge block of ice lay wedged across it,
apparently solid, but only so long as the jaws of the dragon did not
open wider. At its far end it abutted against a short wall of ice: the
upper lip of the crevasse. Here a diagonal line of steps had been cut
—later, we were to fix a handline. We stepped gingerly up it, using
hand-holds chipped in the ice, conscious of the aching void below us
on our right. This was "Hillary's Horror". Some way above this, we
entered the shattered section of steepest ice known as "Hell-fire
Alley". One or two Swiss flags had remained standing since they had
been planted seven or eight months earlier. One stood upright,
perched high on an isolated block of ice, surrounded by unbridgeable
gaps, another was horizontal beneath a massive wall which leaned
inexorably over; they marked a route which had changed out of all
recognition and was utterly impracticable now.

Our track now dodged in and out, up some hundreds of feet,
between, behind, over and even under colossal ice boulders. It is
difficult to give an adequate idea of this section. The ice masses had
fallen recently and had not yet settled down to form a solid slope;
they were, to say the least of it, loose and precariously poised one on
top of another, some in imminent danger of toppling over. Frequent
journeys up and down the Khumbu Icefall have blunted these first
impressions of "Hell-fire Alley", but I always regarded it as a dangerous place. On that first trip it was a relief to move to the right at its
top, towards more open ground. We were now in territory which,
though carved in larger blocks, was in more active movement; this was
the "Atom Bomb" area. We approached a shallow gully dominated by
wobbly-looking séracs and split from side to side by gaping crevasses.
Each, at this early stage, could be crossed by a leap or a long stride,
but later, as they changed shape and multiplied, two bridges were
required in this section. The "Atom Bomb" area was in constant
and audible movement. No day passed without some striking change
occurring, calling for a fresh reconnaissance of the route up to the
plateau where our tents of Camp II were pitched. In general, the
shelves of ice between cracks were subsiding, making big steps, but
in time the movement became more violent, the changes more significant. Their sound could be heard from Camp II—a dull, ominous
"wumph"—fortunately they seemed usually to occur at night.
Marker flags in this area seldom remained visible for many days after
they had been placed; they might be seen, fixed and upright, deep in
some new cavity, or they might have disappeared for ever.

It was about 12.30 p.m. when Ang Namgyal and I reached Camp

II. The tents were empty, but we needed to rest and shelter, for a violent wind was blowing in gusts down from the Western Cwm. We crawled in and lay there, perhaps for half an hour, before starting to follow the tracks leading upwards. About three hundred feet above the tents we met a jubilant trio descending. Ed and the Georges had reached the edge of the Cwm. They were eloquent about the many objective dangers ahead and the technical problems which they had faced. Although it could not yet be certain that we should, even now, find an entrance into the Western Cwm, this was indeed great news. Our first big problem was solved and we could begin to exploit our opportunity, improving the route and sending up loads to the top of the Icefall on the date planned for this operation to begin—24th April.

Although I was tired after coming all the way from Lake Camp, I was very keen to go on and have a view of this upper part of the route. Despite his great efforts, not only on that day but during four successive days, Ed Hillary insisted on joining my rope and returning some distance upwards, to point out the features of the route. The weather was bad and we could only see a certain distance, but I could appreciate that the track was menaced for hundreds of yards by ice cliffs higher up on the right. The big shelf on the edge of the Cwm which they had reached was just visible and apparently not very far above us. We returned to Camp II where a hot drink was being prepared by George Lowe. Later, the whole party went down to Base Camp.

To complete our happiness that day, we found a large mailbag awaiting us. Roberts had arrived at Thyangboche only two days earlier, and Greg had sent on the trusty Ang Norbu in all haste to give us this treat. Except for a small batch which had come up during the early part of the march, these were the first letters we had received since leaving Kathmandu.

I continued on my weary way to Lake Camp that evening and heaved yet another sigh of relief. One more milestone had been passed on the road to the summit.

*   *   *

We must now return to follow the activities of Charles Evans and his party, whom we left at Dingboche, busy teaching the use of oxygen to our Sherpas. They had gone up into the wide basin at the head of the Imja, in the centre of which stands an attractive peak of over 20,000 feet, its base surrounded by some of the several glaciers which converge here. It had been observed the previous year by Shipton's party on their way to explore the Barun gorge and they had given it the descriptive name of Island Peak.

One of the summits of this they proceeded to climb, increasing to no less than six our "bag" of peaks of about 19,000 or 20,000 feet. It was now time for this party to return to Base Camp at Thyangboche, for there was much to do. A large number of coolies was required to move our camp and all our gear to its new location up the Khumbu glacier: Roberts was about to arrive with sixty loads of oxygen; four-teen Low Altitude Sherpas were due to join the party. They went back. In three very full days they were ready to start off again for the new Base Camp, moving once more in two convoys, on 18th and 19th April respectively.

Like Hillary's party before them, they ran into bad weather and suffered much the same discomforts. Charles Wylie reported some interesting records for tent capacities—sixty Sherpas in a twelve-man Dome, eight in a two-man Meade. I went down to meet the first of these convoys as they arrived, laden with firewood on top of their other burdens, at Lobuje, one stage below our Lake Camp. It was some time since Charles Evans and I had met and there was much to hear and tell. With him were Greg and a newcomer to the party, James Morris of *The Times*, who had been sent to provide a first-hand account of our doings; he was to remain with us until the end of the expedition. He would thus relieve me to some extent of the burden of writing dispatches, for which I was to be most thankful during the period of the Assault.

While these rear parties approached Base Camp under Evans and Wylie, my party moved up to join Hillary, having had our allotted rest period beside the glacier lake. Wilfrid Noyce and Mike Ward went on ahead to re-site Base some hundreds of yards down the stony avenue in the centre of the glacier, for we were not happy either about the space available on the Swiss site or its state of sanitation. I hasten to add that this is no reflection on the Swiss, for we were to find the same trouble in our own camp later; despite the most stringent rules laid down by the doctors and insisted on by the rest of us, it is well-nigh impossible to enforce the principles of hygiene in these conditions of cold and dis-comfort. By the time I returned from Lobuje I found a number of plat-forms for the tents had been skilfully built upon the ice, from the stones which littered the surface; a general lay-out of the various departments had been prepared by Michael Ward.

We at once started our task of improving the route up the Icefall, continuing the splendid work of the Reconnaissance party, which was now having a well-earned rest at the Lake Camp. Reinforced by Mike Westmacott, now partly recovered from his sickness, Wilfrid Noyce and Mike Ward, later joined by myself, spent two days between Base and Camp II, cutting many new steps, chopping down dangerous ice impending over the track, preparing a safer deviation across and up

89

the big crevasse to avoid "Hillary's Horror", fixing new ropes at this and other places.

On the afternoon of the second day, 21st April, Mike Westmacott and I remained at Camp II for the night before moving up to the top of the Icefall, in order to choose a site and set up the first tents of Camp III. I had with me five Sherpas carrying equipment for this camp, and later that evening was joined by Hillary and Band. Hillary and Westmacott were to remain at Camp III to improve the track between the two Icefall camps. George Lowe had started with them from Base, but he was still not recovered from his illness and had to turn back; it would be some time before he was fit enough to take a full part in the work.

On 22nd April we set out, Ed Hillary and George Band going ahead to remake and flag the track while Mike Westmacott and I escorted the Sherpas at a slower pace. There had been a good deal of fresh snow —nine to twelve inches—since we had last gone over this ground, and no signs remained of their earlier route, which had not been flagged during the preliminary reconnaissance on 17th April. For the two leaders it was a gruelling task, wading knee-deep in new snow. Even for my party, more heavily laden and endeavouring to clear off more snow and stamp out a firm track, it was exhausting enough.

Except for the lower part, which I had climbed with Ed, this was new ground to me and I was intrigued to see this upper section of the Icefall for the first time. As had appeared from below, the nature of the ice was very different from that of the lower part. Whereas below Camp II the glacier was shattered into crumbling ruin, here we were moving through ice blocks of bigger dimensions; there was a general impression of subsidence rather than of a vast dynamited quarry. From the tents of Camp II, the line taken led us for some distance through another gully at the head of the small plateau, then swung steeply up to the right to reach the first of many characteristic obstacles, a sérac some 250 feet above the tents. We had to get on to a square-topped section of ice cliff which leaned out from the mountainside, half-detached from the parent block. Climbing this with the aid of large ice steps and a handline, we dodged round to its far side in order to bestride the gap and reach the terrace behind it.

A little farther on there was a huge trough. It must have measured at least sixty feet wide, partly filled with chunks of bare ice, and with a narrow platform some twenty feet down, which had sunk from the level of the terrace on which we stood. Here again a staircase had been cut, and we added a fixed rope to make the descent more easy. The exit was perhaps the most dangerous part of the whole journey between Base Camp and the Cwm, for the steep slope on the far side of this trough was covered by blocks of ice of all sizes, piled in indescribable confusion on a wide frontage and extending over some 200 feet up the slope. The collapse of any one of these would have spelt disaster to a party below. This avalanche must have come to rest not long before Ed's party had first negotiated it, for the débris was completely unstable, even more so than in the "Hell-fire Alley" area. And there was no avoiding it. First we had to cross a gaping fissure to reach the lower edge of these menacing boulders at the only feasible point, where a thin tongue of ice, unsupported from below and attached only to the lower lip of the crevasse, had to be relied upon for three anxious steps before it was possible to set foot on the upper edge. Three days later I noticed that this fragile bracket had disappeared into the blue depths below; I learned that it had disintegrated when Bourdillon gave it a light prod with his axe. The crevasse had widened by at least a foot. By then we had available the logs asked for by Westmacott, and we improvised a single-log "bridge" and handline, later to be replaced by two sections of the metal ladder. As an indication of the state of movement of the Icefall, I should add that, a week after this, the 12-foot ladder was in danger of falling into the chasm in its turn. Before we went down to Base for the last time at the end of May, Noyce had found it necessary to lash two wooden poles under the ladder to lengthen it.

After climbing directly upwards through the dangerous band of wobbly ice blocks we were able to turn left in the direction of the Cwm. We were now on the crest of the débris from the collapse of the cliffs above us, which marked the foot of the west ridge of Nuptse. The obvious line was to continue along this shelf, threatened though it was by the flanking cliffs, which would sooner or later disgorge more ice on to the mounting pile; indeed there was no other way. It led upwards in a slanting line, across the tops of countless loose ice boulders, until at last it was possible to pass through a gap to reach the foot of the first really solid line of cliffs at the very brink of the Western Cwm.

Here the risks were only too obvious, for this is just where the Cwm spills into the Icefall, and freshly fallen masses bore witness to the sudden change in gradient. The cliff is too high and steep to climb direct at this point—it rises forty feet sheer—so we contoured round its base to the right, passing between the main "berg" and a large block, about twenty feet high, which had recently split off without disintegrating. This passage, which we named "the Nutcracker", was particularly unpleasant both on account of the peculiarly shaky condition of all the ground at the top of the Icefall and the ever-present possibility of another slice peeling off the cliff and crushing a party in the act of passing through it. There was evidently a hollow space of unknown depth beneath the cliff, perhaps because the shelf of ice was jutting far out over the underlying rock base. In carving a climbable route through it, the ice fragments would not merely fall into the dark abyss but would set up a prolonged rumbling noise, accompanied by tremors of the surface, as if an underground train were passing beneath our feet. It was an eerie and frightening sensation.

The view round the corner was no more encouraging, for the cliff line continued unrelenting, as though to force the intruder right under the fire of avalanches from Nuptse. But there was one weakness in the ice: a narrow, sloping shelf leading to a vertical crack. This crack, which showed where a huge mass would later become detached from the Cwm ice, had been brilliantly led by Hillary on the day I had first met them above Camp II. Already it was noticeably wider, but aided by the steps he had cut we found much less trouble than he in wriggling up the fifteen feet until our heads appeared suddenly and dramatically on to the level shelf above. This was the highest point reached so far, but it was too near the unreliable edge to make a safe site for Camp III. Rather than bring our Sherpas farther, we hauled the loads up the cliff at a lower point and went on ourselves, together with Da Namgyal, to find a good spot. The plateau which we had reached was itself slowly toppling over the edge, a wide crack dividing it from another and higher level of ice; but this was still spanned at two points by snow bridges, apparently solid. We crossed the more durable of the two and found a shallow scoop in a wider area, not immediately overlooked by other cliffs. It would do admirably for the camp. The height was about 20,200 feet.

Impatient to find the answer to the question uppermost in our minds, Ed, George Band and I went straight on for some distance beyond the camp site, to prospect the route into the Cwm. Would we be confronted by a gap too wide to bridge, and, if so, could we climb down and out at the other side? These were burning questions whose answer could brook no delay. After steering a route around and over a number of big crevasses, we were soon stopped by one which could only be avoided if we would accept the risk of climbing right under the hanging ice adhering to the flanks of Everest's west ridge. By remarkable luck we reached it at its narrowest point; the gap was only about sixteen feet. Beyond, the Cwm began to level out. As far as this, the prospect was encouraging, and the next need was to bring up the ladder so as to reconnoitre even farther. It must be sent up without delay.

*   *   *

If I have dwelt at some length on the Icefall, it is because it loomed so large in our activities on Everest and for so long a period. However well prepared the track, the frequent movement of men and stores up and down it would always be a source of anxiety, and we must count ourselves most fortunate that no accident occurred during the six weeks our traffic was upon it.

The first ascent of the Icefall by Shipton's party in 1951 had been a very fine piece of route-finding and ice work. According to Hillary, the condition of this obstacle this year was incomparably worse than it had been two years ago, and the Swiss made no secret about the serious and dangerous nature of the problem as they had found it last spring. Each year, indeed, each month, it becomes transformed. Fresh surprises occur within the space of a few days. In a certain sense, every ascent will always be a new one, a "première". Our Icefall reconnaissance party had done a wonderful job in forcing and finding this particular route.

Leaving Hillary, Westmacott and Da Namgyal to improve the upper part of it and, if possible, find a means of by-passing the worst places, I returned to Base on 22nd April with George Band. In the two days since I had left it, Base had come to present a very different picture. Both the rear parties had now arrived and the place was a hive of activity, with a tent perched on each available level space. Tom Bourdillon, who had left my party over a week before on the bank of the Khumbu glacier in order to meet Roberts and take charge of the oxygen consignment, had erected for himself a workmanlike shelter as an equipment store, using the boxes as pigeon-holes. One of the several tree trunks ordered by Mike Westmacott had been set up as a flagpole for our large Union Jack. As usual, Thondup was efficiently established in a large stone-built kitchen, paved with card-board from empty ration boxes. A novel feature was a capacious ice cave tunnelled into one of the big pinnacles just behind the tents. It was Tom Stobart's idea for alternative living quarters, and a good one. Base seemed to be a well-organized and thorough-going concern. Roberts had come up to wish us luck. He had done an inestimable service to the expedition by delivering to us the oxygen by the date required, though it had meant sacrificing a part of his leave.

One of the first people who came forward as we approached the tents was a small, slightly-built figure with a wizened face and stubbly grey hair. He looked old, but his grin was youthful. It was Dawa Thondup. He had taken part in Himalayan expeditions since 1933, when he was a member of the porter team on Everest. He was decorated by Hitler in 1934 for his gallantry during a storm on Nanga Parbat, when six Sherpas and three members of a German expedition

93

lost their lives. Among numerous other battle honours figure Anna-purna in 1950 and the South Col of Everest in 1952.

Dawa and I were very old friends. We had been together in an attempt to climb Saltoro Kangri in the Karakoram many years ago, since when we had taken part in two expeditions in the Sikkim Hima-laya, as well as several treks in that area. I had last seen him in 1940 and had specially asked the Himalayan Club to persuade him to join us this year. Now in his late forties, Dawa was unfit when Tenzing had left Darjeeling with the others, but arrangements were made for him to come with Roberts a month later, together with another "Tiger", Ang Nyima. Thus enlisted, partly for reasons of friendship and sentiment, we could not guess what splendid service this little man was to perform on Everest.

Part IV

BUILD-UP

CHAPTER NINE

STOCK-PILING

IN London we had calculated that a period of about three weeks would be necessary for lifting our stores into the Western Cwm before making a bid for the summit. At intervals during the march-out and training periods, Charles Evans, Ed Hillary and I had been busy with more exact estimates, based on a number of alternative plans for the Assault and taking into account other related problems. I was most concerned to reduce to a minimum the amount of time actually spent on the mountain and to ensure that everybody should enjoy a rest at lower altitude at least once before the Assault started. We could not know at this stage when to expect the monsoon—the weather forecasts were to be given only from 1st May—but it was wise to assume an early onset of bad weather conditions; there was no reason to postpone the target date for readiness, which was 15th May. The weather was as yet unpredictable. It might well force us to wait for some time after that date before giving us our opportunity. In recognizing this, I had to consider the ill-effects of physical deterioration at high altitude, combined with the strain on morale of tedium and tension resulting from protracted waiting in a high camp. And there was another point. Although the plan of assault could not yet be determined, it was obvious that we should not be able to make more than two successive attempts and must then pause, rest and reorganize if these should not succeed.

With all these factors in mind, I now explained to those concerned with the various items of equipment and rations the main points regarding the stock-piling of supplies at the head of the Western Cwm to last us until the end of May. Should we be delayed after that date, we would have to send down Sherpas for replenishments later. The sum of these weight calculations showed that, provided there were no hitches—bad weather, unforeseen changes in the route, or sickness in the carrying parties—not only should the lift of baggage have been completed as far as our proposed Advance Base by mid-May, but it should be possible to fit in a rest period as well.

On the evening of 22nd April, therefore, I was able to outline the "Build-up" plan to all members of the expedition, as we ate supper in our Mess tent. Everyone was there except Mike Westmacott and Ed Hillary, whom I had left that morning at Camp III. The period was to be divided into two halves. During the first of these, we should mainly be occupied with shifting loads from Base Camp to Camp III at the top of the Icefall; during the second, the centre of activity would be in the Western Cwm. Between the two periods there would be a break for the majority of the party, with the possibility of getting well down the glacier, either to Lake Camp or Lobuje, to enjoy the pleasures and obvious benefits of lower height and a change of surroundings.

To lift the loads, twenty-eight out of our total of thirty-nine Sherpas would be required. They were to be divided into four parties, each of seven men; three of these parties were to be engaged during the first period in the Icefall and only one in the Cwm. This period would last from 24th April until 2nd May. To each party were assigned two members of the climbing party, who would take turns in escorting their team up and down during their journeys, and deal with the recurring need to renew the track and find a way round fresh obstacles as they occurred. The Low Level carrying parties, "Ferries", as they came to be called, would be in the charge of Bourdillon and Wylie, Ward and Westmacott, Band and Tenzing. George Lowe was still sick, but later he was able to take a full part. I was most anxious that, in negotiating the known dangers of the Icefall and the expected hidden crevasses in the Cwm, the Sherpas should not be exposed to risks which were not shared by ourselves.

In the second period after the break, which was to take place between 3rd and 5th May, three out of the four teams would be operating up the Cwm, in the first place from Camp III, but later partly from Camp IV upwards to the foot of the Lhotse Face, while only one would be moving up and down the Icefall. These "Ferries" should enable us to move the whole climbing party up to the Advance Base (i.e. Camp IV) by 14th May, and to establish a dépôt of stores at a Camp V at the foot of the Lhotse Face, ready for carrying to the South Col. In this we were departing in only one important particular from the "Basis for Planning" drawn up in England, for there remained the second and final stage of the Build-up, the "carry" to the South Col. But there was as yet no firm plan from which we could decide the exact quantities of stores required at the South Col; the Lhotse Face which leads to it had still not been seen, much less reconnoitred, and the amounts which could be lifted up this section of the climb would be strictly limited, for this was expected to be the crux of the whole ascent. In these circumstances, it would have been foolish to make assumptions so far ahead, and I now preferred to consider the whole of our eventual operations up the Face of Lhotse as falling within the Assault period. After speaking to the members of the expedition, I spoke, at Tenzing's suggestion, to each group of Sherpas chosen for the various ferrying tasks. All were cheerful and willing.

At this stage in our progress, with important and urgent events ahead, I invited Charles Evans to be prepared to take over as leader in case of sickness or mishap affecting myself: all members of the party were asked to accept this position should it arise. The need or otherwise of a deputy leader had already been discussed in London before we left; there was a precedent in pre-war Everest expeditions. It had seemed to me then that it was undesirable to set up a hierarchy of command and that there was always a danger of over-organizing. In any case, we always looked upon the leader's job as merely one among the many responsibilities which we shared out between us.

*   *   *

Before entering upon this very full and important period, two things remained to be done. A number of crevasses in the Icefall had still to be bridged, and we did not know yet how many others might bar our way up the Cwm; the Cwm had not yet been entered, and a route up it must be made, a site for Advance Base chosen. These things must be done at once.

Next morning Charles Wylie set out with a party of Sherpas carrying an awkward load of 12-foot poles, cut from the forests around Thyangboche. His task was to bridge all the big gaps as far as Camp II and release the ladder sections which had been laid temporarily over some of these, so that they should be available for the major crevasse above Camp III, discovered by Hillary, Band and myself on the 22nd. He had an adventurous day. Having spanned with big logs the chasm over which two sections of the ladder had previously been placed, he went across this narrow and much less convenient bridge —only two poles lashed together with rope. Following him was one Pasang Dorji, a shy, almost furtive lad whose normal job was assisting Thondup in the cookhouse; he had begged to try his hand at more exciting work. Half-way across, the void beneath him doubtless began to prey too heavily on Pasang's mind. The inevitable happened. He lurched sideways and dropped like a stone into the abyss. Charles had perhaps some premonition of this, for he had just bidden Pasang leave behind his load. Both he and the Sherpa whose turn it would be to cross next had, of course, taken the normal climbing precaution of belaying the rope over their ice-axes, buried deeply in the snow. Despite all, Charles had an exhausting time hauling with all his

99

strength on the rope before Pasang arrived, utterly breathless and very frightened, at the far edge of the crevasse. He finally landed, flopping on the snow, in Charles's words, "like a dead seal". Both he and his rescuer remained in this position for some minutes to recover; it had been a remarkable feat of strength on the part of the leader. After this incident, Pasang returned to his chores in the cookhouse.

Only a short distance above, Charles was startled to see another "rope" of three Sherpas, led by Annullu, an experienced man, hurtling down a steep slope above him. Very fortunately they came to rest without being swallowed up by one of the many waiting crevasses. Annullu had broken a crampon, but had decided with jaunty confidence that not only could he climb up these ice slopes with one crampon, but could safely continue to lead his rope. These two incidents, among many which occurred almost daily in the following weeks, demonstrated the need for members of the climbing party to accompany Sherpa carrying teams and share the hazards with them.

Accidents were not confined to the Sherpas, nor were they necessarily due to inexperience. On his way down to Base Camp on 26th April, Ed Hillary had a narrow escape in company with Tenzing. While descending the "Atom Bomb" area, he jumped down one of the several big "steps" dividing crevasses in that zone of constant movement. The whole mass of ice on which he landed collapsed beneath him and he fell towards a crevasse below. That no harm came of it was due to the foresight and skill of Tenzing, who was strongly placed against a slip on the part of his companion and held him brilliantly on the rope.

The other task, that of entering and finding a route up to the head of the Western Cwm, was undertaken by Charles Evans, Tenzing, Ed Hillary and myself. Ed was already at Camp III, so the remaining three of us went up there on the morning of 24th April, ahead of the "High Level" or Cwm Ferry party of seven Sherpas, led by Wilfrid Noyce and Greg, who were on their way up to start work from Camp III. Snow had fallen heavily during the night, and because of this I spoke to Ed Hillary at Camp III during the 8 a.m. wireless call—we now had our wireless sets distributed one to each of the Icefall camps, working to a control set at Base. "Hullo, Ed at Camp III—this is John speaking from Base—Tenzing, Charles Evans and I are coming up to join you today for Cwm reconnaissance—owing to yesterday's heavy snowfall we'll be very grateful if you and Mike will work downwards towards Camp II and remake the track—Over."

Hillary, in acknowledging this, gave an interesting summary of his work the day before at the top of the Icefall. "Hullo, John—this is Ed at Camp III—Mike and I had a pretty tough day casting round for an alternative approach to Camp III and also for another way into the Cwm—Line of cliffs to right towards Nuptse quite hopeless and much more dangerous than direct route—We'll have to stick to this one—Mike and I have done quite a lot of work on the Nutcracker —bloody dangerous place—fixed pitons for handline on the lower wall—Also put rope ladder down the cliff for the boys to bring loads up here avoiding the ice crack—Looking forward to seeing you, John —Whack-o—Over."

The track as far as Camp II was a most fatiguing struggle. For myself the difficulties were increased, for I was suffering from a sudden bout of diarrhoea which had left me very weak. It was snowing as we plodded on our way and this continued for the rest of that day. We reached the camp very tired and decided to rest there until the following day, unable to take advantage of the track so laboriously renewed for us. Camp II was full that night, for besides ourselves there was the High Level Ferry and also a Low Level team making a normal stage here for the night on their way to Camp III.

In spite of Ed's efforts in stamping out the track through deep new snow on 24th April, our party had another hard struggle up to Camp III next day. It was far worse for the High Level Ferry party who had to carry two sections of the ladder the whole way to Camp III from Camp II, where they had been left by Charles Wylie on the 23rd. Since they had not the necessary spanner, they had had to continue up the Icefall carrying these sections as a 12-foot length. It was easy to imagine the nightmare which this proved to be, in the labyrinth of ice boulders above that crevasse and at many other points of the way. Indeed it called for all the great reserves of Wilfrid's patience to finish the journey.

It was good to spend that first night at the threshold of the Western Cwm. Already we had a first consignment of stores outside the tents, carried there by the first Low Level Ferry; the High Level team was in position and, provided we could force the way into the Cwm, they would follow our reconnaissance party up to Advance Base on the morrow. So anxious was I to put an end to our remaining uncertainty on this point that Ed, Charles Evans and I started upwards at four o'clock that afternoon, followed by Tenzing and Wilfrid, to have a preview of the prospects. We took with us three ladder sections, which we had estimated would be sufficient for bridging the big crevasse. Putting them together at the 16-foot gap, with the assistance of Tenzing and Wilfrid, we lowered the ladder carefully across and crawled over one at a time. There still remained many obstacles, yet unseen, to getting up the Cwm, let alone the mountain, but somehow this moment when we stood together on the far side of that crevasse made

a special impression on me. It symbolized our entry into the Western Cwm. The unpleasant fears of operations with complicated ropeways, to which the Swiss had been compelled to resort, vanished. We felt sure we were through.

In this elated mood we went on, late into the evening. There was some difficult route-finding to do, for the crevasses in this lowest part of the Western Cwm were numerous and large; a short section of the route lay unavoidably exposed to bombardments from the tottering ice cliffs above the north edge of the glacier. One interesting passage, later known as "Hunt's Gully", consisted of a very steep descent into the shallow depths of a crevasse, crossing the crack in the ice by a snow bridge and climbing out along a narrow terrace on the far side. We fixed a rope to assist us in getting in and out on the lower edge. Gradually we were able to work away towards the centre of the glacier. Its wrinkled surface smoothed out. As we went on we could see more and more up the Cwm until the whole of Lhotse was revealed, its rocks, heavily powdered with snow, bathed in the evening light. We continued, drawn as though by some irresistible force, until at last we could look upon that scene which had been the object of so much study and conjecture during our London planning—the South Col of

Everest and the great slope below it. There it was, still distant but dramatic, familiar as though we had known it for a long time. We turned back as the sun was setting behind Pumori across the Khumbu glen, and went down excitedly to our tents to tell the others.

Aided by sleeping-pills, I slept well that first night at over 20,000 feet, untroubled by the rumbling avalanches which peeled off the cliffs below the Lho La. 26th April was a brilliant morning. From the edge of our balcony on the ice cliff we looked down some 800 feet on to the little group of tents half-way up the Icefall and could watch minute figures moving about; they were the two Low Level teams, fourteen Sherpas and two Sahibs getting ready to do their scheduled run for the day from Camp II up to Camp III and down to Base. Across the valley stood the ring of peaks enclosing the Khumbu glacier at its bend: Pumori, tall, tapering like a pencil point, Lingtren One, square and steep-ridged, Lingtren Two, thin as a wafer at its top, looking incredibly fragile. We were all in great spirits as we made our way that morning into the Cwm, the reconnaissance party with Evans and myself leading on one rope, followed by Hillary and Tenzing, now starting to form a team which was to strengthen in the coming weeks into a match-winning partnership. After them came Gregory and Noyce with their Sherpas, carrying the high-priority stores for Advance Base and beyond. It was brilliantly fine—indeed it would soon be stiflingly hot. New snow sparkled dazzlingly in the sun, but it was a foot deep here in the Cwm and we did not have easy going. The previous day we had seen signs of a camp some two hundred yards away from our route and guessed it to be the Swiss Camp III. This was confirmed by Tenzing, who now led Hillary off to collect any food and other stores which might be useful to us.

Charles and I continued to move right-handed towards the south edge of the glacier, across a wide expanse of comparatively level ground. We were forced in this direction, partly by the huge crevasses which split the surface from side to side, and partly also because we had noted that there was a "step" or minor icefall, marked by a group of monster crevasses and ice walls, in the Cwm some distance farther up, which could best be circumvented on this flank. Planting flags as we went on, we rose up beside this "step" and reached the upper part of the Cwm, again smooth and stretching almost without break to a second "step", guarding the foot of the slopes beneath the South Col and Lhotse—the distance might be one and a half miles. As we sat there, we could now see not only Lhotse and the South Col, but the great bulk of Everest itself, its west face falling over 7,000 feet to the floor of the Cwm on the opposite side. The rocks of this vast precipice, so black when we had first sighted them from below Namche a month

before, were now sprinkled with snow, which was being torn off in clouds by the west wind.

Tenzing and Hillary had now caught us up, and during a rest we shared some Swiss cheese, chocolate and Vita-Weat which they had found, among many tins of pemmican, at the old camp site. This pair now went ahead, slanting back to the left above the smaller icefall to reach a point beneath a prominent snow shoulder on the west ridge of Everest, where the Swiss had placed their Camp IV last autumn. We arrived at about 12.30 p.m. after a three and a half hours' journey from Camp III, and spent a happy hour digging. Numerous containers of various shapes and sizes were seen half-buried beneath the winter snow; their contents were exciting to surmise and no less satisfactory to discover. Bacon, wafer bread, cheese, jam, pemmican, porridge, chocolate, milk powder, solid "Meta" fuel—all these were brought to light. The food and delicacies would be useful to supplement our own rations and provide a welcome variety. There was also some clothing and equipment, including a large but badly damaged tent.

The weather had already closed in as we descended the Cwm that afternoon. The Ferry party had carried their loads to the top of the first "step", within about three-quarters of an hour's walk of the Camp, and had therefore done very well on this, their first trip up the Cwm. We found them in excellent form when we returned to Camp III, proud of being chosen for the High Level work, and ready for the "carry" on the next day. Indeed, there was no lack of stores for them to take. The two Low Level parties had piled their cargo outside the tents and had already gone down, for they would also have to turn round and return to Camp II next morning. There was thus exactly twice as much to carry as the Camp III party at their present strength could lift in one day, and this disproportion would increase progressively during the first half of the Build-up period. They were a fine crew, wonderfully led by Noyce and Gregory: fat little Gompu, now in his element, always seeking helpful jobs to perform; Kancha, tough and cheerful; Pasang Dawa, quiet, experienced and sensible; Tashi Phutar, Ang Tharke, Pemba Norbu, Phu Dorji.

So the work went on, day after day, for nine days. At the end of this time, each Low Level team had made no fewer than five complete trips to Camp III and back, staging regularly at Camp II for the night. The High Level men had made six long journeys to and from Camp IV. Always the morning heat, both in the Icefall and the Cwm, was stifling, inducing a heavy feeling of lethargy, known as "glacier lassitude". Each day fresh snow fell; each morning the track, wiped out overnight, had to be remade. Floundering in loose snow was terribly exacting work, especially in the Icefall, where with a false step one was likely to slip between two blocks of ice, perhaps waist deep, and have to struggle out encumbered by a 40-lb. load. It was a labour shared by Sahib and Sherpa alike, even if not in equal proportion. The climbing members went less frequently, although they often carried loads to help a tired man. This was simply because our energy had to be spared as far as possible for the tasks which would fall to each of us in the Assault, and it should be remembered that, despite newspaper reports to the contrary, no decisions had yet been made as to which climbers might have the supreme rôle of going for the summit.

By 2nd May we had moved approximately ninety loads, each weighing an average of 40 lb., to Camp III, and, of these, about forty-five loads onwards to, or towards Camp IV, our Advance Base. These stores had been selected as of high priority by Charles Evans, our "Quartermaster", in consultation with those responsible for each commodity. Before leaving Base Camp, where they were weighed and made up into loads by Tenzing and Evans, they were marked with a painted "III" or "IV" or "V", according to their destination. Some had been dumped by more energetic Low Level teams as far as one hour's journey above Camp III, so as to ease the heavy task of the Cwm Ferry party. Bearing in mind the weather conditions with which we had to contend, remembering too that this was a period of "trial and error" regarding many of our men, particularly those working in the Icefall—a number not unnaturally were found unsuitable and had to be changed—and that sickness also depleted the strength of the parties, this was a noteworthy achievement. Moreover, we experienced during this time a crisis with the crampons, essential for the Icefall. At least twelve pairs had broken beyond repair and despite an urgent message transmitted from the wireless station at Namche to the Himalayan Club, replacements could not be expected for several weeks. It was strenuous and anxious work for all, and especially for the Sherpas. It was frightening for some of the novices. It was a routine which became increasingly monotonous by its constant repetition. Yet there were no complaints. The scheduled Ferries ran to an almost clockwork timetable. The Low Level Ferry would leave Base at 1200—arrive Camp II, 1500—spend night—leave Camp II, 0800—arrive Camp III, 0930—leave Camp III (down), 1030—arrive Base, 1400. The High Level Ferry would leave Camp III 0800 —arrive Camp IV, 1100—leave Camp IV, 1200—arrive Camp III, 1330; and so on. Our Ferry trains and their guards had well earned their rest on 2nd May.

*   *   *

Base Camp was not a beautiful place. Situated at about 17,900 feet, above and beyond the region of the highest vegetation, yet hemmed in by the glacier pinnacles and overshadowed by the great bulk of Nuptse, it was lifeless without the compensation of stark grandeur to impress the mind. Breathlessly hot on a still, windless morning, it would become chill and drear as the clouds billowed up the valley and the snow began to fall—a depressingly regular occurrence during the first three weeks of our occupation. The ice was melting visibly all around, and our tent platforms soon stood comically and uncomfortably high above the general surface level of stony wilderness. An unpleasant odour permeated the close surroundings. Fortunately most of us only visited the place infrequently and for brief periods, for it undoubtedly tested the happy relations which existed between us all. It seemed also to give rise to sudden bouts of diarrhoea, which might have been caused by the growing insanitation around us. George Band, George Lowe and Mike Westmacott were more or less seriously sick with this complaint for many days. I have already explained the almost insuperable difficulties of keeping the camp clean, mainly owing to the intense cold at night. This should not, therefore, be interpreted as an aspersion on our three able and assiduous doctors, who were constantly examining patients and handing out interesting new drugs. Even Michael Ward, whose recommendation of the pills he dispensed was once heard to be: "Try some of these—they do no good at all", inspired implicit confidence.

Yet there were times when we appreciated Base Camp despite its drawbacks. It was a haven of luxury to the weary climber coming down from a reconnaissance up the Cwm, or even from a shorter routine Ferry trip up and down the Icefall. There was good food from Thondup's skilled hands; during this period we actually ate fresh beef, for thanks to the initiative of our caterers, George Band and Griff Pugh, and the stoicism of our butcher, George Lowe, a yak had been lured up from the distant pastures and slaughtered in the precincts of the camp. Potatoes were a luxury we could enjoy at Base, whereas in the Cwm they were quickly spoiled by frost. There was usually a choice of accommodation, whether a Meade tent to yourself, the convivial atmosphere of the Mess tent or the constant temperature of an ice cave—we had by now carved several from the ice hill to make up for the steady drift of our tents upwards into the Cwm. Above all, perhaps, there was the chance to rest and relax; to sleep, write or read; listen to Radio Ceylon. And there were other moments when Base Camp was enshrined in a certain beauty. At night the snow would often cease and the clouds disperse. There was a full moon during the Build-up, and to leave the Mess tent after supper on your way to bed was an unforgettable experience. The moon was lighting the top of Pumori and Lingtren, making the slippery sides of the near ice pinnacles shine like polished silver; towards Everest the Icefall was plunged in deep shadow. It was grippingly cold— $-23°$ C.—and utterly quiet, save for an intermittent murmuring from some Sherpas' tent where a lamp was glowing dimly through the canvas, or a sudden dull roar as ice broke from the cliffs of the Lho La. At moments such as these it was possible to feel more kindly towards the camp on the Khumbu glacier.

None the less, when the opportunity came to rest—for most, this was between 2nd and 5th May, for others, shortly after these dates —the chosen holiday camp was Lobuje. At a distance of barely two and a half hours' journey from Base Camp down the west bank of the Khumbu glacier, Lobuje is indeed a delectable spot. It was still early in the year for the grass and flowers to be fully up, yet even the dead grass and dry pods of last year's glory, aided by a little imagination, gave an impression of greenery. The place consists of a couple of yak-herds' shelters upon a small mound, in the trough between the glacial moraine and the mountainside. A spring of fresh, clear water bubbles out strongly from the turf just below the huts; weeds wave lazily in the current. The earliest flowers were beginning to blossom in early May: tightly cushioned moss campion and mauve primula. A magenta-coloured azalea was also in scanty bloom on bushes among the boulders. The valley wind, blowing up-glacier, spared this sheltered nook. Bird and animal life were a delight after living for a time in a dead world. Tibetan tail-less rats, looking for all the world like grey guinea-pigs, and a pair of martens played among the rocks; there was always a variety of birds—snow pigeons, white-capped redstarts, rosefinches, a wren, an enormous lammergeyer drifting listlessly overhead, and various hawks. Surrounded by this atmosphere of peace and comfort, you could once more look upon the high peaks as things of beauty, indeed they inspired a feeling of friendship once more. There, above the far edge of the boulder-strewn glacier, stood Nuptse, the near end of its long ridge assuming the form of a sharp snow cone, perched in isolation above a plunging precipice of rock, blue ice cliff and shining slope.

From 2nd May until about the 12th, there was a small but continuous population at Lobuje. One and all benefited enormously in both physical health and renewed zest for the tasks ahead of them. For any future venture as serious and on as large a scale as Everest, a rest camp of this sort is highly to be recommended.

It was while resting here that Charles Wylie received news of the birth of his son, in a telegram passed over the Indian wireless link at Namche Bazar; an earlier mention by the B.B.C. had not been received by us. In forwarding these glad tidings, our friend at the Namche wireless station added his own congratulations: "I am transported with great exultation to announce the birth of your son. I hope that you have cause for similar rejoicing at least once a year. Please pay bearer one rupee."

CHAPTER TEN

LHOTSE FACE: ONE

W HILE the work of ferrying loads came to a temporary stop in the early days of May, an event of great significance was in progress. This was a reconnaissance of the Lhotse Face, the third major reconnaissance to be undertaken in the course of our expedition. In fact, this excursion was also a dress rehearsal for Everest, for experiments were to be carried out in the use of both types of oxygen apparatus at higher altitudes than had been possible hitherto. These dual aims—first, the reconnaissance, to push up as high as possible on the Face, find a practicable route and report on the nature of the problem; and, second, the testing of the oxygen equipments—had to be achieved before I could decide on the plan for the Assault.

When we were discussing the project earlier, Charles Evans, Ed Hillary and I had hoped that we might get very high on the mountain even at this early period; indeed I dreamed of getting above the South Col, using Closed-Circuit apparatus. But it was clear that we must not expend undue effort on this rehearsal at the expense—in terms of human exertion, time and equipment—of the Assault itself. Before briefing the team selected to carry it out, therefore, I decided to go with them myself to make a preliminary reconnaissance of the upper Cwm and lower slopes of the Face and try out the Closed-Circuit oxygen once again.

The main reconnaissance party, using Closed-Circuit oxygen, consisted of Charles Evans and Tom Bourdillon, who would camp as high as possible up the Lhotse Face and continue next day, if possible to the South Col. Charles Wylie and Michael Ward would be in support of them, using Open-Circuit equipment. Their task was to help in establishing the camp in the Lhotse Face and render any other assistance that might be needed. In addition, they would be able to report on the efficacy of their own oxygen equipment; Michael also undertook to make certain physiological observations for Griff Pugh. To carry the loads for the party, the seven élite Sherpas were to participate, and Charles Wylie would have an opportunity of watching the performance of these men, his team-elect for the Assault. For them, too, it would be a "trial match". I had hoped that they also would be able to use oxygen, thus increasing their understanding of it and confidence in its value, but it would have greatly increased the loads, and we were already finding the need to economize on oxygen, owing to the leakage of a number of cylinders on their way from England, so we had to abandon this plan. A final briefing would be given only after the preliminary reconnaissance had taken place, but the general intention was that it should be completed during the rest period.

I escorted the special Sherpa team from Base to Camp III on 30th April. Tom Bourdillon followed with Charles Evans, both making a low-level trial of the Closed-Circuit system. Others on the Icefall route that day were Griff Pugh himself with his retainer, the boy Mingma, son of Da Tensing. They were to come up to Camp IV or, alternatively, stay at Camp III during the reconnaissance. This was Mingma's first experience of the Icefall or any other serious climbing, and it was perhaps too severe a test for a youngster of thirteen, carrying a considerable load. Griff had a great affection for little Mingma. He arrayed him in some of his own clothing, and Mingma—height 4 feet 6 inches—would proudly go about his duties draped to the knees in a sweater suitable for a 6-foot man. It was charming to listen to them conversing each in his own language, incomprehensible to the other, and it was hardly surprising that Mingma would occasionally make mistakes in carrying out his instructions. One would hear the fatherly reproof of Griff, in slow, pedantically clear English: "Mingma, how many times have I told you not to do that?" And the boy would gaze at him, contritely accepting a rebuke which he did not understand, in respect of some misdemeanour of which he was unaware. On one occasion, Griff had put aside a packing-case purporting to contain important physiological equipment, test tubes and the like, to be carried up the Icefall. His feelings were understandable when, on arrival at Camp III after a most tedious journey with a weary and stumbling Mingma dragging at the end of a tight rope (or vice versa—I forget who was the more in need of assistance) Griff eagerly opened the box to extract his treasures, only to find that instead of test tubes it contained bottle upon bottle of mango chutney.

At Camp III that afternoon we issued for the first time the so-called "Bradley" High Altitude boots with their accompanying crampons. These had been carried there in the first part of the Build-up for use in and above the Cwm. By leaving our normal mountaineering boots and crampons at Camp III, we were able to ease the acute shortage of these latter items of equipment for use in the Icefall. The new boots were rather warm at this lower altitude, but they proved very comfortable to wear.

On 1st May, Charles Evans, Tom Bourdillon and I went up the Cwm to establish Camp IV—so far it was no more than a dump of stores—on our way to get to grips with the Lhotse Face. We were to make a preliminary acquaintance of the Face the next day and would then be joined by Wylie and Ward for the main reconnaissance. With us were six of the seven élite Sherpas; Topkie, a young boy of no great experience who had nevertheless reached the South Col last year, had fallen out soon after leaving Base the previous day, suffering from the prevailing hacking cough. Everyone in the party was carrying a heavy load, for not only did we start short of one porter, but Da Namgyal, one of our most outstanding men, had to drop out not more than one hour's journey from the camp. We divided his load between us, carrying about 50 lb. each. We three were using the Closed-Circuit apparatus; the heat of this in the intense glare of the morning sun, beating down into the windless basin, made it a trying trip. Despite this and the usual heavy going, making a fresh track in the snow which had fallen the day before, we eventually reached Camp IV in two and a half hours, an hour less than the time taken in the Cwm reconnaissance a few days before. The Sherpas returned to Camp III the same afternoon in order to carry further stores required for the reconnaissance. They were to come up with Wylie and Ward the next day.

Camp IV provided a perfect viewpoint for an examination of the problem which the reconnaissance party were about to tackle. Sited in a sheltered hollow, close beneath the immense cliffs falling from the summit ridge of Everest, it stood back less than a mile from the head of the Cwm. Enclosing the Cwm on the far side, the long ridge of Nuptse ran its level course, rising 4,000 feet from the valley floor: steep, striated by rock bands below its jagged crest. Even at this distance, the wall enclosing the head of the Cwm seemed to be on a huge scale, the prospect of climbing it almost desperate. A vast expanse of steep snow, bared in places by the wind to reveal long streaks of shining ice, its smooth uniformity is broken by two significant features. Taking its origin directly from the wide opening of the South Col, a rib of rock stands out from the Face, falling obliquely from left to right, and flattening into the snow surface at about half height. This was christened by the Swiss the "Eperon des Genevois" and called by us "the Geneva Spur". There is neither shelf nor change of gradient on which to place a tent along the flanks of this spur, and the rocks themselves are uncomfortably steep. Farther to the right and directly beneath the turreted top of Lhotse, the surface of the Face is again interrupted by a succession of shallow, shelving terraces, separated by crevasses and steep ice walls. This, known as the Lhotse glacier—it might more aptly be described as a glaciated slope—starts about 3,000 feet below Lhotse's summit, or some two-thirds of the way up towards the South Col from the head of the Cwm. Except in the area where this Lhotse glacier spills into the Cwm, the Face itself is severed from the steepening upper slopes of the Cwm by a horizontal crevasse, a "*Bergschrund*", which skirts its foot. Evidently the most direct way to attain the Col is to force a crossing over this *Bergschrund* and make for the Geneva Spur, climbing by the slopes on one or other of its flanks. But the slope is unrelentingly steep and much of it is ice-covered. There is virtually no natural resting-place for a tent between the Cwm and the Col, over a height of 4,000 feet. This is the route taken by the Swiss last spring. They followed close beside the right edge and made straight for the Col; their success in reaching it although nearly at the end of their strength was an astonishing performance.

By contrast with this, the Lhotse glacier provides a succession of giant "steps", each liable to hold deep snow, each only to be reached by climbing up a steep or vertical ice wall: frequent deviations have to be made to find the least difficult passages. It leads towards Lhotse; at its highest point, therefore, a long traverse must be made away to the left, towards the Geneva Spur, in order to reach the Col. It is thus a considerably longer route.

Comparing the two alternatives before us, one point stood out and was underlined by the hard experience of the Swiss. This was the absolute need to make at least one resting-place for the night in the eventual journey to the South Col. In this way, the ascent could be made in two stages; indeed we might need to find two camp sites and break the journey into three stages. This was due to the difficulties of the climbing, combined with the altitude at which these difficulties must be tackled—from 22,000 to 26,000 feet. Only by discovering a route via the more devious Lhotse glacier could such resting-places be found. Viewing this problem from the distant slopes of Pumori in 1951, this was also the opinion expressed by Shipton. It had been almost a foregone conclusion before we left London. The Lhotse Face reconnaissance party were expected to find the best way up the Lhotse glacier; they hoped to find the camp sites used by the Swiss in their autumn attempt, but it was not by any means certain that they would retrace in detail the route taken by our predecessors.

We continued upwards on 2nd May, still using oxygen. It was sultry and the heat seemed almost unbearable in our masks; as usual, we were sinking deep into new snow, and we were now climbing over untrodden ground. A second and final "step" or small icefall defends the last hollow at the head of the Cwm, but by keeping to the north side of the glacier it was easy to dodge this obstacle, and we were

A	First Step	J	The Bergschrund
B	Second Step	K	Point reached by Hunt, Evans
C	Lhotse Glacier		and Bourdillon on 2nd May,
D	The Traverse, 25,000 ft.		1953, 22,500 ft.
E	Eperon des Genevois (Geneva Spur)	△IV	Advance Base (or Camp IV), 21,200 ft.
e	Eperon Couloir	△V	Camp V, 22,000 ft.
F	South Col	△VI	Camp VI (Temporary Camp), 23,000 ft
G	Lhotse, 27,800 ft.	△VII	Camp VII, 24,000 ft.
H	General line of South-East Ridge	△VIII	Camp VIII, 26,000 ft.

By W. Heaton Cooper, based on the line drawing by Robert Anderson in
The Story of Everest by W. H. Murray, published by J. M. Dent & Sons, Ltd.

scarcely troubled by crevasses. Above this "step", and standing mid-way between the direct line of the South Col and the summit of Lhotse, we found traces of the Swiss Camp V; a few sticks marking the limits of the camp and several food boxes half-hidden in the snow. We had taken two hours, about twice as long as the average time required to make the journey later on. The height of this camp was approximately 22,000 feet by our reckoning.

We now examined the foot of the Face and chose a point away to the right where a shelf running up and across an ice step seemed to afford lodgment on the steep slopes above; it seemed a weak link in the defences. Long before we reached this, it began snowing heavily and our pace became even slower. For the first time while using oxygen equipment I experienced a feeling of effort and had to rest fairly frequently when taking my turn to lead; indeed we were all reduced to much the same state. One and a half hours after leaving the Swiss Camp V, we had climbed the first steep rise above the foot of the Lhotse Face, finally cutting steps up bare ice to reach a typical terrace, which was dominated by a big ice wall, partly overhanging. It might have been no more than 600 feet above Camp V, for we had averaged, even at this moderate altitude, less than 500 feet an hour. The traverse which we had seen from below started leftwards from this point, and we rested for a while. The weather was now very bad. The Cwm was filled with heavy clouds. From where we sat, the ground was so steep above that it was not possible to discern the line which we had selected from below. It seemed best to return rather than expend effort which it would be better to reserve for the main reconnaissance in the following days. We had removed our masks and the effect of oxygen lack was very marked. Our movements were noticeably sluggish, as I was to realize when walking a few paces along the terrace to take a photograph. But it was interesting that in this state of anoxia the mind was still conscious of this slowing-down effect.

Going down towards the Cwm, my oxygen bottle was soon empty, and Tom removed it as well as the soda lime canister to lighten the load. Charles Evans likewise threw away his bottle and canister soon afterwards. Though we were relieved of 30 lb. from our backs and descending over easy ground in the tracks we had already made, both of us were very tired. I found it a great effort even to place one foot in front of the other, and I believe Charles's experience was similar. Tom still had a reserve of oxygen and continued to use his set; he was therefore in better shape than we, but it was a very weary party which reached Camp IV at about 4 p.m. that afternoon.

While we had been thus engaged, another oxygen experiment, also planned to take place just before the rest period, was in progress at a lower level. Leaving Base Camp that morning and using Open-Circuit sets at a flow rate of 4 litres a minute, Ed Hillary and Tenzing had climbed directly to Camp IV in exactly five hours, including a total period of forty-five minutes spent in rests at Camps II and III. The state of the track up the Cwm had not been good owing to the prevailing weather conditions the day before. This was a truly remarkable achievement, an indication both of the going powers of these two exceptional men and of the efficiency of the equipment they were using. Both were quite fresh and anxious to start on the long journey back to Base. I had arranged to go down with them at the conclusion of the preview of the Lhotse Face, but I was too tired to join them and they left almost at once, for the tracks were already disappearing under fresh snow, they were heading into a snowstorm and there remained only two hours of daylight. They had a terrible time going down the two miles of the Cwm, staggering over a fearful breakable crust on the snow surface, frequently losing the route through the Icefall. In spite of all they had accomplished that day, blinding snow and the fact that it was now dark and the track masked by new snow, they reached Base Camp soon after 7.30 p.m., less than three and a half hours after leaving Camp IV: "Tired"—to quote Hillary's diary —"but by no means exhausted".

The whole reconnaissance party moved up to Camp V on 3rd May. I left them with instructions to establish a camp as high as possible on the Lhotse Face, and from there the Closed-Circuit party would push on next day. From our experience on 2nd May, it was now clear that in the present condition of snow there was very slight chance of their getting to the South Col, but it was hoped that they might reach the top of the Lhotse glacier and be able to inspect at close quarters the beginning of the traverse towards the Geneva Spur; this part of the route had seemed to me to be a danger-point for avalanches. In view of the great effort which we had had to make in reaching a point but little above the foot of the Face, I stressed that the whole operation should be limited to forty-eight hours; we decided that the reconnaissance party should be back at Base Camp by 6th May. I then left them in this, our highest camp so far, and returned with three Sherpas, Da Tensing, Gyaljen and Ang Dawa II, who were unwell, first to Camp IV and then to Camp II, arriving at dusk. We spent the night there before descending to Base Camp on 4th May; the Lhotse Face reconnaissance was safely launched and we must now await their report.

The weather continued to be dismally bad; more snow piled up in the Cwm as Charles Evans's party started up the Face on 4th May.

Instead of following the possible lead on the right flank which we had inspected, they cast more over to the left at the prompting of Ang Temba, who remembered the Swiss route. It all looked most unpromising: steep, bulging séracs hanging over the topmost terrace of the Cwm, beneath the Lhotse glacier. There was one possibility—a gully slanting diagonally to the right, set at a high angle and filled with thigh-deep, powdery snow. Charles Evans chanced to see a piece of thin rope on the surface and, pulling it, revealed a handline; it was the beginning of the Swiss autumn route. They struggled up it. Vertical ice then forced them to traverse left and round another bulge, up between further ice cliffs, always on exceedingly steep ground. In some ways this intricate route-finding, pitch by pitch, might be compared with a complex route on a rock face, rather than a problem of ice and snow.

On the way up Ward, climbing on Open-Circuit equipment with Evans, complained of breathing difficulties. On examining his set, Bourdillon discovered that he was getting only just over 1 litre a minute instead of 4. He was found to be in some distress and nothing could be done about the fault, so Ward stopped to await the return of those who would later be descending to Camp V.

For a time they were able to climb directly upwards, breasting a gully whose angle rose to over 50 degrees, until, at the moment when it became unacceptably precipitous, they could make an awkward step out to the right, on to another terrace and along it. Then a short ice chimney, indicated by more Swiss rope pegged into the ice by pitons, led them by a zigzag movement up and across some of the steepest ground yet encountered: first right, then a long swing back and up to the left. They cleared a thick layer of loose, unreliable snow overlying the ice as they went, in order to cut steps. It was extremely exhausting, especially for Bourdillon, who was then in the lead.

At this very time while they were engaged upon this severe passage there was a minor crisis, serious enough in the circumstances. As Tom Bourdillon was clearing away the snow and cutting steps in the ice beneath it, he heard a faint shout: "I am getting no oxygen." It was Charles Wylie, immediately behind him on the rope, crouched over his axe and obviously in difficulties. Here was an awkward situation. On such steep ground there was no security; it was no easy matter to turn round in his steps and go back to see what was wrong; nor was it easy for Charles, delicately balanced and breathless as he was, to swing his heavy equipment off his back to find out the cause. Yet it was done. Charles's oxygen bottle was empty. His mask removed, he was for some moments in distress, gasping in the thin air after being for so long dependent on his oxygen supply. In a little while, however, though still decidedly groggy, he managed to continue, very slowly now. They were in sight of a tiny shelf just above, on which were the tattered remains of a tent and signs of other equipment. This was the Swiss Camp VI. They struggled up to it, cleared a space and pitched their own tent upon it. Leaving the food, oxygen and other equipment for their stay, Wylie and the Sherpas now turned and went down to find Ward, who was suffering badly from anoxia. The weary little party plodded very slowly back to Camp V, leaving Bourdillon and Evans alone on the Lhotse Face.

At Camp VI Evans and Bourdillon made a most valuable dis-covery. Four charged oxygen bottles, mentioned by the Swiss but believed to be at their Camp VII higher up the Lhotse Face, had been found in good condition. Among their tasks had been that of looking for Swiss stores, and Tom Bourdillon had been prepared for this treasure. With the aid of the adaptors manufactured specially for us by our oxygen assembly firm and other tools which he had found at Camp V, he broached these bottles. Thanks to this, he and Charles Evans spent a restful night there, sleeping with the aid of oxygen, while still leaving enough to be useful for later operations in the Assault.

With Ward still feeling the after-effects of his unpleasant experience, Charles Wylie returned, this time without oxygen, to Camp VI on 5th May with Ang Temba and Pemba, while Bourdillon and Evans pushed on up the Face. The snow and weather conditions were alike atrocious. I had hoped that they would be able to take a central line up the glacier where a slope apparently clear of ice steps and crevasses seemed from below to present straightforward climbing. In the present conditions at any rate this proved to be out of the question. They were forced to remain in the more complicated zone on the left. Even on the short slopes the deep snow appeared to be unstable, and both felt that there was a considerable risk of starting avalanches. More-over, they could not get a clear view of their whereabouts owing to poor visibility; for it was snowing. They were probably little short of 24,000 feet when they decided to turn back. No very definite point had been reached, but in the circumstances there was no advantage and considerable danger in pushing the reconnaissance farther than this.

It was in fact a fine effort and a useful one. Clearly the Lhotse Face would be as tough a problem as we had expected and much time must be devoted to the tasks of preparing a route upwards, establishing camps and getting up stores destined for these and the highest camps on and above the Col. Equally valuable was the ex-perience gained in the use of oxygen, particularly the still experimental

Closed-Circuit type. When I questioned the users two days later at Base Camp, they both surprised me by their enthusiasm; after our common experiences in the Cwm I had not expected this. However, in the colder weather and at the greater height it had given a very satisfactory performance. Charles Wylie was well pleased with those of the special Sherpas who had been able to continue after their comrades had fallen sick; it looked as if we had a choice of outstanding men for the final phase.

Two other impressions had been gained from this preliminary reconnaissance. The first was that the hope, on which planning in London had been based, that we should be able to climb from an Advance Base in the Cwm directly to a camp half-way up the Lhotse Face, was likely to be a vain one; in fact, the London forecast proved to be quite feasible in the event. The second impression was that we must delay the administration of oxygen to the climbers until the moment of leaving the Swiss Camp V, at the foot of the Lhotse Face. This was due partly to the discomfort of wearing the masks in the Cwm, and partly because, when accompanying the reconnaissance party up to Camp V on 3rd May I had not used oxygen, although carrying about 30 lb. of the equipment. I had travelled at least as well as the others and with much greater enjoyment. Here again, we were proved wrong later on.

CHAPTER ELEVEN

THE PLAN

B ASE CAMP was strangely empty and silent when I returned with the three sick men on the morning of 4th May. Apart from Tenzing, who came out to greet me with his usual warm handshake and ready smile, there were only James Morris of *The Times*, Griff Pugh, George Band and one or two Sherpas. Everyone else was on holiday at Lobuje. There was plenty of news; best of all, there was a new batch of letters. By now our mail runners were coming and going regularly at intervals of about a week. The average time between Base Camp and Kathmandu—over 150 miles across rugged mountain country—was about nine days, but the swiftest of them all, who was working for James Morris, actually made the journey in six days; an astonishing achievement.

I learned that James had been up to Camp III in company with George Band and Mike Westmacott—a remarkably good perform- ance for one who had never climbed before nor become acclimatized to such an altitude. Weather bulletins had started on 1st May, and we had been able to pick them up on both the All-India Radio and the B.B.C. Overseas networks. They had foretold daily "snow showers" with accuracy but monotonous regularity, useful to our- selves but giving little idea to other listeners of the trials and handicaps which these "showers" were proving to be to the toiling carriers in the Icefall and the Cwm. We were also very glad to learn of the weather conditions as they affected two other big expeditions which had by now taken the field: the Japanese were attempting to climb Manaslu, and the Swiss were on Dhaulagiri, the taller neighbour of Annapurna which had been the original objective of Maurice Herzog's expedition in 1950. In this season these mountains, situated to the north-west of us, could be expected to receive the prevailing weather on its way towards Everest. There was still no mention of the approach of the monsoon, so I asked George Band to cable a request that it should be referred to, if only in the negative.

A number of Sherpas appeared to be casualties, mainly from a tiresome dry cough very prevalent just then amongst us and familiar to all who have been to Everest. It would seem to be due to the dry, cold air, although Tenzing attributed it to the spell of bad weather, which he assured us is normal for this time of year. Anyway, I hoped that the warmer conditions at Lobuje would help to put right the many invalids, for our ranks were seriously depleted. More serious still was the illness of Tom Stobart. Just before the break he, too, had made a first journey to the top of the Icefall in order to take action pictures of our Ferries, but had been unwell when he got back to Base. At Lobuje he was running a high temperature and was having difficulty in breathing. Griff was anxious to receive a first-hand report before making a professional visit—Mike Ward and Charles Evans being on the Lhotse Face—so we sent a wireless set down at once to the lower camp by a mail runner, with instructions to open communications at 6 p.m. George Band was very doubtful whether the reception would be satisfactory, for the distance—six miles—was unduly long for the power of our sets and the two stations were screened from each other by intervening high ground. It was therefore a surprise and a relief when we heard George Lowe's voice, at first indistinctly but later well enough to enable Griff to obtain some particulars about his patient. Pneumonia was suspected and this was confirmed after Griff's visit next day.

I went down to see Tom on 6th May and was greatly relieved to find him much better, already fretting over the opportunities he would be missing to "shoot" film in the Icefall and the Cwm. For some time, however, George Lowe had been understudying him as a reserve photographer, using one of several small cameras intended for taking pictures above the Western Cwm, when this work would have to be carried out by members of the Assault parties. Yet Tom, always conscientious, was most anxious not to fail in his mission, and it is a very remarkable tribute both to his physical powers of recovery and to his determination that by the middle of May he was back with us at Advance Base, his camera set up in a strategic position and Tom himself waiting in his tent like a spider at the centre of its web, quick to emerge and catch every interesting episode that occurred.

The Build-up started again on 5th May. Since about half the total stores we required had now been shifted to the top of the Icefall, for a time Camp III would be the focus of our activity; indeed, it became an advance base for the next ten days. Two High Level teams were sent up there, in charge of George Lowe and George Band; Michael Westmacott, who was still unfit, was to join them a few days later. It was the task of this trio and their fourteen men to shift all loads to their respective destinations at Camps IV and V, setting up Camp IV as the Advance Base by mid-May. In giving him this important job, I said to George Lowe, ever anxious to play a full part in whatever had to be done and eager now to make up for the days he had missed through illness: "Don't worry; it's quite likely I shall be asking you to do some route-making on the Lhotse Face as well as all this, depending on what the reconnaissance party have to report when they get back tomorrow." Little could either of us realize then how significant these words would be to George's future rôle on the mountain. For the time being, there were only Tenzing, Gregory and Noyce to lead the two Low Level teams, but others would become available after the reconnaissance party had returned and rested. The stacks of crates and food boxes had already shrunk encouragingly and it was expected that all stores would reach the camps for which they were intended by 15th May.

Charles Evans's party got back on the evening of 6th May, tired but with a certain indefinable air of assurance, which momentarily surprised me when I learned of the appalling conditions on the Face and the height, under 24,000 feet, at which they had been stopped. I soon realized, however, that they had very good cause to be satisfied and proud of their achievement in face of the handicaps of weather and bad snow. Indeed, it had been a fine performance to climb those steep slopes to Camp VI, and even more creditable to have pressed on beyond. The information they were now able to disclose left me in no further uncertainty either regarding the plan which we should now adopt or the tasks which should be allotted to each and all of us in order to carry it out. I asked all the climbing party to assemble in the Mess tent next morning so that I might outline the programme. Just before this most important meeting, Ed Hillary, Charles Evans and I sat in the morning sunshine outside Tom Bourdillon's oxygen shanty on 7th May to exchange views on the plan.

For some weeks we had realized that, while we must always remain capable of making a third and last attempt should this become necessary, our resources in men and material would only allow us to make two consecutive Assaults; after this we must necessarily wait for some days in order to recover our strength and replenish our camps. Accepting this conclusion, I had first toyed with the idea of putting most of our combined effort into one powerful thrust—a thrust equivalent to two lesser ones—and then, if this were not successful, falling back in order to prepare to launch two more in quick succession. Later, it had seemed to us that the great weakness of such "one up" tactics was that our Assault would tend to be inflexible and unwieldy; and that it was ill-designed to take advantage of the weather. On balance, it seemed wiser to plan on the "two up" principle: that is, to put in two attempts in close collaboration and quick succession. A near failure by the first party might then be exploited by the second without losing time and suffering an incalculable moral setback by retiring from the South Col, which had called for such great effort on behalf of so many to reach. The third attempt would, I hoped, not be needed; if it had to be made, we would then take time to prepare it thoroughly.

Two successive Assaults, then, it was to be. How should they be launched and what oxygen equipment should we use? These questions were really linked, for the tactics of each Assault were to some extent governed by the type of oxygen equipment. It had long been realized, in theory at least, that the peculiar advantage of the Closed-Circuit system was the benefit of greater endurance it should confer on the climber; that is, of being able to climb for a longer time with a given supply of oxygen than a colleague using a similar bottle would be able to do with the Open-Circuit system. There was also a good chance that, at very great heights, the Closed-Circuit user might move appreciably faster than if he were using the Open-Circuit equipment, despite the weight of his set. Indeed, it was confirmation of these two assets which we were seeking in the experiments just carried out on the Lhotse Face. As applied to the final pyramid of Everest, it was hoped that with the Closed-Circuit system the summit might be reached directly from a camp on the South Col, 3,000 feet below and about a mile distant.

In contrast with this, there was virtually no hope of reaching the top on the Open-Circuit apparatus without interposing a further camp. Its endurance was appreciably less and, while still enjoying great advantage over a man without oxygen, the climber must expect to move progressively more slowly as he rose higher. The economy achieved, in time and effort, by avoiding this extra camp needs no stressing. Moreover, the more protracted the period of the climb, the greater the risk of being overtaken by bad weather—speed spells safety on any mountain, but most especially is this true of Everest. It was for this particular reason that I had encouraged Tom Bourdillon in pursuing the tests of his special equipment, despite its more obvious drawbacks; despite, too, the apparent unsoundness of employing two types of equipment, since success in the usage of either depended on the most thorough understanding and drill-like efficiency in handling it. My persistence was also due to the fact that our carrying problem over the final 3,000 feet, from the South Col to the top of Everest, would clearly be critical and we must reduce to an absolute minimum the baggage to be taken up by our few specially chosen men.

There were, in effect, only two acceptable alternative combinations in this "two up" plan. Either we must send up two Assault parties each using Open-Circuit equipment, or one party must use the

Closed-Circuit type and the other the Open-Circuit. A third possibility, that of two "Closed-Circuit" Assaults, I ruled out owing to the risks involved in this equipment: the danger of unconsciousness overcoming the climber in the event of a failure in the mechanism, exposing him to the sudden contrast of breathing the rarefied surrounding air after having been dependent on 100 per cent oxygen. The mechanical efficiency of the equipment could not be fully established until it was tested on the final climb. Of the two acceptable alternatives, the second would, for the reasons I have explained, be the more economical in time, stores and human effort, and this was important because of the need to conserve enough of all these three resources in order to face an eventual challenge to enter the ring for a third round. It was also safer from the weather point of view, as it would save a day. On the other hand, the first alternative, if we could succeed in mounting it, would be safer from a no less important viewpoint; namely, that the equipment was well-proven and unlikely to break down. Even if it did, the climber would be less prone to succumb to the sudden effects of exposure to high altitude, as he would already be receiving a percentage of the surrounding air mixed with the supplementary oxygen supply which he was carrying. It was a nicely balanced choice.

Whichever system was adopted, the main features of both types of Assault would follow a common pattern. The summit parties should each be two in number. There were good reasons for increasing this to three and even four, but the ever-dominant supply limitations ruled this out. Each summit party must be supported by other climbers below, helping to carry the loads, ready to receive them on return from their climb, capable of replacing them and going to their help in emergency. The second Assault must follow closely on the first. The size of, and supplies at, the highest camps on the mountain being restricted by the carrying problem, the minimum time interval between the Assaults must be twenty-four hours. Thus the second party would in a sense be in support of the first, as well as preparing to carry through to the summit if the first party failed. The second party must be larger; it must contain its own support group in its ranks.

Both Assault parties would start from Advance Base which, it will be remembered, was to be our present Camp IV at 21,200 feet, and climb to the South Col at 26,580 feet, according to a similar schedule: first, to Camp V at the foot of the Lhotse Face; the next day to a camp half-way up the Face of Lhotse—at that time we referred to this as the Lhotse Face Camp; from there, on the third day, to the Col, where another camp would be set up. There would be no pause on the Col unless this were forced on either party by wind or weather;

the risk of physical deterioration and the additional food stores involved by delays made this point a most important one.

As regards the employment of oxygen, again, both types of Assault were to be similar in certain respects. At that stage of our thinking, strongly influenced by unpleasant experiences in the preliminary reconnaissance of the Lhotse Face in the first two days of May, we proposed to use oxygen only from Camp V rather than from Advance Base. From that point onwards, both the summit parties would use oxygen for climbing. It was also planned to supply the camps above the Cwm with bottles of "night oxygen", including the Swiss bottles for this purpose; equipped with a special light mask, the summit climber would be able to take oxygen at a low rate of flow (1 litre per minute) during the night and thus maintain his physical condition. In particular, he would be able to sleep more restfully and withstand the cold better.

All these main points had long been settled. Detailed load tables (shown in Appendix VIII) had been prepared for either plan and only two matters remained for me to decide on the morning of 7th May: which of the two plans to adopt, and the tasks to be carried out by each member of the climbing party. These were the matters which Ed Hillary, Charles Evans and I were now busy discussing in the growing heat of that memorable day. Our deliberations were brief, for we found ourselves in complete agreement. We walked over to the Mess tent and everyone gathered within.

*   *   *

There was an unmistakable atmosphere of expectancy and tension. This was, after all, one of the moments everyone had been waiting for. It was the biggest event before the bid for the summit itself. The occasion had an inescapably personal interest: "What is my job to be?" I looked briefly at each of my companions before starting to speak. Some were sitting on boxes, others lying on their sleeping-bags; James Morris was waiting to make notes from which he would write an important dispatch for his newspaper; Tenzing was near me, at the entrance to the big tent. In the mind of everyone there was this unanswered question. It was still and sultry.

The main points which I had to make were as follows. We would continue the work of building up the stores so as to be ready to make our attempts at any period after 15th May. During this time there was a great deal of work to be done in preparing a route up the Lhotse Face, which would probably take longer than we had thought earlier; but this too must be finished by the same target date.

We would go for the Closed-Circuit/Open-Circuit plan. The

Closed-Circuit attempt would be made first because it was in itself quicker and more economical; if it succeeded it might not be necessary to make another attempt—indeed the weather might not last long enough for both—and a camp on the South-East ridge might thus be obviated. This first Assault was to be made by Tom Bourdillon and Charles Evans, now so successful in partnership and well versed in the handling of this equipment. In speaking about this Closed-Circuit attempt, I made it clear that because of the experimental nature of the equipment and the great distance to be covered, partly over ground which we had not been able to see, the primary objective would be the South Peak. Only if the oxygen apparatus and supply were alike satisfactory, the weather fair and the terrain between the two peaks such as to allow them time to get there and back within safe limits, should they attempt to go farther. This leading team would be followed immediately by Tenzing and Hillary using the Open-Circuit equipment; they had by now established their claim beyond any doubt. This second summit party would have a support group consisting of myself and Gregory with four, possibly five, of the élite Sherpas whom we had trained and kept in reserve for this special purpose. We would follow the advice given me by Norton and Long-staff; our very special responsibility being that of carrying the last camp up the South-East ridge to the highest possible point. I had in mind 28,000 feet, although this of course depended on unforeseeable matters, not the least of them the finding of a platform large enough to accommodate the little tent.

I must digress for a moment to explain that later the support arrangements were altered. There were strong arguments for keeping together all those who would be carrying the material for the highest camp, but I felt that this was outweighed by the need to have a supporting party close behind the first summit pair, particularly as we could not be sure that the interval between the two attempts might not become greater than twenty-four hours, due to bad weather or other causes. Wishing to be in position on the Col throughout both Assaults, I decided to attach myself, with two Sherpas, to the first pair; Gregory was to remain in support of Hillary and Tenzing, with three Sherpas.

Assuming that there were no hitches in the progress of these parties from the Cwm to the Col, the second party should arrive on the Col on the same day as the Closed-Circuit pair came down after reaching, or attempting, the summit; a decision would then be arrived at on the spot whether to continue with the second attempt. It was my hope that it would be made in any case. It would take place over a period of two days, the first day being spent in taking a tent and stores for one night as high as possible up the ridge towards the South Peak.

But there was much to be done leading immediately up to these events. First we must stock our Camp IV with stores sufficient to enable us to await an opportunity offered by the weather; we were already planning to besiege Everest for a fortnight. If the mountain held out for longer than this, then we should be forced to replenish from Base Camp. At the same time, we must place the stores required for the Assault—all those to be carried above the head of the Cwm —at Camp V, which would thus, in effect, be a dépôt of the Assault stores. The exact amounts and their weights were already known, and consequently the number of High Altitude Sherpas required was established. At least twelve men were needed, and reserves must be added. These would climb in two teams, each under the leadership of a member of the climbing party. The two leaders chosen for this most important part of the Assault plan were Charles Wylie and Wilfrid Noyce; both had a quite exceptional understanding of our men. This final "lift" to the South Col might take place independently of the timing of the Assault, although, if weather conditions continued to be good at its completion, the first Assault party would follow immediately these South Col Ferry parties. In order to avoid an unnecessarily large camp on the Lhotse Face and to limit the effects of a setback, it was preferable for Noyce's and Wylie's parties to go up separately, like the Assault parties, at a twenty-four-hours' interval.

And there would be yet another task to be done even before the South Col "lift" could start: the preparation of a route up the Lhotse Face, at least as far as the traverse from the head of the Lhotse Glacier leftwards towards the Geneva Spur. Some idea of the magnitude of this problem had been given us as a result of the reconnaissance, but on 7th May we had still not realized its true difficulty. This job I had decided to give to George Lowe, a master of ice craft, with George Band and Mike Westmacott and four of our best Sherpas to assist him. This team, except for Westmacott, was already at Camp III and therefore half-way to the foot of the Face; their work must begin at once if it were to be completed by 15th May, and their place at Camp III must be taken by others. Ed Hillary and I would go up the following day, Ed to lead the main Ferry party on its journeys between Camp III and Camp IV, I with four men to be chosen from those at Camp III, to take station at Camp IV and start to move loads to the site of the Swiss Camp V. For the time being, Gregory and Tenzing would continue to conduct the Low Level Ferries in the Icefall. The reconnaissance party was due to go down to Lobuje for a well-merited rest.

It will be seen that these many tasks absorbed practically the whole of the climbing party. This was ambitious in that it assumed complete fitness on the part of everyone from this time onwards in order to have the best chance of success. I had one reserve from outside the climbing party proper—Michael Ward. In the Assault itself it seemed to me important that Michael should remain at Base in case of casualties from frostbite, exhaustion or other causes. But in the preliminary stages he might be very useful to replace tired or sick men.

I was no less anxious than before that we should not stay longer on the mountain than we must. If the weather went on being as bad in mid-May as it had been for the past month, and if the weather forecasts predicted a continuation of this state of affairs, then we would probably withdraw off the mountain, staying well down the glacier in comparative comfort, until there was an improvement.

Thus was the plan unfolded. If I am any judge of these things, I would say that the air of expectancy and tension had now been replaced by one of confidence and satisfaction. Doubts about the future intentions had been removed; everyone knew the course we were steering, what his particular task was to be, and how the various jobs would be dovetailed together towards the attainment of the ultimate aim of the expedition. Everyone felt he had an important contribution to make towards that aim.

The conference was over and we dispersed, Charles Evans and Tom Bourdillon to sort and label their remaining loads to go up the Icefall, Tenzing and Charles Wylie to discuss the selection of the Sherpa teams, Wilfrid Noyce, just down from a Low Level carry, to make calculations of rations on behalf of George Band, who was at Camp III. Only the Georges had not been present, but I would be able to tell them the plan shortly when I went up to join them.

Yet our purposeful mood was tempered by serious concern next evening. At the time of the 5 p.m. wireless call I spoke to George Lowe, telling him of the intended arrival next day of Ed Hillary and myself to take over from him, bringing with us Mike Westmacott in order that he, with the two Georges, might be released for "other important jobs"; it seemed better to leave explanations until we met. George had a tale of woe to unfold. "Hullo, John at Base—this is George Lowe at III—George Band is ill—bad throat and temperature—has been laid up all today—little chance of his recovering up here—he ought to go right down as soon as possible—Over." So our spearhead on the Lhotse Face was already one man short; for some days at any rate neither Mike Ward, just back from the reconnaissance, nor any other member of the party, could be spared to make up the numbers. I agreed at once that George Band should come down to recuperate at Lobuje. George went on: "Got to IV at midday after plugging solidly since half-past eight—it began to snow an hour after we set out—got off again soon after twelve—followed steps half a mile, then wind and snow so heavy all tracks went—impossible to see flags sixty yards apart—Topkie fell down a crevasse—some Sherpas panicked, but not good old Dawa Thondup—Gompu was absolutely finished—everyone iced up and lost—snow nearly knee-deep—we were casting all the time for flags—Hunt's Gully crossing was tough—crawled over the ladder and staggered back to III—all of us dead beat."

I asked George to give everyone at Camp III a day's rest to recover from this ordeal.

It already began to look as if we might not have enough men to carry through the plan. This was the beginning of a period of mounting anxiety for us all.

CHAPTER TWELVE

LHOTSE FACE: TWO

D URING the brief respite in the work of stock-piling, the Icefall
had undergone some surprising changes. Making our way up to
Camp III on 9th May, in order to release George Lowe for his new
task on the Lhotse Face, Ed Hillary and I missed a familiar feature,
an elegant, finger-shaped ice pinnacle at the brink of the terrace where
the tents of Camp II were pitched, piercing the skyline as you
approached the steep section of the route beneath "Hell-fire Alley".
In a way, it was a relief that this sérac no longer remained, a standing
threat to topple over while a party was passing up or down the route,
but it had served as a useful guide-post when searching for the right
direction in the labyrinth, through a blanket of freshly fallen snow.
As though to make up for this, however, a nearer menace in the form
of a tall ice pillar now leaned over just above "Hell-fire Alley", making
its fell intent only too clear. Something would have to be done about
this, and soon.

The "Atom Bomb" area was unrecognizable. We spent some
minutes casting around for a new line through this chaotic scene,
noting the need for a log bridge across one of the newly-opened
chasms. A little later, when I was resting at Camp II before tackling
the second section of the journey to the top of the Icefall, Greg arrived
with a Low Level team. Without any attempt to dramatize the incident, he told me how they had been very lucky to escape when, just
below Camp II, a mass of ice crashed from above their party, passing
behind Greg and grazing the man next on the rope. This was probably
the nearest moment to disaster which any of us experienced throughout our stay on the mountain.

The dangerous gap overshadowed by loose ice boulders above
Camp II had now stretched so wide that the two-sectional span of
metal ladder barely touched at either edge; we noted this, too, for the
evening wireless call to Base Camp. Along the traverse on the top of
the débris slope we found ourselves on unfamiliar ground, moving on
pulverized ice between blocks of all sizes, from pebbles to vast boulders twelve feet high, blue and freshly split from the parent cliff above
us.

That evening at Camp II I spoke to Wilfrid Noyce on the wireless. He was due to conduct a Ferry party upwards the next day, and I asked him to deal with the two most urgent problems: the sérac menacing "Hell-fire Alley" and the bridge above Camp II, now in danger of falling into the crevasse beneath it. I learned later that he had a hard job of it, hacking away for three-quarters of an hour at the base of the sérac until, prompted by a hefty shove with a bridging log, he had the satisfaction of watching it totter, unbalance and lurch like a felled tree, breaking into countless fragments across the very path by which our many parties made their toilsome way.

As the work of building up our final requirements of stores went on through the Icefall in this first fortnight of May, Camp II itself, sited in an apparently peaceful zone amid the surrounding turmoil, became unsafe. The noises of underground movement increased in frequency and eeriness; splits appeared, admittedly small but none the less tell-tale, in the ice beneath the tents during one anxious night. After that the porters preferred to carry their loads directly to Camp III and descend again to Base in one day, great though this effort was, rather than make the overnight stop in the Icefall.

Mike Westmacott also came up on this day to join George Lowe. He had never really recovered from his bout of sickness in the early days of reconnoitring the Icefall nearly a month before, but had stoutly continued to help there. Now, at the moment when his opportunity to fulfil this important mission on the Lhotse Face had come, Mike was evidently not fit to play a full part. Despite a painful cough, bad throat and queasy stomach, he insisted against all the evidence that he was much better. Unconvinced, I could not but admire his spirit, and so badly did we count on his services now that George Band had fallen sick that I did not suggest that he should return to Base.

Camp III was a large camp that night, with four Sahibs and no less than nineteen Sherpas, for we had with us additional men to complete George Lowe's team for the work on the Lhotse Face. Ed Hillary and I had decided that for some days at any rate he should conduct the Ferry from Camp III to Camp IV, while I should take four men from the fourteen now located at Camp III and move up to Camp IV, in order to form the dump of Assault stores at Camp V.

By the evening of 10th May, George was already in position at V; Mike had been obliged to rest with my party and hoped to join him next day. I was at IV and Ed had returned to III after delivering a first consignment of stores in this, the second half of the Build-up.

So the work continued for the next eight days in the Icefall and the Western Cwm. If there were no incidents, it was nevertheless a depressing period, for the weather, which had been bad ever since we had taken up our programme of acclimatization again on 9th April, relentlessly went on hindering our preparations. If anything, it got worse. On 10th and 11th May it snowed heavily from about midday until after dark, leaving a mantle of snow over a foot deep to be ploughed through in the intense heat which filled the Cwm each morning, unrelieved by the faintest breeze. On the second of these days, Ed Hillary's party took no less than four and a half hours between Camps III and IV, a journey which in fair conditions would be covered by a laden man in under three hours. In my diary for 12th May I find the words: "It is difficult not to feel bitter disappointment in these atrocious weather conditions. Today it has snowed another seven inches or so, and this evening I found the tracks up and down the Cwm obliterated." Even down at Base this was having its effect on the spirits of the party. Somebody else noted: "A most depressing afternoon. Three inches even down here." Above us on the Face of Lhotse, George Lowe was waist-deep in loose and dangerous snow. Considering everything, the cheerful willingness of everyone—and especially our Sherpas—was amazing. Charles Wylie reported that, despite the conditions in the Icefall, the teams had settled down; the number of men falling out through sickness was much less than before the break. Everest's weapon of weather slowed us down but did not hold us up.

Then there was a change, dramatically sudden. We had heard of it through the weather broadcasts but had hardly dared to credit it. The "snow showers" ceased, the afternoons remained clear. The long trail up through the Icefall and the Cwm to the foot of the Lhotse Face became a well-worn path; parties moved up and down it more speedily, with far less toil and trouble than before. In fact, the whole outlook brightened, for the news from the party on the Face was at that stage most encouraging. But I will shortly be telling of their activities. First I must finish the story of the Build-up.

By 15th May this was still not complete. On that day, following the arrival on the 14th of a fresh party consisting of Charles Evans, Tom Bourdillon, Greg and Wilfrid Noyce, I went down the Cwm, changing places with Ed Hillary, as we had previously agreed. After carrying loads and conducting the Ferry party between Camps IV and V for five days, the time had now come to organize the final move of the whole party to Advance Base. This could best be done from Camp III, where most of our activity had been focused since 6th May. Griff Pugh was there, and there were two others on their way down: Mike Westmacott, now forced to go down for a rest, and James Morris, who had not only climbed the Icefall for a second time, but had accompanied Charles Evans and the others as far as Advance Base that morning. We all admired his enterprise: he had well earned his place as a full member of the expedition. That evening I was able to speak to Charles Wylie at some length on the air. I asked him to wind-up the Low Level Ferry service, pay off the surplus men and come up, with Tenzing, to Advance Base by 18th May. The news from George Lowe, speaking on the air from his perch at Camp VI, seemed to warrant this, and with the welcome change in the weather we must now line up at the start. The tent distribution plan had always been complicated and I asked Mike Westmacott, whose job this was, to make the final dispositions with Charles Wylie before leaving for Lobuje. It had proved impracticable to have direct communication between Camp IV and Base, although it may be of interest to mention in passing that while at Camp III I had managed to have two-way communication with Camp IV via George Lowe at Camp VI.

A less successful wireless conversation took place about this time between Da Namgyal, now recovered from his illness and at Camp III, and Tenzing at Base Camp. Tenzing was anxious to give Da Namgyal an important message and he was persuaded to use the Walkie-phone set for this purpose. An unwilling Da Namgyal was handed another instrument at Camp III. Neither had tried these gadgets before and both, for some unaccountable reason, got stage fright. The conversation went something like this: "Oh—Da Namgyal"—"Oh—Tenzing"—"Oh—Da Namgyal"—"Oh—Tenzing." It never got any further and two very discomfited Sherpas had to abandon the attempt.

I stayed two nights at Camp III, conversing each evening on the air with George Lowe and through him with Hillary at Camp IV. While I was there, Griff Pugh arranged to let me try out "sleeping oxygen", an experience which was both useful and pleasant. Specially light masks, of the type used by the British Overseas Airways Corporation for non-pressurized aircraft, had been brought for this purpose, and these were connected with an oxygen bottle in the same way as our large masks. Normally one bottle is shared by two men, the oxygen flow being imparted in equal quantities to each through a light rubber tube dividing at a "T" joint. We used 1 litre a minute each. I found no discomfort in wearing the mask and enjoyed a really restful night and pleasant dreams.

An experiment of a different but no less important nature was at that time taking place in the Icefall. We were keen to do everything possible to ensure that the stores required to support the two Assaults, on which the whole plan depended, should reach their destination.

Michael Ward had in his medical chest some Benzedrine, a drug used successfully in the war to maintain the endurance of troops during periods of prolonged fighting. Its particular property was that of suppressing a desire to sleep. Michael considered that it might be risky to make the initial tests with this on the Lhotse Face itself, so it was administered to two volunteer Sherpas working in the Icefall. When Charles Wylie asked them their impressions on this experiment, one said: "Splendid! it has cured my cough." The other had a different but no more helpful experience. "Fine! it helped me to sleep."

I returned to Camp IV on 17th May, in company with Griff Pugh. The fine weather continued and we were beginning to feel impatient to complete our preparations for the Assault while the mountain remained thus kindly disposed towards us. The most vital of these preparations was that in which George Lowe had now been engaged for a week on the Face of Lhotse. It is time to recount his adventures upon that great barrier of ice and snow.

*   *   *

George had gone up to Camp V on the afternoon of 10th May, accompanied by four of our best Sherpas: Da Tensing, Ang Nyima, Gyaljen and Ang Namgyal. The Sherpas' task would be to replenish Lowe and Westmacott with stores at their temporary camp on the Lhotse Face and, later, to bring up baggage required to stock the Swiss Camp VII, which was to be the half-way house during the Assault period for parties on their way to and from the South Col. George's first move was to establish himself at the Swiss Camp VI, from which he could move both upwards and downwards, stamping out a track, cutting steps and fixing ropes as handlines on the steepest ground. He and his Sherpas went up there on 11th May. Conditions were most difficult, for new snow once again lay deeply on the route followed by the reconnaissance party, and he sank in at least as much as they had. The ascent of 600 feet from the beginning of the steep slope to the camp site took the party five and a half hours—little more than 100 feet of upward progress per hour.

As Westmacott had not arrived at Camp V when George Lowe left, he had asked Ang Nyima, the most skilled and experienced of his team, to remain with him at Camp VI; the others descended to the lower camp. Both Lowe and Ang Nyima were very tired after this gruelling experience and settled down at once to sleep. They slept for fifteen hours. For the next few days the Lhotse Face party worked on two levels. George and Ang Nyima operated from Camp VI, improving or renewing the track downwards and forcing a route gradually farther up towards the top of the Lhotse glacier. Westmacott, with the three remaining Sherpas, was based on Camp V. He would go up to or towards Camp VI, carrying George's daily needs of food, fuel, rope and pitons, and gradually shifting Assault stores to that camp. The really dreadful weather which so afflicted us lower down the line of communication was an even greater trial to this spearhead party, operating on unprepared and much more difficult ground and doing so in a more rarefied atmosphere.

I went up to Camp VI after completing a Ferry trip to V on 13th May. Michael Westmacott was at the lower camp when I arrived; his condition was much worse than when I had seen him three days before, and although he had started out with the utmost determination the previous day, he had not had the strength to reach Camp VI himself. It was obvious that he was approaching a state of exhaustion. Yet he insisted on accompanying me on this occasion. Equally praiseworthy was the devoted work and skilful climbing of the Sherpas, in particular Da Tensing and Ang Namgyal, who had gone on to Camp VI the day before on their own, taking exceptionally heavy loads to make up for the weakness in numbers of the carrying team—for Ang Nyima was doing a climber's job with Lowe, and Gyaljen was by no means well; he had not recovered from the illness which prevented him from taking part in the reconnaissance at the beginning of the month. Taking Ang Namgyal I went up through the deep overnight snow—there was no sign of a track—followed by Mike and Da Tensing. We were very tired when, two and a half hours later, we reached George and Ang Nyima, who that day were busy clearing snow from the final steep ice slope below their camp, cutting bucket-sized steps and fixing a stout hand-rail of manilla rope to replace the frail and weathered Swiss cords. They were both in splendid heart. George was intent on recording our distress with his ciné camera. Ang Nyima, whom we had regarded as somewhat of a spiv when he had first joined us with Roberts towards the end of April, was now in his element. He is undoubtedly one of those few mortals who blossom out only above a certain altitude. Whereas at Base Camp, and even at Camp III, he had not been forthcoming either in demeanour or in his readiness to volunteer his services, here on the difficult slopes of the lower Lhotse Face he was not only giving himself devotedly and skilfully to the task, but doing so with a huge, slow grin. Ang Nyima chainsmoked, and we were at pains to send up supplies to pander to this habit. He deserved it.

After spending about half an hour at Camp VI I went down into the afternoon snowstorm—for once short-lived—and found the other two some distance below. Westmacott was obviously unfit to go any farther, but he told me again how much better he was going today, and somehow he and Da Tensing struggled up another fifty feet to hand over a load to George Lowe. It was indeed a fine effort.

On return that evening I sent a message to Base Camp for Wilfrid Noyce and, later, Michael Ward to come up, in order to reinforce George's party. From my own experience at this time and from the conversation I had had with George, it was evident that the Lhotse Face was an even tougher proposition than we had judged it to be from the results of the reconnaissance. Both Wilfrid and Michael were to some extent prepared for this assignment, for I had spoken to them regarding some such eventuality when the plan was unfolded on 7th May. They were delighted to join the fray.

On 14th May George and Ang Nyima went up 1,000 feet in fine weather and discovered the Swiss Camp VII. That evening I was able to tell George on the air of the reinforcement plan; in reply he spoke enthusiastically of his success that day and of his future intentions. He proposed to rest next day—it would be the sixth since his arrival at Camp V—and on the following day climb onwards to the top of the Lhotse glacier and inspect—perhaps also prepare a route across the Traverse. After that—well, although he may not have said so, it could easily be guessed what was in the mind of the irrepressible George. It was to be nothing short of the South Col. This oration was heard distinctly at Camps IV, III and Base. It was a cheering message and must have set everyone thinking, as it did in my case, that we were virtually on top already.

All available effort was now turned on to the Lhotse Face. Each day two teams went up from Camp IV; one, which often included as porters members of the climbing party, intent on keeping fit, went up to Camp V and back, themselves carrying further stores to complete the Assault dump; another would go to Camp VII, either stopping the night at Camp V or making the journey direct from Camp IV, carrying the stores required for VII and in addition dumping there some of the loads intended for the South Col. By so doing we hoped to lighten the burden of the South Col parties when the time came for them to go up the Face. Following the addition of Wilfrid Noyce to the Lhotse Face party on 15th May—he replaced Ang Nyima, who came down for a much needed rest—first Ed Hillary, then Tom Bourdillon, followed in succession by George Band and Michael Ward, escorted Sherpas up those 2,000 feet on successive days.

George Lowe's optimism had not taken into account the hazards of high altitude. On the night of Wilfrid's arrival at Camp VI, they both took a dose of sleeping-pills. Next day Wilfrid noticed his companion was bemused and had to pummel him into activity before starting. He became more and more concerned as George, moving

135

extremely slowly, climbed towards the site of Camp VII, apparently half-asleep; they took two and a half hours to cover 600 feet. He actually dropped into a sort of stupor several times on the move, and during a pause for rest and food, Wilfrid found him asleep with a sardine hanging half out of his mouth—and George is fond of sardines. It was obviously unwise to continue in this state, and the party turned back—to the dismay of the watchers in the Cwm below. "It was," said Wilfrid, "like playing a drunken man downhill." On arrival at the tents of Camp V, George dropped off into a coma until the following day.

The ill-effects had completely worn off by morning and the pair went far to make amends for this misfortune. Not only did they arrive at Camp VII—the gear for which had been carried up by Ed Hillary during 15th May, when he had made the double journey from Camp IV to Camp VII and back in the day—but their delighted spectators observed them in the afternoon emerging from behind the sérac which conceals that camp and continuing upwards for over 600 feet. This was splendid progress and we waited full of hope for a triumphal advance on the following day. By this time Mike Ward had arrived to join George, thus releasing a reluctant Wilfrid, who would gladly have stayed to continue in the van, but returned in accordance with my request that he should rest in anticipation of the first South Col carry, now scheduled to start on 20th May.

But our hopes, so buoyed up by the previous day's events high up on the Face, were dashed when, on the 18th, three climbers—one of them was Da Tensing—eventually started out from Camp VII only to turn back at a point but little higher than that reached before. This was bitter indeed, and in our state of tension we found it hard enough to understand. Later, we learned from Tom Bourdillon, down from his escort trip to Camp VII, that the wind was very severe—indeed, we could hear it from our sheltered position, roaring higher up like a train. When they had at last ventured out, Michael Ward, tired after his climb the day before, had suffered severely with cold feet, and later George had a slightly frost-bitten hand. In the circumstances they had done well to start out at all.

The drama of the Lhotse Face continued unabated. It was now 19th May and the tenth day of the struggle. The wind continued to batter the rocks of the west face of Everest high above us; it was deflected across the Lhotse Face and rushed through the funnel formed by the sérac guarding Camp VII and the slopes behind it. We waited hour by hour that morning, vainly hoping for signs of movement. There were none. George Band had gone up there and he gave us some idea of the gale; yet the general feeling was one of disappointment. To increase our difficulties, we were no longer able to get any wireless communication with Camp VII. I was anxious to have a direct report from George Lowe himself so as to be able to form a proper opinion of the situation up there; George must be tiring after his astonishing feat of endurance; Griff Pugh was even worried about the effect on the mind of so prolonged a period at over 23,000 feet.

Another cause for concern was Charles Evans, hitherto one of the fittest among us all. He had gone up to Camp V two days before in order to assist in the Ferry to Camp VII. He had dosed himself with aureomycin on an empty stomach and was very unwell at that camp, having to rest there and come back to Camp IV next day. Since then he had been almost unable to eat and I wondered whether he would be well in time to take his place in the first Assault. To complete my woes, there appeared to be an imminent food crisis. George Band had been meticulous in keeping check of our supplies—a most difficult task now that they were widely distributed in several camps. Although the estimates had shortened, it had been expected at the time when the plan was drawn up that we should have sufficient "Compo"— our main food supply—to last until 7th June. While I had originally asked that we should be rationed until mid-June at least, this still seemed adequate. Now, however, I learned that we might run out of "Compo" by the end of the month; had it been so, this would have been a serious blow, for we might well need to wait until the next month before making our Assault, and in any case there would have been difficulty in staging a third and final attempt. Happily, George was later able to reassure me on this point, but we no longer had a comfortable margin.

There was likewise a crisis at this time in the matter of food for the Sherpas. At Advance Base and below, the Sherpa ration consisted largely of their own *tsampa*, supplemented by Assault rations. It was found by Wilfrid Noyce, who was responsible for the Sherpa food, that they were consuming far greater quantities of *tsampa* than he or Tenzing had estimated. Urgent messages had to be sent down to Base Camp for a further 500 lb. to be fetched by Nimmi—an ex-parachutist Sherpa who was one of our casualties and had been given the task of collecting local food. It arrived just in time to save the situation.

The prevailing mood of anxiety was turned, if not removed, with the arrival on 18th May of Tenzing and Charles Wylie with the remainder of our tents and stores. I now decided to fix the start for the South Col "carry" for the following day, when the first party, led by Wilfrid Noyce, would go up to Camp V on the first stage of their

137

journey. They would be followed on 20th May by Charles Wylie and a second team of Sherpas, and if their mission was successful, it would immediately be followed by the Assault. The first Assault party, then, might start upwards on 22nd May.

In making this decision, I reckoned that we could no longer afford to wait for further progress in the preparations on the Lhotse Face. The fine weather, now in its seventh day, must be exploited while it lasted, for it would be tempting providence to delay further. Moreover George Lowe must now be nearing the end of his strength and, weather apart, we had no one else to replace him in his task unless we were to disrupt the parties chosen for the Assaults. This decision was glad news to everyone.

A second and no less joyous event was the arrival with the rear party of our head cook Thondup. I have already mentioned that Thondup, while being an outstandingly good cook, is no climber, nor is he young, by Sherpa standards. Yet Charles had rightly judged that his presence at Advance Base—as we could now call Camp IV —would greatly raise morale. Food continued to be a subject of great interest to nearly all of us; there was no loss of appetite. "A good supper," noted George Band on 16th May. "Soup; stewed steak and peas; tinned peaches and pineapple." Even on the Lhotse Face George Lowe had clamoured for meat and fruit. "What are you chaps eating down there?" he intervened one evening during a serious wireless conversation on supplies, Sherpas and future plans. "Peaches, I expect." He complained loudly when first rationed on the High Altitude scale. It is a pity Greg did not keep a diary; he was well known for his keen interest in the subject of food and his comments would have been worth reading.

Thondup, arriving that afternoon with his somewhat toothless grin, after an adventurous journey through the Icefall—to the delight of his fellow Sherpas, quick to enjoy a joke, he had tried to fix his crampons on to his boots with the spikes pointing towards the soles —was rapturously greeted by us all. Tenzing and he quickly reorganized the whole camp—in particular, the cookhouse—to their satisfaction, and we had pancakes with our tea.

*   *   *

Life in camp during those last few days before the Assault followed a regular pattern. Depending on the population at Advance Base at any one time, you might be lucky enough to have to yourself one of the six Meade tents, or you might prefer the convivial atmosphere of the Pyramid or the big Dome, where we also had our meals; all were within a few paces of each other—about twelve tents of various sizes in an area of ten yards by ten in the little hollow which provided good shelter against the wind.

It is about 8 o'clock in the morning. The walls of your tent are white inside with frozen condensation; the sun has still not reached the camp and it is deadly cold. A cheery Sherpa face appears through the tent opening, with a mug of very sweet tea, heavily dosed with milk powder. Thus fortified, you wait for the warmth of the sun to strike the tent roof; this will happen about a quarter to nine. So intense is the cold that a great effort of will would be needed to emerge earlier. You come out into yet another Everest day; a cloudless sky, a blinding glare which forces you to put on your snow goggles. A quick glance round—first upwards to the slopes of Lhotse: had they started out? Reaching for a pair of binoculars you scan the well-known point half-way up the wall where lies Camp VII. No sign of movement there. You note the amount of snow being blown about on the edge of the Col and the towers of Lhotse's summit ridge. Then over to breakfast in the big tent.

Da Namgyal is carrying over plates of steaming porridge from the cookhouse shelter. The tent is in incredible confusion, with boxes, rucksacks, newspapers and tinned food lying about. In the midst of this débris the resident members are warm in their sleeping-bags, lying on air mattresses. Breakfast is a leisurely affair, for we usually have a good deal to discuss regarding the events for the day. Over our bacon and, possibly, eggs or fried luncheon meat, we wonder when the next batch of mail will arrive; there is a change in the load table for the South Col involving an additional Sherpa to be added to the South Col team; there is an important message to be sent down to Base Camp; how many "Assault" and "Compo" boxes are still down there? This vitally affects our planning and we may have to eat a higher proportion of Assault rations here at Advance Base—a most unwelcome prospect: someone makes a note to try to send a message to James Morris at Base.

During this time Charles Evans has been sitting on a ration box near the tent door, watching the slopes above through a pair of binoculars. "How are they getting on, Charles?" "They are just above VII. They are not getting on very fast. . . . I can just see Tom Bourdillon's party starting up the slopes from V."

Gradually most of us disperse, George Band to see Tenzing about the Sherpas who are to go up with him that evening to Camp V on their way to Camp VII with Assault stores. They will be the same men as those selected for the Assault. Greg, Ed Hillary and I are also going up, carrying loads for Camp V, and we have to divide them among us. Both parties will be starting in the late afternoon, for it is already uncomfortably hot. A pair of boots just sticking out from the sleeve opening of a Meade tent reveal Wilfrid Noyce, who is lying on his sleeping-bag, writing. A few choughs and a single raven are walking around on the snow, looking for scraps.

And so we are occupied till lunch, when everyone again meets in the Mess tent. There is soup followed by cold salami sausage and a huge round of Cheddar cheese—luxuries these; butter from a tin, a packet of Swiss Knäckebrot and our own biscuits. This is washed down with a choice of coffee or lemonade from our Assault ration packs. We take another look at George Lowe and Michael Ward. They are once more sitting down, but are not far below the top of the Lhotse glacier—in fact, tantalizingly close. Will they go any farther? But a little later, with a slight sinking of the heart, I notice that they are coming down. Meanwhile, Tom Bourdillon and six Sherpas are seen crossing the last steep ice slope below Camp VII and soon they disappear behind the sérac—another 200 lb. or so of stores have been carried half-way up the Face.

At 4 o'clock there is tea, jam and biscuits; perhaps a slice of excellent fruit cake from a "Compo" tin. Then the two parties are getting ready, roping up, shouldering loads which have been standing ready since midday, and moving off round the shoulder of our hollow, into the shallow trough in the glacier up which the track, now clearly traceable for several hundred yards, lies like a pencil line in the sun-glazed surface of the snow. Tom Stobart is in action with his ciné camera on a mound above the camp. He takes a few shots and prepares to join us for a trip up the Cwm. It is still hot and the big clouds which have been building up down-valley as far as the entrance of the Cwm are beginning to recede; the wind is getting up, swirling loose snow over the edge of the South Col. The icy cliffs of Nuptse are in deep shadow, and the sun has not far to go before slipping down behind Pumori. Both the parties have disappeared from the Face.

A little later, just as the shadow creeps down the Cwm towards our tents, Tom Bourdillon comes in with his party of Sherpas. He is tired, but obviously delighted to have been up to 24,000 feet without oxygen. "The wind is terrific there" is his comment on our enquiries regarding the progress of the Lhotse Face party that day.

With the departure of the sun it suddenly becomes bitterly cold. The Camp V party has returned after dumping our loads there and we go straight to our tents, put on down jackets and wait for supper. In the Mess Tent, someone turns on the wireless: "This is the General Overseas Service of the British Broadcasting Corporation. Here is the weather forecast for the Everest Expedition, valid for twenty-four hours commencing 12.00 hours G.M.T. or 17.30 hours Indian Standard Time. . . . There will be mainly overcast skies with occasional thunderstorms, accompanied by moderate to heavy snow showers. . . . Winds in free air at 29,000 feet above sea-level will be mainly westerly at 30–35 knots, and the temperature in free air at the same altitude will be −16 to −12 degrees Fahrenheit." This is a time for reading or writing, tucked warmly in a sleeping-bag, until someone shouts "Supper up!" It is getting dark now, but the Mess tent is brilliantly illuminated by a Buta-Gaz lamp. The tent residents have their plates handed to them lying in their bags; the visitors gather round the improvised table and sit on boxes. We close the tent door, for it is cold even in down clothing. For supper there is a mug of soup, tinned steak and kidney pie, eaten with a spoon, a fork or a knife, but not with a combination of these utensils, for most of our cutlery has been lost. Fruit cake and coffee round off the meal.

After supper some interesting conversation is apt to develop. Tom Stobart still has a seemingly endless repertoire of adventure stories. But most of the visitors slip away as soon as they have eaten, to warm up again in their sleeping-bags. I go over to Thondup's shelter and beg a candle; he is an expert hoarder of items in strangely short supply. Sticking this on to a small cardboard box which once contained my oxygen mask, I light it and open my diary. The stylo pen is frozen and will not write; it has to be held over the flame every few seconds to make it flow. First putting my hands into my bag to warm them, I make myself comfortable on one elbow and start to write. "18.5. This has been an important day in the expedition's history. . . . We have set up Advance Base at full strength. . . . Thondup, our head cook, is here, which means good meals for all of us. . . ." Closing the notebook, I reach for a sleeping-pill, blow out the candle and snuggle down for the night. One more Everest day has slipped away. How long will it be before we are finished with this mountain?

*   *   *

I went up to Camp V with Wilfrid and his men on the evening of the 19th carrying a load of oxygen; it was windy, but the track was now stamped and frozen into an excellent footpath, and we reached there in an hour. Before leaving him I said: "In case George and Michael don't manage to prepare the Traverse before they come down tomorrow, you will have to decide whether to carry straight on to the Col with the Sherpas the next day, or whether it will be better to go up there yourself first and prepare the track. If this is necessary, then your party will have to spend a second night with Charles Wylie at Camp VII and you must go up together on the 22nd. You can only judge this on the state of your chaps and the going above Camp VII as you will hear of it from George."

George Lowe and his companion Michael Ward did not give in easily. They made one more attempt to get up to the Traverse on the 20th, the last day available to them before they were to give place to Noyce's party. But the long strain was telling greatly on their endurance. They again made some progress upwards but soon turned back. If they had a sense of failure it was a failure where no other human being could have succeeded. Hindered by weather, his team delayed and weakened by sickness, and in spite of the demoralizing effect of the terrific west wind, George Lowe, supported at intervals by others, had put up a performance during those eleven days which will go down in the annals of mountaineering as an epic achievement of tenacity and skill.

Part V

ASSAULT

CHAPTER THIRTEEN

SOUTH COL: ONE

THE timetable for the "carry" of our Assault stores to the South Col extended over a period of five days. It was on this basis that we had been busy stocking the intervening high camps to cater for the High Altitude teams; their large numbers would make it difficult to increase the period because of the additional food and fuel required, apart from considerations of weather and physical deterioration. Inevitably, therefore, the plan for this final phase of the Build-up was a somewhat rigid one, making little provision for any hitches. When I had told Noyce at Camp V on the evening of the 19th that he might have to leave his party at Camp VII for a second night, I stressed the words "if necessary", for this was bound to create an awkward situation in that camp. There were not enough tents for so many men, and they would use up food and fuel supplies intended for the Assault parties.

During 20th May at Advance Base—another clear day, but with plenty of wind higher up, for the rocks above us were humming under the impact of terrific gusts—Charles Wylie was getting himself and his men ready to follow Wilfrid Noyce. In spite of all the loads which had been carried to Camp VII during the past few days, both Wylie's and Noyce's parties were very heavily burdened. In London we had reckoned that 30 lb. would be as much as could be expected of the Sherpas carrying loads up the Lhotse Face, but here were Wylie's team shouldering nearly 50 lb., and preparing cheerfully to carry this tremendous load to Camp VII at 27,000 feet up those steep slopes without oxygen. It should be explained that a proportion of this baggage belonged to the Sherpas themselves. Apart from their bedding —sleeping-bags and air mattresses—they have a weakness for carrying more personal kit than we considered to be strictly necessary. But when all this has been taken into account, there remained a "useful" load of about 30 lb. to lift. In order to make sure that all the stores were carried up, I had readily agreed with the advice of Tenzing and Wylie to increase by a few reserves the strictly minimum number of thirteen men calculated to be necessary for this "lift". Each of the two parties had two extra men, mainly in case of sickness or other inability to continue the journey, especially over the 2,000 feet of partly unknown ground from Camp VII to the South Col, and also possibly to lighten individual loads during that stage. In any case, their bedding and personal belongings being left at Camp VII, the loads would be lighter in that second part of their climb, and it was proposed to send down any very tired or ill Sherpas from that camp.

That afternoon, two Sherpas were seen descending from Camp VII soon after the arrival there of the first South Col "carry". They were evidently sick or too tired to continue. When they came down to Advance Base, they handed me a disturbing note from Wilfrid who, as in the case of all users of oxygen other than the summit parties, was using "Utility" or training oxygen bottles. According to him, his bottle had been leaking on arrival at the now abandoned Camp VI, but he had found and made use of another bottle which was lying there. This was also leaking and so on arrival at Camp VII he had appropriated two more bottles for the next day, one for himself and another for his leading Sherpa, Annullu who, it had been agreed, should have oxygen to enable him to assist Wilfrid in making the unprepared track upwards next day. Worse still, Wilfrid finished up with the words: "Tell Tom that several of them leak when turned on."

Now this was bad news indeed. Poor Tom Bourdillon, not easily dismayed, was distinctly ruffled. Nine Utility bottles, each weighing 20 lb., had been laboriously carried to that high camp; each had its particular use to match the detailed plan of Assault. Did this mean a failure in our oxygen supply, with possibly disastrous consequences to the Assault? Wilfrid, though gifted in more ways than one, has not a markedly mechanical bent and we hoped that his tests were not conclusive. Tom, however, had a lurking fear that these very tests, carried out by a possibly anoxic Wilfrid at 24,000 feet, might have resulted in the discharging of all nine cylinders. Tom's habitual peace of mind was rudely disturbed. Meanwhile, we still had no wireless communication with Camp VII, which might have reassured us. In the absence of definite information, I decided that we must prepare for the worst and arrange for an additional supply of bottles to accompany the second Assault party. These were urgently ordered from Camp III, and I warned Charles Wylie of the need to send up a replenishment team of Sherpas with the second Assault party. It would be most difficult to find men, as almost all, other than members of the Assault teams, were committed to the present "carry" on the Lhotse Face. They would have to be volunteers and some would already have made the journey to the Col. I then turned to George Lowe, only just back from his ordeal on the Lhotse Face but clamouring for a job, and asked him to be prepared to lead this party. Needless to say, he jumped at the idea. I now suspect that then and there he secretly set his own objective even higher. We were to find later that the state of the oxygen bottles at Camp VII was not as serious as we had feared.

That evening, I was turning over in my mind the possible implications of a hitch in the South Col "carry". Considering the ill-repute which the Col had gained during the Swiss expeditions the year before, remembering that we had not succeeded in climbing much more than half-way towards it in the course of eleven days' hard struggle, could we be sure that all, or even more than the stoutest few among the Sherpas, would agree to go? It would hardly be surprising if many found themselves overawed in the face of the unknown, for Sherpas are superstitious folk; they have many memories of disasters in high places. Or they might in some cases simply not be strong enough to continue to that far saddle, which had so nearly exhausted the Swiss and the Sherpas with them. After all, they would be climbing with heavy loads and without oxygen.

Yet it was quite essential to the success of the plan that each and every load should reach its destination and that it should do so according to the timetable. Ruminating thus, I felt that something more might have to be done to "boost" the action now in progress, and I discussed this with some of my companions that evening at Advance Base. In the end, it was agreed that, should Wilfrid be seen to adopt his alternative plan of leaving his men and going up himself with Annullu, and if he was not able to make satisfactory progress—we should have to judge of this through our binoculars—two of us would go up to encourage and assist both South Col parties. It would mean a considerable sacrifice in the detailed execution of the plan, but clearly first things must come first. So it may be imagined with what intense anxiety we at Advance Base awaited the events of 21st May.

The morning of 21st May dawned fine and there seemed to be less wind higher up. We scanned the white expanse of snow above, our eyes glued to a certain bulge of ice split by a vertical crevasse. Just above this was a sérac concealing the tents of Camp VII. We hoped for an early start by the first "carry". But nothing happened until 10 a.m. Then two tiny dots, barely discernible to the naked eye, but clearly seen through glasses, emerged and moved horizontally to the right, towards the foot of an ice groove by which the small cliff behind the camp is climbed. They were alone. Obviously Wilfrid had adopted the alternative plan. Thinking of the effects this might have on the Assault, we were at first disappointed; we had naturally hoped for the best. Moreover, their progress was very slow at first as they toiled up

147

the slopes leading to the top of the glacier, about 1,000 feet above. Naturally, we did not doubt that there were difficulties up there—finding the route, cutting steps and perhaps fixing ropes.

It was at this juncture that I made up my mind to take the action proposed overnight: namely, to send up a pair of climbers to reinforce the "carry". This decision made, there was the delicate matter of choice of individuals. Everyone in the camp was either part of the Assault teams, ready to start as soon as the "carry" was completed, or resting after recent work on the Lhotse Face. Members of the first summit party I ruled out, for this would have meant either reversing the order of the two attempts or cutting out the Closed-Circuit effort. It might have been possible for myself and Gregory to go up, but, apart from disrupting the composition of the Assault teams, this would have removed from each team those responsible for conducting the supporting parties. From every point of view, there was only one solution, and it was a drastic one; the lot must fall on Tenzing and Hillary. They came last in the order of batting, they were both fresh and quite exceptionally strong. Moreover, Tenzing's reputation among the Sherpas stood immensely high; if any persuasion were needed to support that of our chosen leaders in the South Col "carries", he was the one best qualified to give it. I spoke to them about this at 11 a.m. that morning, pointing out the delay it would probably cause in the timing of the second Assault and the strain it must impose upon themselves, possibly to the detriment of their own chances in the Assault.

Both men were not only willing; they seemed pleased at the prospect of their mission. Tenzing was especially delighted. All through our work of stock-piling he had necessarily undertaken the least exciting tasks of all, leading the Low Level Ferries, organizing ration and firewood parties, sending and receiving mail runners at Base; maintaining order there and helping to keep all his men cheerful. These things he had done well and willingly, for it was in his nature to do so. But I knew that his heart was set on getting higher, and higher still. Always he was happiest when climbing. I had first seen this on Chukhung Peak, and again when we went up the Cwm together to find the Swiss Camp IV. Now, for the first time since his astonishing dash with Hillary from Base to Camp IV and back on 2nd May, he was to have a chance to show his mettle. This was what he had been waiting for. They prepared themselves without more ado and left at midday.

Meanwhile, we continued to watch the progress of Noyce and Annullu. Soon after the departure of Hillary and Tenzing, they had passed the highest point reached so far on the Lhotse glacier and stood at 12.30 on the shelf beneath the final slopes sweeping up to Lhotse, where a traverse must be made to the left towards the couloir beside the Geneva Spur. They were now at about 25,000 feet. Excitement mounted as we watched them move towards this famous Traverse; although we did not know it then, Annullu was now in the lead, "moving", as it seemed to Noyce, "at the pace of a fast Swiss guide".

It was not easy to judge from below, but it had always seemed that a shallow gully just flanking the glacier before the wider slopes of snow or ice could be reached, might harbour loose, dangerous snow. We expected to replace a Swiss rope marked on one of their photographs as having been fixed to safeguard this passage. Yet these two men moved steadily on. They were taking an unexpectedly high line, as though straight towards the top of the Geneva Spur. Although we did not yet believe that this was their intention, it was good enough to see that they found it unnecessary to stop and fix a rope over the doubtful place. Their speed had noticeably increased and our excitement soon grew to amazement when it dawned upon us that Noyce and Annullu were heading for the South Col itself. Our earlier worries quite forgotten, we continued to gaze all that afternoon.

With scarcely a pause they moved on until they were close in beside the rocks of the Spur. They climbed farther, disappearing behind the projecting buttress and I, unable to bear the suspense, left camp alone and moved out about two hundred yards into the centre of the glacier to get a better view. This was probably unwise; only the day before Tom Bourdillon had fallen to a depth of six feet in a concealed crevasse a few yards from the tents, but the occasion must have dimmed my mountaineering judgment. I was able to watch them for some time longer; then after an interval, I caught one more fleeting glimpse, this time a point of blue—the colour of a windproof smock—against some rocks just below the skyline; it quickly merged into the background of sky. It was 2.40 p.m. Wilfrid Noyce and his companion Annullu stood at that moment above the South Col of Everest, at about 26,000 feet. They were gazing down on the scene of the Swiss drama, and they were also looking upwards to the final pyramid of Everest itself. It was a great moment for them both, and it was shared by all of us who watched them. Their presence there was symbolic of our success in overcoming the most crucial problem of the whole climb; they had reached an objective which we had been striving to attain for twelve anxious days.

They descended a short slope—it might have been a mere 200 feet, but it would be an unwelcome feature to an exhausted climber on his way back from climbing Everest. I had asked Wilfrid to fix a handline here to help returning parties up this slope, and on his way back he did this; we were to be thankful for it later on. On the level plateau of the Col they found the remains of the Swiss occupation: battered tents, oxygen frames, climbing gear and food. They helped themselves to a few useful items—Annullu exchanged his oxygen set for a filled rucksack, Wilfrid picked up some Vita-Weat, a tin of sardines and a box of matches, all in perfect condition after lying exposed to the elements for over six months. There was no more than a stiff breeze blowing and they were able to enjoy this unique occasion to the full.

With Noyce still using a bottle of oxygen which, far from leaking, seemed to possess an abnormally long life, they now returned to Camp VII, arriving there relatively fresh at 5.30 p.m. For Noyce, it was "one of the most enjoyable days' mountaineering I've ever had". Wylie's party, followed by Tenzing and Hillary, had by now arrived there. Noyce and Annullu were greeted with tremendous enthusiasm by the group of Sherpas as they descended the fixed rope and approached the tents. There is no doubt that the return of this pair, without distress or injury, after climbing steadily to the South Col that day, had made a profound impression on the waiting men. If these two could do it, so could they. After his arrival, Wylie had spent some time talking to them, sympathizing with their tiredness, their headaches and coughs, handing out pills; they had all promised to do their best on the next day, but it was obvious that they had lacked confidence until this moment. Morale rose suddenly, inspired by a fine example. Spurred by Tenzing's encouragement and clear orders for the morrow, the success of the "carry" was now assured.

But the watchers in the Cwm could not know this. Our anxiety persisted the following morning as we again stared up the Lhotse Face, waiting for signs of activity at Camp VII. This time we had not long to wait. At 8.30 a.m., an unwontedly early hour for so high a camp, two little dots were seen coming out from behind the sheltering ice pinnacle. The atmosphere at Advance Base was tense as we waited to see what would happen. Yes! there they came; we counted aloud, as one after another the Sherpas followed in a long string spread out across the dazzling expanse of snow. Fourteen . . . fifteen . . . sixteen . . . seventeen: a seemingly incredible number were on the move together, at over 24,000 feet. The entire caravan was on its way, carrying our vital stores towards the South Col.

The two leaders remained ahead. We guessed that these must be Hillary and Tenzing, and this was confirmed later in the day, when Noyce and Annullu returned. At first I was disappointed by this for, with his supreme mission in mind, I had asked Ed to do no more than was strictly necessary to ensure the success of this convoy. Supposing any action were needed, it had been hoped that this might be supplied by verbal encouragement alone. At most, I had suggested to them that they should give a lead as far as the top of the glacier. Yet they went on steadily, remaking the track which the overnight wind had quite wiped out from the slopes, acting as a human magnet to the others. Even from below we could realize the toil of this journey; progress was painfully slow. But only those who lived it could fully know the hardships.

There had been nineteen men at Camp VII that night. They had been crammed into tents insufficient for so large a party, and buffeted by the wind. There was an unaccountable dearth of rations, for enough had been sent up and the lack should have made itself felt only after their departure. Moreover, cooking in those cramped quarters was not easy. Knowing that a long day's climbing lay ahead, Tenzing had rightly insisted on an early start; but such are the difficulties, mental as well as physical, of doing even the simplest things at high altitude that, though roused at 6 a.m., the party had managed to prepare only a mug of tea by the time they started at 8.30. A very few added some Grape-nuts to their tea. Most of the Sherpas started out with no nourishment at all.

Many of them were feeling the effects of altitude acutely and were slower than others would have been, but when roped together on a climb the pace of a party is necessarily that of the slowest. Two steps, heavy panting, leaning over the ice-axe for support, then another two steps. After ten paces forward in this way, a few would collapse against the slope and all must wait for them to recover. So it went on the whole day. They sadly lacked nourishment. "We went through all our pockets," said Charles Wylie later, "and finished our sweets." But they stuck to their job.

Almost imperceptible as their progress was from below, the column advanced across the great snow slope until the last man disappeared behind the rocks of the Geneva Spur. All but one. He had reached the end of his tether and had to stop half-way across. Charles Wylie, always solicitous of his men and conscientious about his job, at once shouldered the load of this man and went on. Shortly afterwards, Wylie's oxygen apparatus developed a leak in the 4-litre flow rate connection. It could only be cured by plugging into this coupling and receiving oxygen at the higher rate; for he had been using 2 litres until then. Using twice the amount of oxygen, he soon exhausted his supply, while still some 400 feet below the top rocks of the Spur. In far worse plight than the Sherpas, for as had happened to him during the Lhotse Face reconnaissance, he was now suddenly dependent on the rarefied air for existence, after breathing additional oxygen for a number of hours, Wylie went on, decidedly groggy but determined, until he reached the top. Later, on the Col itself, he found the presence of mind and energy to make a careful stack of the stores, weighting them down with stones against the risk of their being blown away by the fierce wind. He then proceeded to notice the scenery and film the surroundings; such conduct still seems almost unreal.

In their state of tiredness, weak from lack of food, the return journey was almost as much a trial as the climb to the Col. The last stragglers reached Camp VII at 7 p.m. that evening as it was growing dark; they had been out for ten and a half hours. Most elected to spend a second or, for some, a third night there. They had an even more uncomfortable night than the previous one. The wind had risen to gale force and, sweeping across the Lhotse Face, was driven as in a bellows between the sérac and the mountainside. The tents were often in danger of being uprooted from their platform and the occupants had a nerve-racking time sitting up against the tent walls to hold them down.

A few stalwarts preferred to make a dash for the comforts of Advance Base. Five Sherpas, led by the indomitable veteran Dawa Thondup, who had graduated to the select South Col team after setting an outstanding example in the Icefall and the Western Cwm, came down the slopes to Camp V as we of the first Assault party arrived there that evening. Some apparently almost fresh—Dawa was one of these—others staggering with fatigue, they passed straight on towards Advance Base. Each smiled as he went by; more than one boasted of having had only a mug of tea since 7 o'clock that morning. And ahead even of these heroes were Hillary and Tenzing who, having climbed directly from Advance Base to Camp VII the previous afternoon, having led the whole way to the South Col, stamping out a track through difficult wind-crusted snow, now descended that same day from the Col to Advance Base, which they reached after dark. In under thirty hours, these two men had climbed from 21,200 to 26,000 feet and back. When I saw them they were already tired, Ed more weary than I had ever seen him before; so much so that I wondered how long it would be before they would be fit enough to start the second Assault.

When, at about 2 p.m., it was already obvious that the South Col "carry" would reach its destination, we all experienced a tremendous feeling of relief. Although we could not predict the wind conditions, the weather remained fine; the stores we needed were at the foot of the final peak. There was no reason for further delay: the Assault was on. I spoke to Charles Evans, now most fortunately fit once more, and to Tom Bourdillon. We would leave that evening for Camp V on our way upwards. For us, the climax was fast approaching, and we must now live up to the splendid examples set by those who had paved the way.

CHAPTER FOURTEEN

SOUTH COL: TWO

W HEN we arrived at Camp V on the evening of the 22nd, the wind was already active, blowing snow around and increasing the sensation of cold; by the time we had settled into our tents it was strong and getting stronger every minute. We spent an uncomfortable night there; it was of course far worse for the South Col party at Camp VII.

Next morning, Da Tensing looked into my tent while I was getting ready to start. Despite our best estimates, we still found that more stores must be lifted up to Camp VII than we could manage, and I had asked for two men to join our caravan. Da Tensing, always ready to help, had come forward, and here was this fine veteran, with young Changjiu, on their way up. They had preferred to start straight from Advance Base, where they would have a better night, and they were keen now to press on. Da Tensing climbed well and knew the route intimately, so I raised no objection.

I left camp with the two Sherpas of the first Assault team, Da Namgyal and Ang Tensing (nicknamed Balu), at 8.30, using my Open-Circuit set. The route bore no resemblance to the one I had followed ten days before when I went up to visit George Lowe. We were now walking on a hard, well-beaten path leading to the foot of the steep Face. Once on the Face, although some of the technical difficulties remained, conditions were far easier. Deep footmarks had pressed down the snow into comfortable pockets and large steps had been carved in the ice; the insecure Swiss cords had been replaced by stout manilla rope, hanging free from any encumbering snow. In these conditions, we went up as far as the site of our Camp VI in reasonable time—just under two hours; indeed, this was good going for the laden Sherpas without the benefit of oxygen. Yet for some reason I was finding it hard work and remember wondering, as we sat upon the now deserted tent platform, whether I should perhaps fail the summit party, not even getting to Camp VII; it was a disturbing thought. I was almost pleased to note, when Charles Evans and Tom Bourdillon arrived just as my party were getting ready to leave, that they, too, were making heavy weather of it. Whatever the reason for this bad start, the next 1,000 feet proved to be far less tedious. Instead of feeling sorry for myself, I was able to spare a thought for the poor Sherpas, struggling up manfully but now obviously feeling the altitude and unable to climb at my pace.

The route between Camps VI and VII was still very steep, but generally speaking more straightforward. For a short while the line chosen by George Lowe closely bordered the great ice slope of the Lhotse Face on the extreme edge of the Lhotse glacier; I noted that we were about level with the lowest rocks of the Geneva Spur at this point. Then a long traverse was made back to the centre of the glaciated slope, beneath a huge ice cliff, and after a few steps upwards on steep ice we reached the foot of another rope, hanging over a vertical pitch by which the cliff was turned. Looking up as we sat resting above this obstacle, I noticed that the split bulge on which I had so often gazed from Advance Base in the last week was very close above. On we went, up further ice steps, on to terraces, getting nearer to the still hidden camp.

We heard a shout from above, carried away on the wind: the South Col men were coming down, unladen and gay, as if they had just enjoyed a Sunday School treat. There was no room for both parties on this particular traverse, and there was more difficult ground, indicated by another rope dangling a few yards off; so we were glad to stay and rest. Last of the party came Charles Wylie. I congratulated him, although not then aware of the full story of his personal achievement the day before. Shouting against the wind, he said: "By Jove, John, that last part of the ridge is tremendous. With a bit of luck you should get the top camp very high indeed." It was just the sort of encouragement I needed. The last hundred feet to the camp were even steeper than I had expected. A slanting traverse led up to the foot of the cleft bulge and its base, then to be contoured round to the left, up about fifty feet of very steep ground: more rope: more ice steps. The tents remained invisible until the last moment, and it was a relief to sight them on a spacious platform, backed by a big cliff and screened from the Cwm by a tall, wedge-shaped sérac. Da Tensing and Changjiu had deposited their loads and passed us on their return journey as we made a long stride across the crevasse which marks the line of eventual cleavage of that sérac from the parent mountainside. They wished us luck. We had taken under three and a half hours from Camp V.

This balcony is astonishing. Jutting out from the general line of slope falling from Lhotse, it must have surprised the Swiss when they discovered it last November; it is so unexpected and it is the only resting-place large enough to accommodate more than about two tents

155

on the whole length and breadth of the Lhotse Face. Here the party had been able to erect as many as eight tents on the nights preceding our arrival. Walking a few steps to the southern end, I looked across at the ridge of Nuptse, now seen almost in profile and scarcely higher than we were. The blade-like sharpness of its crest was fascinating, almost frightening. There was a certain nick in the arête, at just 25,000 feet, now not more than 1,000 yards away to the south. Often during the acclimatization periods we had looked through this gap—the lowest point on the Nuptse–Lhotse wall. Once, after climbing some 3,000 feet above our first Base Camp at Thyangboche, Michael Ward and I had seen the South Col for the first time and examined the final part of Everest. Now I longed to see the reverse view: to recognize the places where we had stood then. But I was still not high enough.

At its north end, the balcony gave a grandstand view of the upper part of our mountain. Now more foreshortened than ever, the summit ridge above the sweep of brown rocks on the west face seemed incredibly close. There was plenty of wind up there that day—too much to make any attempt possible; a long plume of snow vapour stretched the whole length of the South-East ridge. In contrast with this apparent nearness, the South Col seemed a long, long way off. I now fully understood for the first time that we were only half-way there: a point frequently stressed by George Lowe from this same place, but never quite accepted in my mood of optimism and impatience in the Cwm. I felt comparatively fresh and was busy for half an hour taking photographs before the two "summiters" arrived. They had exchanged the soda lime canisters of their Closed-Circuit sets while resting at Camp VI, using new ones left lying in the snow at this camp site, and they had subsequently had trouble due to the freezing of valves in Charles Evans's set, caused by the coldness of these fresh canisters. It was a portent of later events.

That evening, thanks to George Band's foresight in sending up replacement equipment, we were able to have a good wireless reception with Advance Base, thus reopening communications after an interval of several days. This was most timely, for I was keen to hear the plans of the second Assault party. It was a relief to learn from George Lowe that the party would be moving up to Camp V the next evening and would be only forty-eight hours behind us. After seeing Tenzing and Hillary on their way down from the South Col, this was better than I had dared to hope. Very faintly, I also heard James Morris speaking from Base Camp to some other station up the Cwm —probably Camp III. In the hope of telling him the latest news, I made a long verbal report on our set, but we learned later that this was not heard.

While we were having supper we compared notes on previous experience of this altitude. Charles Evans had climbed to about 24,000 feet on Annapurna three years before; I had been to about 24,500 on Saltaro Kangri in the Karakoram in 1935. For Tom this was the highest he had yet reached.

The wind got up that evening in gale force once more. As on the previous night, the tents bellied and roared, giving us at first little rest, for it is an anxious sensation to be kept in uncertainty whether you and your party are going to be lifted bodily and cast down the mountainside. However, thanks to our oxygen helpers at home and to Tom Bourdillon's skill, we slept well later, using the Swiss cylinders which had by now been transported here from Camp VI where they were found. The usual method was for two men to use one bottle of oxygen for sleeping; the flow rate of 2 litres a minute was then divided equally between them. I, being third man out and the least important of the three of us to the Assault, had a bottle to myself. Having 2 litres per minute to myself, I was better off than they while the supply lasted, but that was only for about four hours.

For me it was a bad start on the morning of 24th May. I found each step an immense labour, even along the level fifty yards of the lower lip of the crevasse dividing us from the cliff above, in order to reach the fixed rope and ice gully. Climbing this very steep pitch, the effort was agonizingly great. I stopped to gasp after every step upwards. Some feet farther on, after moving along a terrace immediately above our tents, I could continue no longer, and for a terrible moment imagined that my day, and in fact my part in the summit effort, was over. I consulted Tom when he and Charles Evans came up to us. The oxygen pipe connecting the economizer with the flow-rate manifold was kinked and I had been carrying a dead weight of over 50 lb. without oxygen and breathing only the air filtered through the valves of my mask; small wonder it had been a trying experience! He put this right only to find that there was a leak in the 2-litre-rate connection, which could only be prevented by plugging into this coupling; it was the reverse situation to that which Charles Wylie had experienced two days earlier in the couloir beside the Geneva Spur. There was nothing for it but to climb at the lower rate of flow—I had been using 4 litres. Apart from the extra effort involved, this might not be a disadvantage, for it would bring down my pace towards that of the Sherpas and economize oxygen; there would thus be less danger of the supply running out.

So on we went, after losing a valuable half-hour on this incident. I thought of the watchers below wondering, as I had done on similar occasions, "What on earth can they be up to, stopping so soon after

leaving Camp VII?" We climbed up to the top of the Lhotse glacier
very slowly indeed; both ropes were moving at much the same snail's
pace. Just before the top terrace is reached, two final obstacles bar
the way: another ice cliff, with a yawning crevasse along its foot.
Fortunately, a shelf of ice ran across this, rising steadily from left to
right. It meant a deviation from the direction in which we wanted to
go, but it led us to the top of the cliff, delightfully. Once again an
old Swiss line lay about loosely, but it was unsafe and in any case
unnecessary to use it.

Above, another big crevasse stopped us; we had to move yet farther
to the right until it narrowed sufficiently for a big upward stride to
be made. An awkward and anxious stride, for the edges on both
sides overhung, and you stepped from one fragile snow bracket on to
another. But we got across, as had many before us, and after climbing
up a few more feet we all sat down to rest at the level of the Traverse.
It was about 1 p.m. The Cwm looked shrunken and very distant; it
seemed to have narrowed to map-like proportions. Below the brink
where the Icefall dropped away, the Khumbu glacier was a black well
of seemingly bottomless depth; a few clouds hung above it in white
blobs. An insignificant blur some way down, under the west ridge of
Everest, was Advance Base. Now at last I could overlook that nick in
the Nuptse ridge to the forest-clad mountains to the south. We saw
beyond the dwarfed cone of Pumori to the level summits of two other
giants, Gyachung Kang (25,190 feet) and Cho Oyu (26,860 feet), and
felt we could almost count ourselves on equal terms with them. We
were very high in the world.

On we went, intrigued, towards the Traverse. There were no signs
of tracks, although the feet of seventeen men had passed this way only
two days before; the wind had rubbed them out, coating the surface
with a treacherous board-like crust. Sometimes it let you sink awkwardly into the underlying soft snow; at other times it bore your
weight. It was a tiring progress. For a while the angle was fairly steep,
more so than I had expected—over 45 degrees at the point where the
gully runs beside the Lhotse glacier; an old rope could be seen 100
feet below us, fixed between the glacier edge and a horizontal band
of rock. Then the gradient relented as we stepped across the huge
slope. I remember Lambert mentioning that it might just have been
possible to ski down. It was in fact about the extreme limit of steepness
for ski-ing turns; it would have made a strenuous but exciting plunge
down those 3,000 feet to the Cwm.

The hours began to drag as we went across this slope. Charles
Evans and Tom Bourdillon were ahead, having a hard time of it
breaking the trail through the crust; the Sherpas behind me were now

tiring rapidly, and our pace was even slower than that of the leading pair. Time seemed endless. We would advance for perhaps four, or even six successive paces. After the third, there would be suggestive groans from behind—Balu wanted to rest. Another pace and he would give clearer expression to this: "Sahib, aram mangta hai", and when I had taken another step forward, I would be forcibly restrained by the rope. There was nothing for it but to stop, watching the agony of these two men as they crouched over their axes, moaning and panting, for a full minute at a time. "Thik hai?" I would ask. A faint grunt from Da Namgyal and we would go on, to the accompaniment of a few encouraging but probably unconvincing words from myself about the nearness of the Col. The performance would then be repeated. About every 100 yards I stopped and carved a large hole in the slope for all three to sit in safety and we rested for a longer spell, our feet dangling out over the great slope, sweeping away beneath us towards the tiny speck that was Camp V.

By about 3 p.m. we had entered the couloir and were close in beside the rocks. We had been going five and a half hours and I glanced at the pressure gauge of my oxygen bottle—300 lb. per square inch. This is almost the point where the effective supply peters out, and I shouted up the slope to Tom and Charles to wait while we crawled towards them. Was I to go on without oxygen? It would certainly give out within the next half-hour. Or should I join the other rope and leave the two Sherpas to come along at their own pace? We were now only about 250 feet below the point where it is possible to traverse out of the couloir to the left and across the upper part of the Geneva Spur; the Col was not far off. I consulted Da Namgyal, who assured me that they were happy to come along slowly; anything was better than being dragged along as at present. So I tied on to Charles's rope and we went ahead, glancing back from time to time to make sure that the Sherpas were following.

It was 4 p.m. when we topped the Geneva Spur and stopped for a minute on a level patch of hard snow. Above us, across the hollow of the South Col, rose the South summit of Everest; no longer a "minor eminence" as I had dubbed it in London, but an elegant snow spire, breathtakingly close yet nearly 3,000 feet above our heads. Right-handed from this peak the South-East ridge descended, very steeply at first and then at a more gentle gradient to a snow shoulder at about half its height. This seemed just the place for that top camp, my task for next day. The ridge then dipped downwards once more, its crest rock and snow mixed, to another and lower shelf. Here there was again a rapid steepening of the angle, as it plunged in a rock buttress towards the far right corner of the South Col, perhaps 700 yards from where we stood, and beyond a pronounced rocky hump rising above the eastern edge of the Col.

The flanks of this ridge facing the South Col are very steep, part rock, part snow, seamed here and there with snow-filled gullies, spilling out into the upper slopes of the Col opposite our viewpoint. We had heard from Wilfrid Noyce that the ridge and the South summit which topped it were impressive; none of us had been prepared for any spectacle quite so sharp, quite so beautiful as this. To me it seemed that a new and unsuspected peak of Alpine stature stood above the South Col; my first reaction was one almost approaching dismay and resentment that we should be confronted with such a problem after struggling so far towards the end of our journey.

And what of the South Col at our feet? We looked down upon as dreary and desolate a place as I ever expect to see: a broad plateau, perhaps as much as 400 yards along each edge, its northern and southern limits set by the steepening slopes rising towards Everest and Lhotse, falling away abruptly westwards into the Cwm and eastwards down the Kangshung Face. The surface of this waste is partly covered by stones, partly with sheets of bare, bluish ice. The edges are snow-fringed, but the snow has been hardened almost to the consistency of ice by the wind. And it is the wind which adds to the sense of dread which possesses this place. It was blowing fiercely as we went down the slope which must be descended from the top of the Spur to reach the level surface of the Col. We were making towards the right where there were some patches of colour among the stones; a splash of orange caught the eye. These patches marked the remnants of the Swiss camp.

It was a queer sensation to go down like this at the end of our long, hard climb, as though entering a trap; and this feeling was heightened by the scene which we were approaching. For there before us were the skeletons of the Swiss tents, three or four of them; they stood, just the bare metal poles supported still by their frail guy ropes, all but a few shreds of the canvas ripped from them by the wind. Around, frozen into the ice, were other fragments of cloth, and lying upon the surface some heavier objects. I noticed two Dräger oxygen frames, a coil of nylon rope. But there was little time to take stock of our surroundings, for it was growing late and we must make haste to get our tents erected before the cold gripped us. Clothed and hooded as we were in every garment we possessed—windproofs, down jackets and trousers, down, silk and windproof gloves: all this over jerseys, woollen shirts and underclothes—it was cold enough. We pulled out the Pyramid tent from the pile left by the South Col party on 22nd May and set to work.

And now began a struggle which none of us is likely to forget. If the wind had been strong on the Spur, it was terrible down here. My oxygen had finished before descending to the Col, and Charles Evans took off his set to leave him more free to work. We were pathetically feeble, far too weak to compete against that fiendish gale. For over an hour we fought and strove with it, playing a diabolical tug-of-war, trying to put up one single tent which can be put up in one or two minutes lower down. All the time the canvas was being snatched from our hands and we were being caught in a tangle of guy ropes. We staggered about, getting in each other's way, anoxic and hopelessly inadequate to cope with the conditions. Tom kept his oxygen set on for a short time and at first could not understand the antics of Charles and myself as we rolled around like drunkards. Once I tripped over a boulder and lay on my face for five minutes or so, before I could summon the strength to get up. But soon Tom's canister gave out, and then his oxygen supply. He too fell down and also lay, more or less unconscious, on the ground.

By now—it might have been 5 p.m.—the two Sherpas had arrived. Balu at once crawled into the half-erected tent; he had completely lost his nerve. But he served at least one useful purpose, even if unwittingly; we were able to pass in rocks and oxygen bottles for him to weight down the inner edges of the tent. And in the end it was up, more or less. The Meade tent took less time, and by about 5.30 p.m. we three were in the Pyramid, the two Sherpas in the Meade, lying amid a confusion of sleeping-bags, mattresses, rucksacks, ropes and oxygen sets, to recover from this ordeal.

It was already getting dark. Charles started to prime the stove; I went out to chip off lumps of ice from the surrounding boulders to melt for water, and I hauled in ration packs from the dump. We sorted out the muddle as best we could and crawled into our bags, clothed in everything, including windproofs. Between 5.30 and 9 p.m. we brewed and drank no less than four mugfuls of liquid each; there was lemonade, soup, tea and cocoa. It was most satisfying. While Charles and I were occupied in this way, Tom was fitting up oxygen equipment for sleeping purposes. We eventually settled down for the night, always conscious of that great wind as it tore at the tent walls as though bent on removing us from this desert where it ruled supreme.

*   *   *

Overnight we had agreed that it would not be possible to make an early start next day, desirable though this was. We were too tired and the confusion was too great. Despite the wind, we three spent a

reasonably comfortable night with the aid of oxygen. I woke abruptly and remained awake when my supply came to an end after four hours; my breathing became laboured and I began to feel cold in my sleeping-bag. But even so, we all agreed that we felt rested and refreshed next morning. It did not take long, however, to reach a certain decision. We would postpone the attempt by twenty-four hours. The implications of this were serious enough. We should be consuming more rations, more fuel; deterioration was bound to make itself felt, and we might be so weakened that this would prejudice our chances. Last but not least, we were taking a big chance with the weather, and especially the wind. Indeed, this was the most tantalizing aspect of all, for on this morning, 25th May, the wind relented, the weather was utterly clear. There was no more than a breeze blowing across the Col.

But we were not ready. Food had to be sorted out; Balu was unable to start, but we hoped that, with rest, he might recover. The decisive factor was that the oxygen had not been prepared, and this is a slow task at this altitude. For it takes infinitely longer to do simple things, let alone intricate jobs such as this. Fortunately, from the viewpoint of the Assault programme, there was time, for instead of following us at a twenty-four hours' interval, as had originally been planned, Ed Hillary's party would not arrive until the afternoon of the next day.

We spent the time restfully. After a late breakfast—I forget what we ate, but remember it included some excellent Swiss honey which I had found on the Col and our own salami sausage—I went out to tidy up around the tents. Da Namgyal came to help, and we put up the third tent—the little 6-lb. "blister". I was in a tidying mood and took a certain pleasure in lining our oxygen bottles in a neat row just outside our tent, stowing all food stores close to the entrance, and placing the Swiss gear separately from our own. I also placed a small packet upon a rock. This contained photographic plates intended to record cosmic rays; it had been given me by Professor Eugster of Zürich University during our visit there shortly before we left for India. These had already been exposed for nearly a fortnight at Camp VII. I very much regret to say that they have remained on the South Col, where they must by now have made a very definite recording of these interesting phenomena.

In addition to four tins of honey, some cheese and Vita-Weat, I found a tin of tunny fish among the Swiss kit. It is an interesting commentary on appetite and animal instincts at 26,000 feet—and a fact which I mention not without a certain feeling of shame—that I was unsocial enough to conceal this tit-bit from my companions. I took it into the little "blister" tent and emptied the tin myself.

After doing these chores, I took a stroll along the Col, still wearing on my feet only a flimsy pair of down socks over two woollen pairs. First towards the western edge, in order to peer down into the Cwm from a huge square block which had been a landmark from below. I moved slowly along, heading into the breeze. Each step had to be carefully considered, but the ground sloped gradually away and the effort was not unduly great. Reaching the brink, I looked down at last on the Nuptse ridge, now quite undoubtedly below me, and beyond it to the lower peaks to the south, an infinite distance away. Directly below, I could see quite clearly three of our camps. Advance Base, a smudge on the snow surface, was there in its hollow. Away to the left and slightly higher, I could see the tiny tents of Camp V, scarcely distinguishable one from the other. Most dramatic, however, was Camp VII, half-way up and also away to the left. I could look, as though from an aircraft, straight into the funnel in which it lay. The general fall of the Lhotse Face dividing me from it looked exceedingly steep. Pumori, which so ruled above Base Camp, was now difficult to pick out from the background of ice and snow; I was looking over its top to the other side, in Tibet. Before leaving the edge on this side, I waved just in case anyone below should happen to be looking in this direction at that moment. As far as I know this gesture was not observed.

And so back up the gradual slopes, the wind behind me. A much greater effort this, stopping every few yards with a slight anxiety lest I should not make the distance. As I approached the tents, I was astonished to see a bird, a chough, strutting about on the stones near me. At every camp we had been visited by choughs; even at Camp VII there were two or three and I had wondered then whether we should find them on the Col. But here the bird was, behaving in the same way at 26,000 feet as his cousins had at Base Camp. During this day, too, Charles Evans saw what must have been a migration of small grey birds across the Col. Neither of us had thought to find any signs of life as high as this.

After a rest to gather strength, I went out again to view the eastern panorama. The tents were more or less in the centre of the Col, and the journey was much the same as the other. There was a good deal of ice to cross before I could stand at the edge. I found this tiresome in nylon-covered down socks; so much so that I did not venture too close in case a gust of wind—it was then increasing in strength—should send me sliding helplessly over the brink. Here was a scene I had been longing to see. Years before, in 1937, I had climbed the south-west summit of a mountain named Nepal Peak, 23,400 feet, close by Kangchenjunga, 28,150 feet, the third highest mountain in the world. From there I had looked north-west towards Everest and Lhotse, beyond the nearer peak of Makalu, 27,800 feet. It was a view I had always treasured in memory.

Now here was the reverse side of the medal. Across the shoulder of near-by Makalu, a great pyramid of snow and reddish rock, soared Kangchenjunga, tent-shaped above the rising clouds, around it a number of satellites, including the Twins and Nepal Peak itself; I looked again on these familiar mountains after an interval of sixteen years. Ten thousand feet below, I saw the snow-free earth, where the Kangshung valley ran its course towards the east. I returned to the camp.

Tom and Charles were getting ready for the next day and it seemed better to give them more space and freedom to make an early start by moving into the little tent myself. I shifted my belongings and spent a restful afternoon, reading Borrow's *Wild Wales*. There was a great urge to do nothing—the danger signal of deterioration.

Among the equipment scheduled to be carried to the Col was a "Walkie-phone" set. This I found and we tried to get it to work in time for the evening call. Most unfortunately one of the batteries had been damaged on the way and we were not successful, but I spoke a message to James Morris at Base Camp, just in case he might pick it up. It would have been interesting to send a message from 26,000 feet to Base at under 18,000 feet.

The Meade tent was only a yard away and I shouted to Da Namgyal to find out how Balu was. The reply was not encouraging and I told Da Namgyal that we should share between us the loads to be carried up next day. With Tom's help we prepared our oxygen equipment and I fetched a bottle to use that night. All was set for our great day.

CHAPTER FIFTEEN

SOUTH PEAK

I HAD decided overnight that, since we would apparently be deprived of the services of Balu, the chances of Da Namgyal and myself carrying our share of the total loads required for the top camp to the Snow Shoulder, probably nearly 28,000 feet, were very small. It seemed best now to take them as high as we could and leave the second support party, Gregory and his three Sherpas, who had rather less than half the total weight of stores to lift, the task of taking on the loads from the point where we left them. I spoke of this to Charles and Tom during 25th May. Our loads consisted of oxygen, a tent, food, kerosene, etc.; my share weighed about 45 lb. in addition to some personal items, including a camera. Gregory's party was to bring up four Assault oxygen bottles and a small Primus stove.

I was astir at 5.30 next morning, still feeling reasonably fresh after another four hours' use of oxygen during the night. I shouted to Da Namgyal in the neighbouring tent, to make sure he, too, was getting ready. Charles and Tom were due to start first, at 6 a.m., as they had much the longer journey. I looked out at about that time, hoping to see them ready to leave. But they were still within and I took no action. Shouting into the wind, I would not have been heard even at that distance—five yards. Meanwhile I went on with my own preparations, putting on boots and crampons, all a deplorably slow business. Da Namgyal brought me a cup of tea and told me that Balu was in a bad way and could not come with us. Just before 7 a.m. the two of us came out on to the Col and roped up, tightening our hoods around our faces against the bitter wind, drawing on our outer gauntlets over down gloves and adjusting our goggles. Our oxygen equipment was ready overnight and I hauled my set out of the tent.

Outside the Pyramid tent was Charles Evans, crouching over his oxygen set and blowing into one of the tubes. Clearly he was having trouble with it. I asked what was the matter; the supply valve had been broken and it had taken over an hour to diagnose the trouble and replace the valve, unfortunately with a less suitable component from the Open-Circuit apparatus. This was not a propitious start.

Some minutes later, Charles Evans and Tom Bourdillon were still by their tent, the technical hitch as yet unsolved. This was serious. Charles came over and asked if he could help by joining me in carrying up loads for the top camp, since in his view the prospects for the Assault were dim. I declined his offer, since it was most unlikely that two climbers who had used oxygen all the way since leaving Advance Base could reach a point high on the South-East ridge without oxygen. I suppose I was too intent on my own coming effort for that day to feel despondent about this bad news of the Assault; it seemed all I could do was to carry on with my job. There was indeed nothing more to say, and words were an effort in the wind. So Da Namgyal and I started off towards the ridge soon after 7 a.m., each carrying about 45 lb. on our backs and using oxygen at 4 litres' flow per minute.

We moved very slowly. In fact, the gently rising ice-slopes seemed just as much of an effort as had my wandering on the Col without oxygen the day before. The ground was bare ice polished by the wind, with scattered pebbles embedded in it. As it steepened, the slope became covered with brick-hard snow on which I found that my short-pointed crampons tended to scrape and slip; it was already tiring. Looking round, I was delighted to see Tom and Charles just leaving the tents and moving towards me; they must have put right the defect, and the first Assault was launched on its final lap.

At the same time it was depressing to note how little progress we had made in the past half-hour—perhaps 150 feet upwards and 200 yards in distance. I was heading for a snow-filled gully or couloir, which had been pointed out to us on a photograph by the Swiss as being the only practicable route to the South-East ridge. The ridge now towered directly above our heads, over 1,000 feet up. Da Namgyal wanted me to move farther to the right, to the foot of the rock buttress which cuts off the ridge before it reaches the edge of the Col, and from the point we had reached the gully appeared to rise so steeply that for a moment I was inclined to agree that we might as well try the alternative rock climb. But it would now have involved a long detour to the right, and there was a compelling urge to economize energy as much as possible. Indeed we already had little in reserve.

Tom and Charles were coming up fast from behind. As Da Namgyal and I stopped to take our first rest, sitting in the shallow groove of an incipient *Bergschrund* which marks a sudden steepening of the gully, they went ahead. It was good to see that they were climbing so strongly, and I admit to feeling glad that I should be spared the labour of kicking or cutting steps higher up.

On we went, still on a hard surface in which our crampons left barely a scratch, but after a while we struck softer patches and these became more frequent as we crept up into the comparative shelter of the rock walls limiting the gully. It was pleasing to note that already we were above the top of the rocky hump which stands near the eastern edge of the South Col. The couloir steepened. At half height it was perhaps 45 degrees, nearer its top it had risen in gradient to about 50 degrees, making the cutting of steps—or kicking them when the snow was soft enough to make an impression—essential to comfort at this altitude.

Tom and Charles were busy with this task; it slowed them down, but they were still gaining ground on us; they were perhaps as much as forty yards ahead, half-way up the couloir. Our progress grew slower, more exhausting. Each step was a labour, requiring an effort of will to make. After several steps at a funeral pace, a pause was necessary to regain enough strength to continue. I was already beginning to gasp and fight for breath. In this distress, I tried a different technique: resting for a minute, then starting forward as fast as I could—it was doubtless ludicrously slow—for eight or nine consecutive paces, without taking account of the need to co-ordinate my movement with breathing. I would then hang upon my axe until once more sufficiently controlled to go on. This was an agonizing performance which, on reflection, I do not recommend to future Everest climbers. That I experimented with it at all, flouting all the tenets of mountain climbing, was a gesture of desperation. Towards the top of the couloir, Tom and Charles had traversed across it to set foot on a steep slope of mixed rock and snow; direct ascent had become awkwardly steep. We followed in the steps they had made, and I sat upon the first rock ledge to take in Da Namgyal's rope as he came towards me. He did not say anything but looked woefully tired.

We went on, for the ridge was now close; up steep but easy ground until we reached the crest. Quite suddenly we had arrived at the little tent left by Lambert and Tenzing almost exactly a year before—or the ragged remains of it. Like those on the South Col below, it had only the struts, held upright still with scraps of orange cloth flapping in the wind. We fell on to the small level space just above the tent. My lungs seemed to be about to burst; I was groaning and fighting to get enough air, a grim and ghastly experience in which I had no power of self-control. But only while it lasted. For, as had happened lower down in the couloir, normality came quite suddenly and with it a desire to go on, an ability to take an interest in the surroundings.

I looked around, first out on to the world, for we were now on its roof. Kangchenjunga and Makalu stood above a sea of cloud, which was rising rapidly all around us; the wind was already strong, but we were fairly well sheltered, for as usual it was blowing from the north-west. Then I gazed down to the South Col. This was highly satisfying:

the tents looked minute, for we had climbed some 1,400 feet, even though it had taken us almost three hours to attain this height. Below the lip of the Col, we could now look straight down the Lhotse Face and upon the top of Camp VII; despite all its 24,000 feet, it looked an infinite distance below, and I wondered how we had managed to climb those apparently precipitous slopes below and above it. Lastly, I glanced up the ridge, now half-hidden in mist. It was snowing and the wind was in my face as I turned. There were Charles and Tom climbing the steeper ground towards the Snow Shoulder. They seemed to be going very strongly indeed, at least 300 feet above us now; I wondered how they managed to go so steadily without taking rest.

Up till now Da Namgyal had, I believe, been climbing with less effort than myself. But now he seemed utterly done up. I spoke of going on and he was apathetic. It is not Da Namgyal's nature to give in, but it was only too clear that we should not be able to continue much farther. Leaving one oxygen cylinder, which I decided to carry back to supplement the supplies for the second Assault, we followed slowly in the track made by the summit pair. The going was not very steep at first, the ridge narrow but not uncomfortably so. But there was a tiresome layer of some three inches of powder snow upon a harder under-surface, masking the rocks on the crest. The track made by the others, where we could trace it, was a help. I resorted to some attempt at achieving a rhythm—a step, four or six gasps, another step, and so on. It was a little less painful than the rush tactics, but we climbed no faster than before.

After about twenty minutes—we might have climbed 100 feet above the Swiss tent—Da Namgyal said he could do no more. I knew him too well to doubt it, for there is no stouter-hearted and less-complaining man. I urged him on, for there was no satisfactory place to leave the gear at this point; a likely-looking shelf could be seen above, another fifty feet up. We got there and stopped. As so often happens, it was disappointing—scarcely room to sit, let alone place the equipment securely. I felt I could manage yet another fifty feet and again saw what appeared to be a better ledge up the now steeper section rising towards the Snow Shoulder—the Shoulder itself seemed to be only some 300 feet above us now. But Da Namgyal could not do it, and I cannot say I was sorry that he had reached his limit; I was near enough mine. So we stopped and built a cairn upon a rock on the crest of the ridge, immediately above a little gap, just big enough for the tent and other stores.

The place is easy to identify from below, for it is but slightly above the direct line of the original couloir by which we had climbed to attain the ridge. There we placed the tent, food, kerosene and our own oxygen bottles. To these I added a candle and matches to provide a small measure of comfort for the second summit party. The height, like others, has yet to be calculated exactly. Taking 27,300 feet as the altitude of the Swiss tent, as they had estimated, I then believed myself to be at 27,500 feet. Later we agreed to a general scaling down of all these heights, and reckoned this dump to be at 27,350 feet.

For no reason that I can now explain, we moved a few yards across the southern slope and began, very feebly, to scrape out a platform. This was not logical, for I had long determined that the highest camp must be in the region of 28,000 feet, and I had in mind the Snow Shoulder. Being short of one Sherpa, it was fairly certain that we must leave the final lift to the second party. We again rested until about 11.30 a.m., when we were ready to start back.

It must have been while we were there that Da Namgyal removed a glove. Two days later, at Advance Base, I learned that he had a badly frost-bitten finger. This was skilfully attended to by Michael Ward and the trouble cleared up without his having to take any drastic measures. This was the only serious case of frostbite during the whole expedition.

Carrying our empty oxygen frames, we went down the ridge, now enveloped in mist, the snow on our backs. We were terribly slow and wobbly, so much so that on reaching the platform where the framework of the Swiss tent stood, I decided to use oxygen from the bottle left there, at any rate for the steepest part of the couloir, to reduce the risk of an accident. But this made matters worse and I quickly took off my mask. So far I had given no thought to the efficient working of the oxygen equipment; it had never failed before and it did not occur to me to check in case there might be some blockage. This worsening effect, when tried only for a few minutes as we descended towards the couloir, may, however, be significant. It was not until twenty-four hours later, when unscrewing the tube connecting the mask with the set, that I discovered this was completely blocked with ice. It is mentioned here, not in any sense as an excuse but simply as a possible explanation of the otherwise quite extraordinary difficulty in breathing and climbing which I experienced going up, an experience quite contrary to that in the latter part of the Lhotse Face, although the difference in height between the two places was not very considerable.

In the couloir we took extreme precautions. Although it has a good run out on to the stone-covered ice-slopes of the Col, the height from the point where we entered it is certainly over 1,000 feet above the Col, and a slip would have had serious consequences. We moved singly, each alternately securing the other with a turn of the rope round the head of the ice-axe, driven into the snow. First Da Namgyal would go down and I would join him, then he went down farther; so it went on, rope length by rope length. Once he slipped and slid for several feet, but only until the slight amount of slack rope was taken up. This was due entirely to exhaustion, for Da Namgyal is a very steady, safe climber; it was a warning for additional care.

As we descended we could see figures spread out across the Lhotse Face, coming up towards the South Col. The second Assault party were approaching to join us; this was a pleasing sight. At last we were on easier ground. When we came out of the couloir and on to the upper slopes above the Col, two of the party arrived at the tents; shortly afterwards they came towards us. We were now sitting down every ten paces or so, although the difficulties were over and the angle was no longer steep. We recognized Tenzing and Hillary approaching us over the icy surface. I suddenly felt as though the strength was leaving me like water. My knees gave way and I collapsed, a ridiculous figure, as they came up. Da Namgyal flopped down also, while we were plied with lemonade from Tenzing's flask. Ed helped me towards the tents, but finding that I could not make the distance, hurried off to fetch his oxygen set. With a boost of 6 litres a minute, I soon revived—I remember very clearly what a full and free flow I was receiving—and we were able to complete the few remaining yards. I shall not forget their exceeding patience and kindness.

*   *   *

On reaching the ledge where we first stood upon the South-East ridge of Everest at 27,200 feet, Tom Bourdillon and Charles Evans were feeling well and confident. They arrived there shortly after 9 a.m., having taken one and a half hours to climb 1,300 feet; only about the same height had to be covered to reach the South summit. At this rate of progress   almost a thousand feet in one hour—they should have time to spare for the suspected difficulties of that final hidden ridge leading to Everest itself. Best of all, the Closed-Circuit sets were functioning well, despite the anxiety caused earlier that morning and the fact that Charles Evans's apparatus had perforce been set at a fixed flow rate of 2 litres per minute. The weather alone was unfavourable, but even this was not a serious hindrance. They set off determined and full of hope.

But from this point onwards the going became worse. The overlay of fresh snow called for greater care, covering the ledges and making it difficult to get a grip with their crampons on the hard surface beneath; they moved much more slowly. In two hours, indeed, they had not covered more than half the distance towards the South Peak.

But they had now reached an important landmark. This was the Snow Shoulder, so noticeable a feature when seen from the top of the Geneva Spur. As Tenzing pointed out later, it is probably about the highest place reached during the attempt by himself and Lambert in the spring of 1952. Clouds were all around them, snow was falling and being blown off the ridge.

As they paused on this less steep ground, an awkward problem arose over the oxygen equipment. The soda-lime canisters which form a part of the mechanism of the Closed-Circuit apparatus have an average endurance of approximately three to three and a half hours. They had now been going at least two and a half hours, and the canisters in use might be expected to have at most a further hour of useful life. Each man was carrying a second canister, and it was now a question whether they should change to the fresh ones at this point. By doing so here, they would have the advantage of a fairly spacious resting-place, and this did not appear to be available higher up; in fact, the ridge steepened very considerably from this point onwards. Equally important was the fact that there is a tendency for the valves in the apparatus to freeze up after a new and cold canister has been connected. This had happened only three days before, when they had introduced new canisters at Camp VI on their way up to the South Col. The risk would be better faced here than on top of the South summit, where a breakdown of this nature might have very serious consequences. Against these arguments was the objection that by rejecting the canisters in use they would be wasting the endurance of their oxygen equipment and would thus shorten their day. If I have gone into this problem in some detail, it is merely to stress what a dilemma it must have been for Charles and Tom, at 28,000 feet on the South-East ridge of Everest; hardly the most congenial place in which to consider and discuss such a nicely balanced problem, especially wearing oxygen masks.

They decided to change the canisters and went on. Charles was now having trouble again with his set, resulting in rapid laboured breathing, which may or may not have been due to the new canister; he was making a tremendous and gallant effort to keep going. They arrived at the foot of the final steep rise, a great slope tilted abruptly at a high angle sweeping up towards the South Peak. The snow was unstable, a fragile crust overlying loose deep snow underneath, and Tom, who was ahead at this point, doubted its safety. Away to the left were rocks, bordering the South face where it falls away towards the western brink of the South Col. They traversed across to these, half-expecting the slope to break away beneath them. The angle of the rocks was also steep and they were somewhat crumbling, but the strata dip favourably to the climber on this side of the mountain, and the ledges, small though they were, tilted so as to provide accommodating holds. On and on, up those last 400 feet they climbed, very slowly now, Charles Evans in considerable trouble with his breathing but determined not to give up. Then quite suddenly the angle eased, and almost at once they found themselves standing upon the South summit of Everest, at over 28,700 feet. It was 1 o'clock. Charles Evans and Tom Bourdillon had climbed higher on Everest by many hundreds of feet than anyone had ever climbed before. Better still, they had reached the highest summit so far climbed.

Clouds were all round them, obscuring the view, adhering like a banner to the tremendous eastern precipice falling away from the final ridge towards the Kangshung Valley. But that final ridge was clear, and they were now gazing upon a problem which had intrigued all mountaineers and which we especially had all been longing to see. It was not encouraging. Viewed thus, end on, it is narrow and apparently rising steeply. On the left, it falls sharply away to the edge of the rocks topping the west face of the mountain, which drops a sheer 8,000 feet into the Cwm above our Advance Base. On the right, or east, is an even more abrupt precipice of even greater height; it was masked now by cloud. Huge bulges of snow hung over it from the crest of the ridge, cornices of Himalayan dimensions formed by the prevailing westerly wind.

Should they go on? For them, here was a unique chance to climb to the top. But unless it were to be a one-way journey, it obviously depended on the factors of time and weather; the question of time was directly linked with that of their oxygen supply. Unless they had sufficient oxygen to last during the traverse along the ridge both ways and also to descend the ridge by which they had climbed, it was not feasible. To estimate the time required to climb an unknown ridge, seen foreshortened in this way so that it is not possible to be sure the farthest visible point is the summit, is not easy. Charles Evans reckoned that it might take three hours to the top, another two hours back to the South Peak. At that rate they would long since have exhausted their remaining oxygen supply and, even had they been able to return to the South summit without it, they would not be back there until 6 p.m., with nearly 3,000 feet to descend to safety. In fact, it was out of the question.

Yet it was with some reluctance that they turned to go down. Both were now very tired, emphasizing, if any further persuasion had been needed, the futility of going on towards the summit of the mountain. The trouble with Charles's set persisted and they stopped while Tom adapted it for use on the Open-Circuit principle—a remarkable feat this, at that height and after all they had done already. Later, they had to stop again and change back to Closed-Circuit, as Charles had been receiving rather less benefit still. They did not fancy the small ledges on those steep rocks and took a chance now on the snow slope to the left, sinking deeply into it through the crust, but probably too tired to think of the possible consequences. The descent of 1,500 feet to the Swiss tent took them about two hours. Their state of exhaustion is shown by the fact that, sound climbers as both of them are, they slipped on a number of occasions on the technically easy part of the ridge above this tent. It was about 3.30 p.m. when they arrived there.

Then they, like Da Namgyal and I a few hours before, had to face the couloir. They too took the usual precautions, but they were understandably even more wobbly than we had been. Tom led down and had just reached the end of the rope and fixed his axe as a belay when Charles came hurtling down the slope from behind, to quote Tom, "like a bullet". As the rope tightened round Tom's axe it was wrenched out of the snow and Tom was dragged from his steps, sliding with gathering speed down the hard surface of the couloir. But the jerk on the rope as the axe checked it had slowed Charles's fall. Tom instinctively took the correct action, turning on to his stomach and jabbing the pick of his axe above him into the snow as a brake. They came to a stop, waited to recover and started on down again.

*   *   *

On the Col, I was resting in the "blister" tent, talking to Tenzing. George Lowe suddenly put his head through the entrance. He was tremendously excited; he was jubilant. "They're up: by God they're up!" he shouted. This was indeed electrifying news, quite sufficient to banish the weariness of my own efforts that day. Everyone was overjoyed. The Sherpas, who had toiled up towards the top of the Geneva Spur behind Gregory and Lowe, were no less thrilled than ourselves. Indeed, perhaps more so, for they were under the impression that the peak rising from the South Col was in fact the highest point. They believed that Everest had been climbed. When they reached the tents, Ang Nyima turned to me and said in slang Hindi: "Everest khatm ho gya, Sahib", which in equally slang English may be translated, "Everest has had it". For them, the spectacle had been particularly dramatic. They had been watching our progress all that morning while they were crossing the slopes of the Lhotse Face, but Bourdillon and Evans had been hidden for some time by the clouds which now screened the mountain. At about 10 o'clock there was a break in the mists around the sharp snow cone of the South Peak and upon it, like insects on a wall, two little dots could be seen. They climbed steadily up that forbidding, impossibly steep-looking snow slope and soon disappeared over the top. It was as if they did not trouble to stop, intent on going farther, to the utmost point beyond.

We spent an anxious afternoon, with a lurking uncertainty lest Charles and Tom might not return. The clouds completely obscured the ridge and the wind had increased in strength. At 3.30 p.m. there was a thinning of the cloud at the top of the couloir, and there they were. They came down slowly and we prepared to receive them. At 4.30 they approached the tents and we went out to meet them; burdened with their cumbersome equipment and bulky clothing, their faces frost-covered, they looked like strangers from another planet. Both were utterly weary.

Later, they told us the story I have just narrated: the story of the first ascent of the South summit of Everest. It was natural that disappointment should have been among their feelings, to get so near the ultimate goal and then be denied it. Yet it must be remembered that they had achieved exactly what had been hoped of them. I had been insistent that the South summit was the objective and that, by reaching it, they would provide invaluable information to the second summit pair; indeed, the two Assaults were intended to be complementary. Their feat in climbing to over 28,700 feet and back in one day from the South Col was a magnificent effort, and a triumph also for the oxygen equipment on which such infinite pains had been taken. They had sighted that last part of the ridge and were able to describe it to Tenzing and Hillary. They had given us all, by their example, incalculable confidence in final victory.

*   *   *

With the second Assault party and their extra stores safely arrived on the South Col, preparations were made for their departure next day up the South-East ridge.

First, the Sherpas who had accompanied them, bringing up these stores, got ready to go down. Da Namgyal decided to join them, in spite of his outstanding and exhausting effort that day, and Balu also left. They were a heroic little band, whose names deserve to be specially recorded in this story of the ascent of Everest: Dawa Thondup, approaching his fifties; Da Tensing, another veteran; Topkie, a mere boy who had sometimes exasperated us in the Icefall and the Cwm by his carelessness and his irritating cough, yet with the heart of a lion; Ang Norbu, sturdy and unshakable; the jaunty Annullu, whose pace was like that of "a fast Swiss guide". For all these men save Da Tensing, this was their second trip to the South Col during this expedition. Da Tensing himself had done exceptional, skilled and

175

strenuous work with Lowe on the Lhotse Face and had made yet another of his many journeys to Camp VII on the day the first Assault party had gone up there. No praise is too high for them.

George Lowe had escorted them up and now asked to stay to assist in the "carry" of stores to the top camp. This I very gladly agreed to. Of the three special Sherpas accompanying this second party, the team to carry the stores up to Camp IX, only one now appeared likely to be fit to continue. This was Ang Nyima, already renowned among us for his work with Lowe in the early days of preparing the Lhotse Face. The other two, Ang Temba and Pemba, my orderly during the March-out, were both feeling ill on arrival. In the second support team, too, it would be necessary for the climbers to become porters.

We were overcrowded that evening at Camp VIII. The Pyramid was occupied by the four members of the second Assault party, while we of the first party, having finished our effort, occupied the Meade, designed for two. The three remaining Sherpas of the second support team somehow managed to squeeze into the tiny "blister" tent. It was a terrible night. For Hillary it was "one of the worst nights I have ever experienced". For those of us whose third night it was on the South Col, packed like sardines, managing without oxygen and exhausted after climbing high on the mountain throughout that day, it was a nightmare. The thermometer indicated $-25°$ C., and the wind, which had been strong all day long, now rose again to gale force. Pressed as we were against the walls of the tents, it was as if we had no protection at all. Constantly buffeted throughout the night, there could be no question of sleep. It continued hour after hour, adding greatly to our existing state of weariness. On the morning of 27th May, there was no longer any doubt that the first Assault party was in very poor shape indeed, especially, I think, Tom Bourdillon.

My diary for this day reads as follows:

"It was no surprise to find at about 8 a.m. that Ed's party had not started. The wind was blowing like mad, so much so that it was a nightmare to go out of the tent. A scene of wild confusion reigned around Everest, which was shrouded in cloud with snow being torn from the South-East ridge. We huddled into the Pyramid and discussed the situation while Tenzing made some attempt to work the Primus—of the Sherpas, only Ang Nyima was showing any sign of life. A postponement of twenty-four hours was imperative; fortunately we have stock-piled enough to make this possible and the important thing is to keep up our strength by eating and drinking enough. For me, this is my third day spent on or above the Col, and I've had three nights of it. But it is interesting to compare our condition with that of the Swiss who spent a similar period here last year, and who

Thyangboche Monastery, where the expedition made its first Base Camp, with the summit of Everest rising on the horizon, behind the Lhotse-Nuptse wall.

A ferry party on its way to Camp IV through the heavily crevassed
lower part of the Western Cwm.

John Hunt on the South Col on 26th May, after descending from the South-East Ridge.

The Nuptse wall soaring above the Western Cwm.

Evans viewing the summit ridge from 28,750 feet on the South Peak which he and Bourdillon were the first to reach on 26th May.

The second assault party, Tenzing and Hillary, check their oxygen equipment before setting off from Camp IV. Note the summit flags wrapped round Tenzing's iceaxe.

Hillary and Tenzing on their way to establish their final camp at nearly 28,000 feet.

scarcely got down alive. Here are we, well supplied with food, fuel and oxygen, sitting at 26,000 feet almost as if at Base.

"At about midday Charles and Tom started off on their way down. Then Charles suddenly reappeared with the alarming news that Tom could not get up the slope to the top of the Eperon [Spur] and was in a critical state. Another of us must accompany him down if he were to get down alive. Here was another difficult decision. My post was here on the Col, to see the big assault safely launched and decide, if need be, on a further postponement or, possibly, a withdrawal. Yet I was supporting the first Assault, and by sending either Greg or George would only weaken the second Assault's chances. I decided I must go. So I rapidly packed, with much willing help, and plodded very slowly up the slopes of the Spur, Ed carrying my sack.

"Left Ed with parting instruction not to give in if avoidable, and promising to send up a reinforcement party. We (Charles, Tom, Ang Temba and self) started slowly—so painfully slowly—down the couloir and across the big slopes beneath Lhotse. We halted frequently and for long intervals, for Tom, and to a less extent Ang Temba, were barely in control of their legs. I led, Charles brought up the rear. So it went on until, very nearly at the end of our strength (except, perhaps, Charles), we staggered down the last few feet to Camp VII. To our relief and delight, here we were met by Wilf Noyce and Mike Ward, who helped us in. Just as we were coming down the ice pitch above Camp, Temba slipped and fell into the big crevasse. He was held by Charles, and Wilf managed to get his sack off (he was upside down) and get him up. It is indicative of my state of exhaustion that I could not find strength to lift a finger throughout this incident."

Wilfrid Noyce's presence at Camp VII was very fortunate. Without him, Tom Bourdillon, Ang Temba and I could not have managed for ourselves that evening; he looked after us like a nurse and prepared our supper. Moreover, he was half way to the Col and, unbeknown to him, I had told Ed Hillary before leaving there that I would send up Noyce and three more volunteer Sherpas with further stores, in order to enable them to stay out yet another day of bad weather if necessary. I also had in mind that Noyce and one or more of these men might replace any casualties up there and thus take part in the second Assault. So it was that Charles Evans, who found the energy to continue on down with Michael Ward to Advance Base the same evening, was to arrange for three men to come up and join Noyce here at Camp VII on 28th May.

Tom and I descended to the Cwm next morning. On the way we met Charles Wylie with the three Sherpas. Wylie had rightly decided that they should not go up to the Lhotse Face unaccompanied, and he had also felt that this camp should be occupied until the return of Hillary's party. These rôles he took upon himself: a great contribution to the sound conduct of the Assault. It is typical of Charles that as he passed I noticed in his bulky load an Assault oxygen bottle. This and other items of replenishment he had taken over from a fourth Sherpa who should have been with the party, but who had not been able to go beyond Camp V. Wylie was, of course, climbing without oxygen.

We reached Advance Base in the early afternoon, our immediate task completed. There was nothing for us now to do but await the outcome of the second Assault.

CHAPTER SIXTEEN

THE SUMMIT

By EDMUND HILLARY

E ARLY on the morning of 27th May I awoke from an uneasy sleep feeling very cold and miserable. We were on the South Col of Everest. My companions in our Pyramid tent, Lowe, Gregory and Tenzing, were all tossing and turning in unsuccessful efforts to gain relief from the bitter cold. The relentless wind was blowing in all its fury and the constant loud drumming on the tent made deep sleep impossible. Reluctantly removing my hand from my sleeping-bag I looked at my watch. It was 4 a.m. In the flickering light of a match, the thermometer lying against the tent wall read −25° C.

We had hoped to establish a camp high on the South-East ridge that day, but the force of the wind obviously made a start impossible. We must, however, be prepared to go on if the wind should drop. I nudged the uncomplaining Tenzing with my elbow and murmured a few words about food and drink, then callously snuggled my way back into my bag again. Soon the purring of the Primus and the general warming of the atmosphere stirred us into life and while we munched biscuits and drank hot water flavoured with lemon crystals and heaps of sugar, Lowe, Gregory and I discussed rather pessimistically our plans for the day.

At 9 a.m. the wind was still blowing fiercely, and clad in all my warm clothing I crawled out of the tent and crossed to the small Meade tent housing John Hunt, Charles Evans and Tom Bourdillon. Hunt agreed that any start under these conditions was impossible. Ang Temba had become sick and was obviously incapable of carrying up any farther, so we decided to send him down with Evans and Bourdillon when they left for Camp VII about midday. Hunt decided at the last moment to accompany this party, owing to Bourdillon's condition, and George Lowe and I assisted a very weary foursome to climb the slopes above the camp and then watched them start off on their slow and exhausting trip down to Camp VII.

All day the wind blew furiously and it was in a somewhat desperate spirit that we organized the loads for the establishment of the Ridge Camp on the following day. Any delay in our departure from the

South Col could only result in increased deterioration and consequent weakness. The violent wind gave us another unpleasant night, but we were all breathing oxygen at one litre per minute and this enabled us to doze uneasily for seven or eight hours.

Early in the morning the wind was still blowing strongly, but about 8 a.m. it eased considerably and we decided to leave. However, another blow had fallen—Pemba had been violently ill all night and was obviously not capable of going on. Only one Sherpa porter, Ang Nyima, was left to carry for us out of our original band of three. Our only alternative was to carry the camp ourselves, as to abandon the attempt was unthinkable. We repacked the loads, eliminating any-thing not vitally necessary and having no choice because of our reduced manpower but to cut down vital supplies of oxygen.

At 8.45 a.m. Lowe, Gregory and Ang Nyima departed, all carrying over 40 lb. each and breathing oxygen at 4 litres a minute. Tenzing and I were to leave later so that we could follow quickly up the steps made by the other party and so conserve energy and oxygen. We loaded all our personal clothing, sleeping-bags and air mattresses, together with some food, on to our oxygen sets and left at 10 a.m. carrying 50 lb. apiece.

We followed slowly up the long slopes to the foot of the great couloir and then climbed the veritable staircase hewn by Lowe in the firm steep snow of the couloir. As we moved slowly up the steps we were bombarded by a constant stream of ice chips falling from well above us where Lowe and Gregory were cutting steps across to the South-East ridge. We reached the ridge at midday and joined the other party. Near by was the tattered ruin of the Swiss tent of the previous spring, and it added an air of loneliness and desolation to this remark-able viewpoint. From here Lambert and Tenzing had made their gallant attempt to reach the summit after a night spent without sleep-ing-bags.

It was a wonderful spot with tremendous views in every direction and we indulged in an orgy of photography. We were all feeling extremely well and confident of placing our camp high up on the South-East ridge. We heaved on our loads again and moved 150 feet up the ridge to the dump made by Hunt two days previously. The ridge was quite steep but the upward-sloping strata of the rocks gave us quite good footholds and the climbing was not technically difficult, although loose snow over the steep rocks demanded care. The dump was at 27,350 feet, but we considered that this was still far too low for an effective summit camp, so somewhat reluctantly we added all this extra gear to our already large loads. Gregory took some more oxygen, Lowe some food and fuel and I tied on a tent. Apart from

Ang Nyima, who was carrying just over 40 lb., we all had loads of from 50 to 63 lb. We continued on up the ridge at a somewhat reduced rate. Despite our great burdens we were moving steadily, though very slowly. The ridge steepened on to a slope of firm snow and Lowe chipped steps up it for fifty feet. By 2 p.m. we were beginning to tire and started looking for a camp site. The ridge appeared to have no relief at all and continued upwards in one unbroken sweep. We plugged slowly on, looking for a ledge without success. Again and again we hopefully laboured up to a prospective site only to find that it was still at a 45-degree angle. We were getting a little desperate until Tenzing, remembering the ground from the previous year, suggested a traverse over steep slopes to the left, which finally landed us on to a relatively flat spot beneath a rock bluff.

It was 2.30 and we decided to camp here. All day the magnificent peak of Lhotse had commanded our attention, but now its summit was just below us. We estimated our height at 27,900 feet. Lowe, Gregory and Ang Nyima dropped their loads on the site with relief. They were tired but well satisfied with the height gained, and to them must go a great deal of the credit for the successful climb of the following day. Wasting no time, they hurried off back to the South Col.

It was with a certain feeling of loneliness that we watched our cheerful companions slowly descending the ridge, but we had much to do. We removed our oxygen sets in order to conserve our supplies and set to work with our ice-axes to clear the tiny platform. We scratched off all the snow to reveal a rock slope at an angle of some 30 degrees. The rocks were well frozen in, but by the end of a couple of hours' solid work we had managed to prise loose sufficient stones to level out two strips of ground a yard wide and six feet long, but almost a foot different in levels. Even though not breathing oxygen, we could still work quite hard, but rested every ten minutes or so in order to regain our breath and energy. We pitched our tent on this double level and tied it down as best we could. There were no suitable rocks around which to hitch our tent guys, and the snow was far too soft to hold aluminium tent pegs. We sank several of our oxygen bottles in the soft snow and attached the guys to these as a somewhat unreliable anchor. Then, while Tenzing began heating some soup, I made a tally of our limited oxygen supplies. They were much less than we had hoped. For the Assault we had only one and two-thirds bottles each. It was obvious that if we were to have sufficient endurance we would be unable to use the 4 litres per minute that we had originally planned, but I estimated that if we reduced our supplies to 3 litres per minute we might still have a chance. I prepared the sets

181

and made the necessary adjustments. One thing in our favour was that Evans and Bourdillon had left two bottles of oxygen, still one-third full, some hundreds of feet above our camp. We were relying on this oxygen to get us back to the South Col.

As the sun set we crawled finally into our tent, put on all our warm clothing and wriggled into our sleeping-bags. We drank vast quantities of liquid and had a satisfying meal out of our store of delicacies: sardines on biscuits, tinned apricots, dates and biscuits and jam and honey. The tinned apricots were a great treat, but it was necessary first to thaw them out of their frozen state over our roaring Primus. In spite of the great height, our breathing was almost normal until a sudden exertion would cause us to pant a little. Tenzing laid his air mattress on the lower shelf half-overhanging the steep slope below and calmly settled down to sleep. I made myself as comfortable as possible half-sitting and half-reclining on the upper shelf with my feet braced on the lower shelf. This position, while not particularly comfortable, had decided advantages. We had been experiencing extremely strong gusts of wind every ten minutes, and whenever I received warning of the approach of such a gust by a shrilling whine high on the ridge above, I could brace my feet and shoulders and assist our meagre anchors to hold the tent steady while it temporarily shook and flapped in a most alarming manner. We had sufficient oxygen for only four hours' sleep at one litre per minute. I decided to use this in two periods of two hours, from 9 to 11 p.m. and from 1 to 3 a.m. While wearing the oxygen we dozed and were reasonably comfortable, but as soon as the supply ran out we began to feel cold and miserable. During the night the thermometer read −27° Centigrade, but fortunately the wind had dropped almost entirely.

At 4 a.m. it was very still. I opened the tent door and looked far out across the dark and sleeping valleys of Nepal. The icy peaks below us were glowing clearly in the early morning light and Tenzing pointed out the Monastery of Thyangboche, faintly visible on its dominant spur 16,000 feet below us. It was an encouraging thought to realise that even at this early hour the Lamas of Thyangboche would be offering up devotions to their Buddhist Gods for our safety and well-being.

We started up our cooker and in a determined effort to prevent the weaknesses arising from dehydration we drank large quantities of lemon juice and sugar, and followed this with our last tin of sardines on biscuits. I dragged our oxygen sets into the tent, cleaned the ice off them and then completely rechecked and tested them. I had removed my boots, which had become a little wet the day before, and they were now frozen solid. Drastic measures were called for, so I cooked them over the fierce flame of the Primus and despite the very strong smell of burning leather managed to soften them up. Over our down clothing we donned our windproofs and on to our hands we pulled three pairs of gloves—silk, woollen and windproof.

At 6.30 a.m. we crawled out of our tent into the snow, hoisted our 30 lb. of oxygen gear on to our backs, connected up our masks and turned on the valves to bring life-giving oxygen into our lungs. A few good deep breaths and we were ready to go. Still a little worried about my cold feet, I asked Tenzing to move off and he kicked a deep line of steps away from the rock bluff which protected our tent out on to the steep powder snow slope to the left of the main ridge. The ridge was now all bathed in sunlight and we could see our first objective, the South summit, far above us. Tenzing, moving purposefully, kicked steps in a long traverse back towards the ridge and we reached its crest just where it forms a great distinctive snow bump at about 28,000 feet. From here the ridge narrowed to a knife-edge and as my feet were now warm I took over the lead.

We were moving slowly but steadily and had no need to stop in order to regain our breath, and I felt that we had plenty in reserve. The soft unstable snow made a route on top of the ridge both difficult and dangerous, so I moved a little down on the steep left side where the wind had produced a thin crust which sometimes held my weight but more often than not gave way with a sudden knock that was disastrous to both balance and morale. After several hundred feet of this rather trying ridge, we came to a tiny hollow and found there the two oxygen bottles left on the earlier attempt by Evans and Bourdillon. I scraped the ice off the gauges and was greatly relieved to find that they still contained several hundred litres of oxygen—sufficient to get us down to the South Col if used very sparingly. With the comforting thought of these oxygen bottles behind us, I continued making the trail on up the ridge, which soon steepened and broadened into the very formidable snow face leading up for the last 400 feet to the southern summit. The snow conditions on this face were, we felt, distinctly dangerous, but as no alternative route seemed available, we persisted in our strenuous and uncomfortable efforts to beat a trail up it. We made frequent changes of lead on this very trying section and on one occasion as I was stamping a trail in the deep snow a section around me gave way and I slipped back through three or four of my steps. I discussed with Tenzing the advisability of going on and he, although admitting that he felt very unhappy about the snow conditions, finished with his familiar phrase "Just as you wish". I decided to go on.

It was with some relief that we finally reached some firmer snow

higher up and then chipped steps up the last steep slopes and cramponed on to the South Peak. It was now 9 a.m. We looked with some
interest at the virgin ridge ahead. Both Bourdillon and Evans had
been depressingly definite about its problems and difficulties and we
realized that it could form an almost insuperable barrier. At first
glance it was certainly impressive and even rather frightening. On the
right, great contorted cornices, overhanging masses of snow and ice,
stuck out like twisted fingers over the 10,000-foot drop of the Kangshung Face. Any move on to these cornices could only bring disaster.
From the cornices the ridge dropped steeply to the left until the snow
merged with the great rock face sweeping up from the Western Cwm.
Only one encouraging feature was apparent. The steep snow slope
between the cornices and the rock precipices seemed to be composed
of firm, hard snow. If the snow proved soft and unstable, our chances
of getting along the ridge were few indeed. If we could cut a trail of
steps along this slope, we could make some progress at least.

We cut a seat for ourselves just below the southern summit and
removed our oxygen. Once again I worked out the mental arithmetic
that was one of my main preoccupations on the way up and down the
mountain. As our first partly full bottle of oxygen was now exhausted,
we had only one full bottle left. Eight hundred litres of oxygen at three
litres per minute? How long could we last? I estimated that this should
give us 4½ hours of going. Our apparatus was now much lighter,
weighing just over 20 lb., and as I cut steps down off the southern
summit I felt a distinct sense of freedom and well-being quite contrary
to what I had expected at this great altitude.

As my ice-axe bit into the first steep slope of the ridge, my highest
hopes were realized. The snow was crystalline and firm. Two or three
rhythmical blows of the ice-axe produced a step large enough even
for our oversized High Altitude boots and, the most encouraging
feature of all, a firm thrust of the ice-axe would sink it half-way up
the shaft, giving a solid and comfortable belay. We moved one at a
time. I realized that our margin of safety at this altitude was not great
and that we must take every care and precaution. I would cut a
forty-foot line of steps, Tenzing belaying me while I worked. Then in
turn I would sink my shaft and put a few loops of the rope around it
and Tenzing, protected against a breaking step, would move up to
me. Then once again as he belayed me I would go on cutting. In a
number of places the overhanging ice cornices were very large indeed
and in order to escape them I cut a line of steps down to where the
snow met the rocks on the west. It was a great thrill to look straight
down this enormous rock face and to see, 8,000 feet below us, the tiny
tents of Camp IV in the Western Cwm. Scrambling on the rocks and

cutting hand-holds in the snow, we were able to shuffle past these difficult portions.

On one of these occasions I noted that Tenzing, who had been going quite well, had suddenly slowed up considerably and seemed to be breathing with difficulty. The Sherpas had little idea of the workings of an oxygen set and from past experience I immediately suspected his oxygen supply. I noticed that hanging from the exhaust tube of his oxygen mask were icicles, and on closer examination found that this tube, some two inches in diameter, was completely blocked with ice. I was able to clear it out and gave him much-needed relief. On checking my own set I found that the same thing was occurring, though it had not reached the stage to have caused me any discomfort. From then on I kept a much closer check on this problem.

The weather for Everest seemed practically perfect. Insulated as we were in all our down clothing and windproofs, we suffered no discomfort from cold or wind. However, on one occasion I removed my sunglasses to examine more closely a difficult section of the ridge but was very soon blinded by the fine snow driven by the bitter wind and hastily replaced them. I went on cutting steps. To my surprise I was enjoying the climb as much as I had ever enjoyed a fine ridge in my own New Zealand Alps.

After an hour's steady going we reached the foot of the most formidable-looking problem on the ridge—a rock step some forty feet high. We had known of the existence of this step from aerial photographs and had also seen it through our binoculars from Thyangboche. We realized that at this altitude it might well spell the difference between success and failure. The rock itself, smooth and almost holdless, might have been an interesting Sunday afternoon problem to a group of expert rock climbers in the Lake District, but here it was a barrier beyond our feeble strength to overcome. I could see no way of turning it on the steep rock bluff on the west, but fortunately another possibility of tackling it still remained. On its east side was another great cornice, and running up the full forty feet of the step was a narrow crack between the cornice and the rock. Leaving Tenzing to belay me as best he could, I jammed my way into this crack, then kicking backwards with my crampons I sank their spikes deep into the frozen snow behind me and levered myself off the ground. Taking advantage of every little rock hold and all the force of knee, shoulder and arms I could muster, I literally cramponed backwards up the crack, with a fervent prayer that the cornice would remain attached to the rock. Despite the considerable effort involved, my progress although slow was steady, and as Tenzing paid out the rope I inched my way upwards until I could finally reach over the top of the rock and drag myself out of the crack on to a wide ledge. For a few moments I lay regaining my breath and for the first time really felt the fierce determination that nothing now could stop us reaching the top. I took a firm stance on the ledge and signalled to Tenzing to come on up. As I heaved hard on the rope Tenzing wriggled his way up the crack and finally collapsed exhausted at the top like a giant fish when it has just been hauled from the sea after a terrible struggle.

I checked both our oxygen sets and roughly calculated our flow rates. Everything seemed to be going well. Probably owing to the strain imposed on him by the trouble with his oxygen set, Tenzing had been moving rather slowly but he was climbing safely, and this was the major consideration. His only comment on my enquiring of his condition was to smile and wave along the ridge. We were going so well at 3 litres per minute that I was determined now if necessary to cut down our flow rate to 2 litres per minute if the extra endurance was required.

The ridge continued as before. Giant cornices on the right, steep rock slopes on the left. I went on cutting steps on the narrow strip of snow. The ridge curved away to the right and we had no idea where the top was. As I cut around the back of one hump, another higher one would swing into view. Time was passing and the ridge seemed never-ending. In one place, where the angle of the ridge had eased off, I tried cramponing without cutting steps, hoping this would save time, but I quickly realized that our margin of safety on these steep slopes at this altitude was too small, so I went on step-cutting. I was beginning to tire a little now. I had been cutting steps continuously for two hours, and Tenzing, too, was moving very slowly. As I chipped steps around still another corner, I wondered rather dully just how long we could keep it up. Our original zest had now quite gone and it was turning more into a grim struggle. I then realized that the ridge ahead, instead of still monotonously rising, now dropped sharply away, and far below I could see the North Col and the Rongbuk glacier. I looked upwards to see a narrow snow ridge running up to a snowy summit. A few more whacks of the ice-axe in the firm snow and we stood on top.

My initial feelings were of relief—relief that there were no more steps to cut—no more ridges to traverse and no more humps to tantalize us with hopes of success. I looked at Tenzing and in spite of the balaclava, goggles and oxygen mask all encrusted with long icicles that concealed his face, there was no disguising his infectious grin of pure delight as he looked all around him. We shook hands and then Tenzing threw his arm around my shoulders and we thumped each other on the back until we were almost breathless. It was

11.30 a.m. The ridge had taken us two and a half hours, but it seemed like a lifetime. I turned off the oxygen and removed my set. I had carried my camera, loaded with colour film, inside my shirt to keep it warm, so I now produced it and got Tenzing to pose on top for me, waving his axe on which was a string of flags—United Nations, British, Nepalese and Indian. Then I turned my attention to the great stretch of country lying below us in every direction.

To the east was our giant neighbour Makalu, unexplored and unclimbed, and even on top of Everest the mountaineering instinct was sufficiently strong to cause me to spend some moments conjecturing as to whether a route up that mountain might not exist. Far away across the clouds the great bulk of Kangchenjunga loomed on the horizon. To the west, Cho Oyu, our old adversary from 1952, dominated the scene and we could see the great unexplored ranges of Nepal stretching off into the distance. The most important photograph, I felt, was a shot down the North ridge, showing the North Col and the old route which had been made famous by the struggles of those great climbers of the 1920s and 1930s. I had little hope of the results being particularly successful, as I had a lot of difficulty in holding the camera steady in my clumsy gloves, but I felt that they would at least serve as a record. After some ten minutes of this, I realized that I was becoming rather clumsy-fingered and slow-moving, so I quickly replaced my oxygen set and experienced once more the stimulating effect of even a few litres of oxygen. Meanwhile, Tenzing had made a little hole in the snow and in it he placed various small articles of food—a bar of chocolate, a packet of biscuits and a handful of lollies. Small offerings, indeed, but at least a token gift to the Gods that all devout Buddhists believe have their home on this lofty summit. While we were together on the South Col two days before, Hunt had given me a small crucifix which he had asked me to take to the top. I, too, made a hole in the snow and placed the crucifix beside Tenzing's gifts.

I checked our oxygen once again and worked out our endurance. We would have to move fast in order to reach our life-saving reserve below the South Peak. After fifteen minutes we turned to go. We had looked briefly for any signs of Mallory and Irvine, but had seen nothing. We both felt a little tired, for reaction was setting in and we must get off the mountain quickly. I moved down off the summit on to our steps. Wasting no time, we cramponed along our tracks, spurred by the urgency of diminishing oxygen. Bump followed bump in rapid succession. In what seemed almost miraculous time, we reached the top of the rock step. Now, with the almost casual indifference of familiarity, we kicked and jammed our way down it again. We were tired, but not too tired to be careful. We scrambled cautiously over the rock traverse, moved one at a time over shaky snow sections and finally cramponed up our steps and back on to the South Peak.

Only one hour from the top! A swig of sweetened lemonade refreshed us and we turned down again. Throughout the climb we had a constant nagging fear of our return down the great snow slope, and as I led down I packed each step with as much care as if our lives depended on it, as well they might. The terrific impression of exposure as we looked straight down on to the Kangshung glacier, still over 9,000 feet below us, made us move with the greatest caution, and every step down seemed a step nearer safety. When we finally moved off the slope on to the ridge below, we looked at each other and without speaking we both almost visibly shrugged off the sense of fear that had been with us all day.

We were now very tired but moved automatically down to the two reserve cylinders on the ridge. As we were only a short distance from camp and had a few litres of oxygen left in our own bottles, we carried the extra cylinders down our tracks and reached our tent on its crazy platform at 2 p.m. Already the moderate winds of the afternoon had wrenched the tent loose from some of its fastenings and it presented a forlorn sight. We had still to reach the South Col. While Tenzing lit the paraffin stove and began to make a lemonade drink heavily sweetened with sugar, I changed our oxygen sets on to the last partly filled bottles and cut down our flow rates to 2 litres per minute. In contrast to the previous day, when we were working vigorously without oxygen at this camp, we now felt very weak and exhausted. Far below on the South Col we could see minute figures moving and knew that Lowe and Noyce would be waiting for our descent. We had no extra sleeping-bags and air mattresses on the South Col, so reluctantly tied our own on to our oxygen frames. Then with a last look at the camp that had served us so well we turned downwards with dragging feet and set ourselves to the task of safely descending the ridge.

Our faculties seemed numbed and the time passed as in a dream, but finally we reached the site of the Swiss Ridge Camp and branched off on our last stage down on to the great couloir. There an unpleasant surprise greeted us. The strong wind which had been blowing in the latter part of our climb had completely wiped out all our steps and only a hard, steep, frozen slope lay before us. There was no alternative but to start cutting again. With a grunt of disgust I chipped steps laboriously downwards for 200 feet. Gusts of driving wind whirling down off the ridge tried to pluck us from our steps. Tenzing took over the lead and cut down another hundred feet, then moved into softer snow and kicked a track down the easier slopes at the bottom of the couloir. We cramponed wearily down the long slopes above the South Col.

A figure came towards us and met us a couple of hundred feet above the camp. It was George Lowe, laden with hot soup and emergency oxygen.

We were too tired to make any response to Lowe's enthusiastic acceptance of our news. We stumped down to the Col and slowly ground our way up the short rise to the camp. Just short of the tents my oxygen ran out. We had had enough to do the job, but by no means too much. We crawled into the tent and with a sigh of sheer delight collapsed into our sleeping-bags, while the tents flapped and shook under the perpetual South Col gale. That night, our last on the South Col, was a restless one indeed. The bitter cold once again made any deep and restful sleep impossible and the stimulating effects of our success made us so mentally active that we lay there for half the night re-living all the exciting incidents and murmuring to each other between chattering teeth. Early the following morning we were all very weak and made slow but determined preparations for our departure.

The 200-foot slope above the South Col was a great trial, and even when we commenced the long traverse down towards Camp VII we found it necessary to move very slowly and to have frequent rests. The upper part of the Lhotse glacier seemed very steep to us and as we came down the ice steps towards Camp VII our main wish was to rest. We were only thirty yards from the camp when a cheerful shout attracted our attention and there to greet us was Charles Wylie and several of the Sherpas, all looking fresh and strong and with the same question trembling on their lips. The hot drinks they pressed into our hands and their joyful acceptance of our news were a great stimulant in themselves, and we continued on down the Lhotse glacier mentally if not physically refreshed.

As we approached Camp IV, tiny figures appeared from the tents and slowly drifted up the track. We made no signal to them but wearily moved down the track towards them. When only fifty yards away, Lowe with characteristic enthusiasm gave the "thumbs up" signal and waved his ice-axe in the direction of the summit. Immediately the scene was galvanized into activity and our approaching companions, forgetting their weakness, ran up the snow towards us. As we greeted them all, perhaps a little emotionally, I felt more than ever before that very strong feeling of friendship and co-operation that had been the decisive factor throughout the expedition.

What a thrill it was to be able to tell them that all their efforts amongst the tottering chaos of the Icefall, the disheartening plunging up the snowy inferno of the Western Cwm, the difficult technical ice work on the Lhotse Face and the grim and nerve-racking toil above the South Col had been fully rewarded and that we had reached the top.

To see the unashamed joy spread over the tired, strained face of our gallant and determined leader was to me reward enough in itself.

Part VI

AFTERMATH

CHAPTER SEVENTEEN

RETURN

I T had been an anxious day waiting for news at Advance Base. The weather seemed perfect; it was cloudless and there was apparently little wind up there on the Col. We were watching the Lhotse Face all day, observing Noyce and his three Sherpas going up from Camp VII—he in the lead, much slower than on his epoch-making first climb.

At the top of the Lhotse glacier one man dropped out; shortly after, we noticed another of the remaining trio go back to join this one. Two only continued, two started down again towards Camp VII. It no longer looked a very promising aid for Ed Hillary, whether as a reinforcement or a rescue party. Meanwhile, three others were coming down from the Col; the two groups passed, and later the descending caravan reached Camp VII. It was all most intriguing and kept our minds from brooding too much on the unseen drama higher up. Some time later, no fewer than five men emerged from Camp VII and came down to the Cwm; evidently this must now include the two men who had broken away from Noyce's reinforcement party. All this activity gave rise to much conjecture.

That afternoon we had some indication of the outcome when Gregory arrived with four Sherpas—Ang Nyima and the sick Pemba from the South Col, Ang Dorji and Phu Dorji, two of the three men who had been with Noyce. Greg had great news. He told us the wonderful story of the placing of Camp IX on the previous day and added the Stop Press information that he had seen Ed Hillary and Tenzing at 9 o'clock that morning, just as he had seen Tom Bourdillon and Charles Evans three days before as they climbed the final snow slope towards the South Peak. They were going well while he watched them. This news and, in particular, the time of day when he had seen them, gave us good reason to be confident, and we waited impatiently for the evening, when it was hoped we should have a certain signal which Wilfrid Noyce and I had arranged between us. While I was at Camp VII on the way down, I had discussed with him some means of letting us have news from the Col so as to put an end to the suspense and tension. We had agreed that he would place sleeping-bags on some suitable snow slope either above or just below the edge of the Col, clearly visible to ourselves at Advance Base. The placing of one bag would mean that the summit party had been unsuccessful; two bags placed side by side would spell the second ascent of the South summit; two bags placed at right angles in the form of a "T" would give the glad news of complete success—the summit itself.

Our feelings may perhaps be imagined when, towards evening, light mists came up the Cwm, veiling the slopes below the South Col. In vain we strained our eyes, searching those snow slopes during an occasional thinning of the cloud; no sign could be seen. The sun went down behind Pumori. After that, we could not expect that Noyce or anyone else up there would have the fortitude to remain outside the tents. The suspense continued.

We waited on next day, hoping for success, not daring to contemplate a setback. Westmacott had come up overnight, after doing splendid work for the past ten days in the Icefall; according to his report, later confirmed by our own observations, the ice was undergoing rapid change and he had been kept continually busy on this thankless, risky but essential task. Our numbers, apart from those engaged in the second Assault and Charles Wylie, waiting in support at Camp VII, were completed next day when James Morris came up the Cwm with two Sherpas from Camp III. The sense of expectation gripped us all and it was difficult to keep even outwardly calm.

About 9 a.m. we saw five figures appear from behind the screening rocks of the Geneva Spur, in the couloir. A sigh of relief escaped me. At least the whole Assault party were complete and safe; although they were moving slowly, no one appeared to be in distress. Hillary, Tenzing, Lowe, Noyce and Pasang Phutar were on their way down. All we could do was to wait. Considering what they had been through, they did not keep us long. Soon after disappearing into Camp VII, three of them emerged, coming down the Lhotse Face for the last time. Tom Stobart, with one Sherpa, set out for Camp V; he was intent on an early "shot" of the returning party, whatever their fortune.

At 2 p.m., just after the Indian Wireless News bulletin had informed the world that we had failed, five men could be seen at the top of the shallow trough about 500 yards above the camp. Some of us started out at once, Mike Westmacott and myself ahead, while our Sherpas crowded outside their Dome tent, no less eager than the rest of us to know the result. But the approaching climbers made no sign, just plodded on dejectedly towards us; they did not even wave a greeting. My heart sank. In my weak state, this plod up the track was already an effort; now my feet felt like lead. This must be failure; we must now think of that third and last attempt.

Suddenly, the leading man in the party—it was George Lowe—raised his axe, pointing unmistakably towards the distant top of Everest; he made several vigorous thrusts. The others behind him were now making equally unequivocal signs. Far from failure, this was IT! They had made it!! Feelings welled up uncontrollably as I now quickened my pace—I still could not muster the strength to break into a run, and Mike Westmacott was now well ahead. Everyone was pouring out of the tents; there were shouts of acclamation and joy. The next moment I was with them: handshakes—even, I blush to say, hugs—for the triumphant pair. A special one for Tenzing, so well merited for him personally, this victory, both for himself and for his people.

Amid much chatter, we escorted them into camp, where the Sherpas, grinning broadly, crowded round, shaking Ed warmly by the hand, offering a more respectful, indeed reverent welcome to Tenzing, their great leader. We all went into the Mess tent to hear the great story. Devouring an omelette, draining mugfuls of his favourite lemonade drink, Ed Hillary described the events of 28th and 29th May in graphic yet simple terms, while James Morris scribbled in his book the notes for his message to the world. He, perhaps more than the rest of us at that moment, realized the faint but glorious possibility of getting the headlines home in time for the Coronation of Her Majesty the Queen. At this time, the climax of his mission also, James was at the top of his professional form. He wasted no time in starting off down the Cwm, this time in company with Mike Westmacott, who was to escort him safely down to Base Camp that night.

A little later on during that unforgettable afternoon, I went out to greet Wilfrid Noyce, Charles Wylie and Pasang Phutar. They too had put up a great show. Noyce and Pasang Phutar had both been twice to the South Col. On this second trip, they had each carried a double load—at least 50 lb.—from the point where the other two Sherpas had given up, about half the height and distance between Camp VII and the Col. Noyce and Wylie were the only two members of the climbing party to reach the South Col without oxygen, as well as carrying heavier loads than our Sherpas. Wylie had covered the last 400 to 500 feet without it on 22nd May; Noyce on 28th May must have climbed some 1,400 feet after his supply gave out.

I asked Wilfrid about the agreed signal. Yes, he had made it. Although he had only reached the South Col an hour or two before when Hillary and Tenzing came down from the South-East ridge, Wilfrid had set out again with a very puzzled Pasang Phutar to the top of the Geneva Spur, carrying two sleeping-bags. What could this eccentric Sahib be doing at this hour of the day, starting off so soon after getting to the Col, apparently determined to sleep out? The mystery deepened for him when, on arriving at the slope which seemed to Wilfrid most likely to be seen from below, he arranged the sleeping-bags in the form of a "T" and proceeded to lie down on one of them—the wind was strong and this was essential to prevent the bags being blown away—bidding the astonished Sherpa to do like-wise. Surely, thought Pasang, this was carrying hardihood too far? So they were not even to get inside the bags? Thus they remained, shiver-ing, for ten long minutes as the sun went down behind Pumori, until Wilfrid decided they had done their best to pass the great news down to us. Thankful that the ordeal was over, they went down again to the tents.

After supper we brought out the expedition rum and toasted the Patron of the Expedition, H.R.H. The Duke of Edinburgh, who had followed our progress with such keen interest and sympathy. We also drank the health of Eric Shipton who, among others, had done so much to bring about this event.

That evening we thought again of those many earlier climbers, of their struggles, their skill and courage, of all they had contributed towards the ascent of Everest; we knew how tremendously glad they would be to know of the triumphant outcome of this long struggle. And I looked around the tent at these men who had finished the job, all of them now relaxed, happy, exuberant. How well they deserved it and how fully they each and all had shared in the achievement so brilliantly concluded by Tenzing and Hillary! I felt an immense pride in these companions of mine.

*   *   *

The mountain had been climbed and we lost no time in getting away. We had an overwhelming urge to return to more congenial surroundings, and, as we had only provisioned ourselves in the Cwm until the end of the month, we were now running short of supplies of food and fuel. Anxious to salvage as much serviceable equipment as possible, I asked Charles Wylie to stay behind in the Cwm with a rear party to carry loads down to Camp III. Parties descending from Camp VII had brought back tents and stoves from there the day before, and another party of Sherpas under George Band had gone up to collect stores from Camp V. The rest of us started down to Base Camp on 31st May.

No one had any regrets about this leave-taking of Everest. Indeed, the Western Cwm and the Khumbu Icefall no longer held any glamour for us now that the job was done; the beauty of the Cwm was much impaired by the hot sunshine of the past fourteen days which had fretted and furrowed the snow. It now had a rough and dirty surface from wind-carried dust and badly needed a new coat of snow. Camp III we found to be a scene of squalor, a mess of abandoned boxes, food-tins and other rubbish, reminiscent of some much-frequented ski-ing haunt in early summer. Farther down, in the Ice-fall, there were remarkable changes and part of the route was unrecognizable; it was melting like a big sugar cake. On the neglected site of Camp II, the tent platforms were fissured with small crevasses, and the same filth as at the higher camp surrounded it. An entirely new variant of the original route had been made in the "Atom Bomb" area, itself obviously precarious; I wondered what would have been the solution to this recurring problem if we had stayed much longer. Of all the many flags we had planted between Camp V and Base Camp, not a single one was standing; they lay in deep melt grooves or at the bottom of crevasses. It was as if the mountain was bent on showing us, before our departure, how ephemeral was our intrusion into its territory.

I was travelling with Greg, Ang Norbu and Balu; Greg and I were still suffering from the after-effects of our climb above the South Col and were in a very feeble state. Indicative of my own weakness was the fact that during the descent of the steep section of "Hell-fire Alley", I twice slipped and fell some distance, being well held on the rope by Ang Norbu. At the bottom we missed our way on ground which was now quite new to us, for a big river ploughed its way through the ice pinnacles where there had been flat ice alleys before. The others had similar experiences. We reached Base very late and very tired, but it was a relief to be down for the last time.

All were gathered at Base Camp by the afternoon of 2nd June, after much good work on a reverse Ferry service to bring back our gear; Mike Westmacott led a final party up to Camp III on the morning of the 2nd to assist Charles Wylie's party with the last loads. It was a typically unselfish act on his part, to spare the remainder of us and to observe to the last the policy of accompanying our men through this section of the route. Mike Westmacott's name will always be closely associated with the Khumbu Icefall; having taken a leading part in the reconnaissance, he also participated in its preparation, in leading Ferry parties through it and in its maintenance during the whole of the Assault period.

In our Mess tent after supper we turned on the wireless to hear the Coronation news; George Band tuned in to All-India Radio. In the second headline of the news summary, the announcer said: "The wonderful news broke in London last night that Everest has been climbed by the British Expedition. . . ." We were dumb-founded. Before leaving us in the Cwm, James Morris, now on his way to Kathmandu, had said that he hoped to be able to get a brief message back quickly, but none of us had seriously imagined that it could already have been known at home twenty-four hours ago. Great though my private hope had been that we might have climbed the mountain in time for the Coronation, this hope had gradually receded as the days passed, and I had finally contented myself with the thought that it would be nice to have the news follow as closely as possible after that great event.

With growing excitement and amazement we listened further. The Queen and the Prime Minister had sent telegrams of congratulation to us via the British Ambassador in Kathmandu; the news had been announced over the loudspeakers along the Coronation route; the crowds had cheered; and so on. It all sounded like a fairy-tale. Although we were still far from grasping the full significance of the event, we already knew quite as much as was good for us in one evening. Another jar of rum was called for and a second celebration took place. There would be many more to follow. The Sherpas naturally shared in the revelry. We drank a loyal toast to Her Majesty the Queen, assuming the privilege of drinking it seated upon the ground or on ration boxes, for space forbade otherwise. A runner was summoned to carry urgent messages to Namche, to go thence by the good offices of the Indian wireless station to Kathmandu. Cables of humble appreciation were sent to the Queen and the Prime Minister, another to the Himalayan Committee saying that I proposed to bring Tenzing and Hillary to England—George Lowe had already planned to come. At the same time, I tentatively suggested that we might all be allowed to come home by air, together if possible. Still dazed with our success and possibly a trifle bemused by the excellent rum, we tottered off to our tents very late that night.

Tenzing had already sent for coolies, and when these came up next morning we moved off down-glacier, bidding an unreluctant farewell to Base Camp. We were more than ready to turn our backs on this dead world of ice and rock and reach out towards the life-giving earth.

At Lobuje we heard more glad news on our wireless set; a most generous message from the Chairman of our sponsoring committee, Sir Edwin Herbert, another, most precious to me, from my wife. In our light-hearted mood, we remembered our 2-inch mortar. It had not been called upon to clear a path up the mountain for us, but it would carry out a no less appropriate function now. A salute should be fired, a *feu de joie*. We had twelve bombs, a gift from the Indian

Army. With each of us taking turns, these were duly loosed off, to the delight both of ourselves and of the whole of our numerous retinue. This was followed by some practice with our equally neglected .22 rifles, the targets being some spare mortar-bomb detonators; in this some of the Sherpas also tried their hand. After dark the Sherpas and Sherpanis, who had fully caught the general spirit of rejoicing, started a dance which continued into the early hours. Linking arms, they formed a long line, the men at one end, the women at the other and, to the accompaniment of strange and melancholy singing, swayed and stamped their feet in intricate rhythm. Some of the party joined in and managed to get the hang of it. In pauses between dances, we obliged with a chorus of songs—"Uncle Tom Cobley", "Ilkley Moor", "John Brown's Body".

Below Lobuje next day, we had to cross the now swollen Lobuje Khola, and some of us chose to do so where the torrent was fairly wide. Last to cross at this spot was little Greg, decorated as usual like a Christmas tree with several cameras and light-meters. Having struggled about half-way across, he was in danger of losing his balance in the foaming water. He shouted something to this effect to Tom Bourdillon, the largest and strongest of those who had reached the far bank. Quite unimpressed by the plight of his companion, Tom callously yelled back: "I can't help you, I've just put my boots on." Luckily for Greg, his leader had a softer heart and strode back into the stream, boots and all, to lend him a hand in his distress.

The expedition returned to its original base at Thyangboche on 4th June. We again went to pay our respects to the monks, and I was happy to be able to make a donation towards the repair of the Monastery roof after all. The promised dance was arranged for the same evening. We arrived at the appointed hour and were seated along a gallery overlooking the inner courtyard in the growing dusk. After a long pause, conch shells were blown and grotesque figures came down the steps from the sanctuary. The performing monks, robed in richly coloured garments, wearing masks of terrifying ugliness, proceeded to whirl and gambol in a strange and undignified manner around the prayer flag marking the centre of the courtyard. Others provided some very rudimentary music with horns and cymbals. It was quaint, sometimes comic, but quite unbeautiful. It went on for a very long time. While I was at the Monastery, I told the elderly acting Abbot that we had climbed Everest. He was plainly incredulous and nothing would shake his unbelief. But his natural courtesy forbade him to give expression to this in so many words, and when we left he graciously congratulated us on "nearly reaching the summit of Chomolungma".

While we were at Thyangboche, the early telegrams reached us, transmitted over the Indian wireless network. We began to realize that with the completion of our mission on Everest, tasks of a different but, in their way, equally arduous nature lay ahead. Among the many messages received at this time was a most generous one from our Patron, H.R.H. The Duke of Edinburgh. Another which specially delighted us was from the kindly official in charge of the Namche wireless post, who congratulated us on "your thumping Victory over the King of Adventure".

Next day an Advance party consisting of myself, Gregory and Bourdillon left Thyangboche to reach Kathmandu as quickly as possible. There was clearly a great deal to do. The main party, in the charge of Ed Hillary, was to start as soon as the coolies had been mustered, not an easy task in this season when every man is busy in his fields. With our departure from Thyangboche, Charles Evans left us. He had always planned to remain in Nepal until the autumn and now, though very tempted to return with us and take part in the popular rejoicings, he decided to carry on with the programme which he had always had in mind. This started with the collecting of further data for the making of a map of the Everest area; he was to return for some days to the valleys in which we had trained before going to Everest. Annullu and Da Tensing stayed with him.

Our start was inauspicious. There is nothing Sherpas enjoy more than a good "party"; the occasions come easily to them, and what better excuse could there possibly be than the ascent of Everest? They wasted no time in making merry, from the moment they reached the highest village in the valley onwards. In these circumstances we found Namche Bazar a difficult place to get away from. On 5th June, after we had waited there most of the day for our Sherpas and the few coolies to catch us up, they eventually arrived in an advanced state of inebriation. This condition quickly grew worse in the next hour, so much so that three very impatient "Sahibs" eventually left the village accompanied only by Dawa Thondup, whose head is even harder than that of most Sherpas. In our eagerness to press on—double marches were planned throughout our return journey—we were hardly disposed to take a lenient view of this lapse. Indeed, I sent back an urgent message to Charles Wylie to dispatch a reliable Sherpa forward at utmost speed to catch us up, for we did not then expect to see these men again.

We heard later the result of this request. Charles chose Pemba, a quiet and solid type of man. To ensure that he should travel fast, he hired a pony for him; he was to carry an urgent message to me from Charles. The following day, as the main party approached Namche, they came across a sad accident on the track. Sitting on the bank nursing a twisted ankle was a glassy-eyed and befuddled Pemba; lying across the track itself was another Sherpa, sleeping it off. There was no sign of the pony. Diligent in the duty bestowed upon him by Pemba before the fumes of alcohol had overcome him, the recumbent Sherpa sat up and solemnly handed Charles his own urgent message. "It's very important, Sahib," he said.

As we descended the Dudh Kosi the rain started; it rained most of every day for several days as the Advance party hastened back along the homeward track. The way was long and tiring, climbing across the big ridges in thick, clinging mist, with the rain teeming down. Sometimes we made a rough shelter with our two tarpaulins and slept out. More often, to escape the leeches and the rain, we begged the hospitality of some Sherpa family and spent a comfortable night on the upper floor of a solid stone and timber house. As we marched we rapidly recovered from our state of weakness and with this recovery our appetites grew. Pasang Dawa, quite himself again and back with us, together with Ang Temba, was our cook. We ate rice, eggs and sometimes a chicken, supplemented by pemmican, biscuits, jam, coffee or tea from our dwindling Assault rations—the "Compo" was long since finished. We bathed in the rivers, delighting in getting clean again for the first time in three months. Usually we reached the end of a double stage only at dusk and were on the move again next morning soon after daylight. Always we slept blissfully well; a great treat this, after the long period of drug-assisted slumber.

If the long views were usually denied us by the monsoon clouds, it was all the more startling when the high peaks were unveiled in some sudden break, unbelievably high and distant now, withdrawn from us, no longer intimate and real, and we found the more delight in our immediate surroundings, especially during the first few days of the march, when we were still moving in the region of 10,000 to 14,000 feet. Approaching the mountain, the countryside had been arid, now it was green. The path was bordered by big purple orchids, magenta and pale yellow azaleas, saffron and pink rhododendrons; ripe wild strawberries carpeted the ground. We caught glimpses of exotic birds. None of us will ever forget those little miracles of beauty, the yellow-backed, fire-tailed sunbirds, flitting above the rhododendron scrub in their bright red-yellow plumage and singing a high-pitched, plaintive song. Nor were the clouds themselves without a certain majesty, as they rode inexorably northwards in stately procession, heavily laden with their burden of moisture.

Shortly before we climbed up the vast mountainsides to leave the Dudh Kosi, we were surprised to hear a large aircraft overhead, and soon we caught sight of its shining fuselage in a break in the clouds.

It was flying northwards, towards Everest, and we wondered whether it might be looking for signs of us on the mountain. It was only on return to Kathmandu that we learned that this was a photographic reconnaissance flight sent by the Indian Air Force, whose Commander-in-Chief had most considerately delayed this mission until it was certain that we were safely off the mountain, lest the reverberation of the engines might dislodge avalanches or otherwise disturb our concentration on the job of climbing.

Returning runners now began to pass us daily, bringing huge piles of telegrams and the first congratulatory letters. We continued to be astonished—almost incredulous—at the reactions all over the world to our success. Pushing on still with all speed in the heat of the lower hills, a very weary Advance party eventually arrived at Kathmandu on the evening of 13th June, nine days after leaving Thyangboche. Our Ambassador, Christopher Summerhayes, gave us a warm welcome; we had been thinking of this moment for some time.

*   *   *

The main party followed at a more leisurely pace, for they had with them the whole of our remaining gear, amounting to about one hundred loads. They also experienced difficulty in getting clear of Namche, not only on account of the *chang* and *rakshi*, but also owing to the Sherpa mothers—determined women who rule sternly in the home. Young Mingma, Griff Pugh's devoted assistant, whose father Da Tensing had remained with Charles Evans, had made up his mind to travel with the party and see the big world outside Khumbu. But his mother not unnaturally thought otherwise. Arriving on the scene early on the morning of their departure from Namche, she railed at the would-be abductors of her child. "You have taken my husband," she said, "now you would snatch my son away from me too. Mingma, come here!" and the weeping fourteen-year-old was led unwillingly back to his home.

Another lad, Ang Tsering, aged seventeen, the youngest of our team who went to the South Col, was more cunning when his parent also appeared on the scene with the same intentions as Mingma's mummy. He persuaded her to let him go with the party as far as Ghat, one march distant down the valley, promising to come back from there. She was guileless enough to agree with this entreaty. Needless to say, Ang Tsering is now in Darjeeling with all the other boys.

After a journey lasting fourteen days, the main party arrived at Banepa, at the eastern end of the Valley of Nepal.

*   *   *

A week after our return to Kathmandu, I set out with my wife, who had flown out from England to greet me, and James Morris of *The Times*, to meet the main party as they approached the Valley of Nepal. We spent a night with them at Hukse, their last staging-place before reaching the end of the motorable track. There was wild commotion now throughout the Valley, mingled with some political opportunism, mainly over the achievement of Tenzing, a native of Nepal, whom they rightly hailed as a national hero. Amid the tremendous rejoicings all along our route on the following day, which ended with a triumphal procession in a flower-bedecked state coach along streets thronged by dense masses of shouting and excited people, who showered Tenzing, Hillary and myself with rice, red Holi dust and even coins, we were escorted to the Palace, to be most graciously received by the King.

The scene at the Reception was a moving one; it was also not without a touch of humour. There was the Nepalese Court, attired to do us honour, seated along the walls to witness the ceremony of Investiture of decorations by His Majesty the King to certain members of the expedition. There were the members of the expedition, at the end of their three weeks' journey from the distant mountain, bedraggled, unshaven, dirty, dressed in filthy clothes—shorts, gym shoes and the like. Pugh, standing, I was glad to notice, somewhat in the background, was still wearing pyjamas, the same pair of pyjamas which he had worn throughout both the March-out and the return journey.

But in all these rejoicings, I could not help feeling sorry that the nature of our enterprise was so misinterpreted by many of these good people. In their rightful pride and joy over Tenzing, they quite neglected the other Sherpas and most members of the expedition, his comrades in the great achievement.

After four days during which we were busy packing our baggage, attending receptions and enjoying the generous hospitality of the Court and Government, the Indian Embassy, the Indian Military Mission, our own Ambassador and many others, we left Kathmandu.

At the airfield we bade farewell to our friends Thondup, Dawa Thondup, Pasang Dawa and Ang Temba. They and others who had returned with us were leaving for Darjeeling next day. Some had stayed behind in Khumbu. Among many other friends and kind people of Nepal, His Excellency the Prime Minister, Mr M. P. Koirala, who had been most appreciative of our success, was also present to see us off.

Temporarily, the party divided. Charles Wylie and Michael Ward undertook the hardest job, that of escorting our baggage by road and rail to Lucknow, where it was taken over by a representative of the

Shipping Agency, who had kindly come all the way from Bombay to oblige us. Hillary, Gregory, Tenzing and his family, and my wife and I flew to Calcutta, where the Governor and the City authorities were anxious to do honour to the expedition, and especially to the great citizen of their State, Tenzing. The rest of the party travelled via Patna to Delhi, where we were all reunited on 27th June.

In three hectic days, we received a wonderful welcome from the public of Calcutta; everywhere we were entertained with the utmost kindness and hospitality, and especially by the Governor and Srimati Mookherjee, Mr Shannon, our Deputy High Commissioner, members of his Staff, and members of the Himalayan Club. It was impossible not to be touched by the genuine thrill our adventure had given to so many ordinary folk, and particularly the youth of Bengal. For my wife and myself, this was a specially pleasant interlude on our journey home, for we had been stationed in Bengal before the war and many old Bengali friends came to see us.

No less joyous, despite the heat, were the mammoth receptions in Delhi. The highlight of this triumphal tour was a most impressive ceremony at Rashtrapati Bhavan, where the President of the Indian Union, Sri Rajendra Prasad, decorated some members of the party and presented engraved silver shields to us all. Nor shall we forget the graciousness and hospitality of the Prime Minister, Sri Jawaharlal Nehru, Mr George Middleton, our own representative, his wife, the Staff of the High Commission, Major-General Williams, and very many others.

It was a particular delight in Delhi to meet again George Finch, veteran of the 1922 Expedition and pioneer of the use of oxygen for climbing purposes. His presence among us at this time was the more welcome in that we were so anxious that the tributes with which we were being showered should be shared with those who had shown us the way. As one of the two outstanding climbers of the first expedition to make a definite attempt to reach the summit of the mountain in 1922—the other was George Mallory—and as the strong protagonist of oxygen at a time when there were many who disbelieved in its efficacy and others who frowned upon its use, no one could have better deserved to represent the past than George Finch. We saluted him.

We had regretfully to decline many requests to visit other Indian cities—official invitations came from Madras, Bombay, Patna, Dehra Dun and Darjeeling. The generous enthusiasm of the Indian people for the Everest adventure was indeed a revelation to us. But we were wanted at home as quickly as possible, and we were naturally no less eager to be there.

And so, at last, we set out homewards by air, thanks to the generosity of *The Times*, in an aircraft of the British Overseas Airways Corporation. To our great delight, Tenzing and his family came with us. Everywhere we touched down—at Karachi, Bahrein, Cairo, Rome and Zürich—we met with the same expressions of spontaneous enthusiasm; everyone was most kind. Of particular interest to us was our meeting at Zürich with members of the Swiss Everest Expeditions and of their sponsoring body, the Foundation for Alpine Research. No climbers could have been more generous in their appreciation of our success than the Swiss team who so nearly succeeded last year. In the short time we spent with them, we were able to discuss with our Swiss comrades, Raymond Lambert, Gabriel Chevalley, Herr Feuz and others, the problems of the climb we all knew so well, for our ascent was linked at almost every step with their attempt. I also gladly take this opportunity to mention the warm acclamation given to the ascent of Everest by the French party who were busy preparing to go out themselves next year, should we not get to the top.

On 3rd July we landed at London Airport, where we received the most longed-for welcome of all: that of our own people here at home.

The adventure was over.

CHAPTER EIGHTEEN

REFLECTIONS

W HAT were the reasons for our success? How was it that we succeeded in getting to the top when so many others before us had failed to do so? I am adding the second question only to give what, in my mind, is the one reason transcending all others which explains the first. For I wish once again to pay tribute to the work of earlier expeditions.

The significance of all these other attempts is that, regardless of the height they reached, each one added to the mounting sum of experience, and this experience had to reach a certain total before the riddle could be solved. The building of this pyramid of experience was vital to the whole issue; only when it had attained a certain height was it within the power of any team of mountaineers to fashion its apex. Seen in this light, other expeditions did not fail; they made progress. They had reached this stage when we prepared to try again last winter. By that time, but not before, the defences by which the mountain had so far withstood assault were well enough known; it only remained to study them and draw the right conclusions in order to launch yet one more party which would have every weapon—material and human—with which to do battle against Everest. We of the 1953 Everest Expedition are proud to share the glory with our predecessors.

Above all, and independent of their lessons, we were inspired by their example, their persistence, their spirit of quest, their determination that there should be no surrender. For this compelling urge to continue the struggle, we have above all else to thank the earlier Everest climbers.

With this just tribute to the past, I would link the names of those who served on the Committees which launched them and of others who generously contributed the funds which, alone, made possible each successive enterprise.

Next in the order of events I would place sound, thorough, meticulously detailed planning. On Everest, the problems of organization assume the proportions of a military campaign; I make no apology for this comparison, or for the fact that last winter we planned the ascent of Everest on these lines. It was thanks to this that we were able not only to foresee our needs in every detail—guided by previous experience provided by others, we judged aright—but to have constantly before us a clear programme to carry out at every stage: the March-out; acclimatization; preparation of the Icefall; the first and second stages of the Build-up; reconnaissance and preparation of the Lhotse Face; even, in outline, the Assault plan itself. These were the aims to be achieved by given dates, and achieve each and all of them we would, and did.

I would once more pay tribute to the excellence of our equipment and the fact that it stood up to the severe testing on the mountain and did what was required of it. Those firms, those zealous hands both in this country and abroad, which took such great pains to produce all we needed, which worked, often against time, to do this, and those who gave us financial support, they must also share the triumph.

Among the numerous items in our inventory, I would single out oxygen for special mention. Many of our material aids were of great importance; only this, in my opinion, was vital to success. In this department perhaps more than in any other, those who worked to satisfy our requirements had the hardest task of all, for time was so short. But for oxygen, without the much-improved equipment which we were given, we should certainly not have got to the top.

The chance of success of big Himalayan expeditions has often been adversely affected by ill health among the climbers. Unless allowance was to be made for this by making the size of the party so large as to be unwieldy, it seemed to be a matter of the first importance to avoid this handicap of sickness. The number in our party was sufficient to carry out the kind of plan which I had in mind, but there was not a large margin. The plan adopted was an ambitious one in that it depended on the active participation high on the mountain of almost the entire team; if several of us had been sick when the opportunity for the Assault occurred, it is very doubtful if we should have got to the top. That we were so fit was due initially to careful selection of the party. In the field, the training and acclimatization carried out in the period allotted for this purpose were an outstanding success. We have also to thank those who furnished our sound and sufficient diet and advised on the need for drinking large quantities of liquid daily throughout our time on the mountain, and especially while at high altitude. Nor must we forget the care we received from our doctors.

A few figures may be of interest to illustrate this matter of fitness, combined with the use of oxygen. No fewer than nine of the climbing party went to the South Col; three of these climbed twice to that place. Of the nine who reached it, seven went to a height of well over

27,000 feet on the South-East ridge; four climbed the South summit, over 28,700 feet; ultimately, two went on to the top. Of those nine, three remained at or above 26,000 feet for four days and nights; three more for three days and nights. Although some of us were very weak on return to Advance Base, none was in a state of collapse.

Before leaving the question of diet, I must add one other point: the effect of our rations on morale. After allowing for the fact that individual tastes in the matter of food can never fully be catered for, even within the ample limits of baggage of a large expedition such as ours, I am certain that the rations so carefully calculated and provided had much to do not only with our good health but also with our general contentment.

Above all else, I should like to stress our unity as a party. This was undoubtedly the biggest single factor in the final result, for the ascent of Everest, perhaps more than most human ventures, demanded a very high degree of selfless co-operation; no amount of equipment or food could have compensated for any weakness in this respect. It would be difficult to find a more close-knit team than ours. It is a remarkable fact that throughout the whole four months that we were together, often in trying circumstances, I never heard an impatient or angry word passed between any members of the party. This made my own task infinitely easier, and most particularly when the time came to decide on the individual tasks to be undertaken during the period leading up to and during the Assault. It could not fall to everyone to attempt the summit, and for some there must have been disappointment, made greater by their fitness to go high. But everyone rightly believed that he had a vital part to play in getting at least two members of the team to the top, and it was in this spirit that each man carried out his job—whether it was finding and preparing the route up the Lhotse Face; leading Sherpas to the South Col with Assault stores; carrying heavy loads to establish the final camp; or the less conspicuous tasks of maintaining our communications with Base Camp, supervising the catering and other chores at Advance Base. All these things were done without complaint, and they were done well. In this, and in the work of our Sherpas, lies the immediate secret of our success.

And the Sherpas were magnificent. Their co-operation in the essential teamwork of the whole party, their own individual performances, are beyond praise. I can give no better proof of this than by saying that of our total team of twenty-seven Sherpas chosen for the work above the Western Cwm, nineteen men went to the South Col and, of these, six did so twice. In terms of stores this means that we lifted some 750 lb. up to 26,000 feet; this it was that enabled our Assault teams to remain there in good spirits and without suffering undue deterioration over a longer period than had been expected. The happy relationship between the Sherpas and ourselves was brought about by everybody in the party, but most particularly was this the work of Tenzing and Wylie.

The combined efforts of the Sherpas and ourselves are summed up in the placing of our highest camp at just under 28,000 feet. Here was the supreme test of support for the two who were to make the final attempt to reach the summit; on those two days, 26th and 28th May, the tasks of Sherpas and Sahibs were no longer complementary, they were identical. All were sharing the same burdens, all, equipped with the same aids, were sharing the difficulties of the climb and the height. Thus it was that we achieved what Norton and Longstaff had so strongly advocated as an essential preliminary step to final success.

Lastly among the matters contributing to our success, there was the weather. After hindering our preparations to no small extent for five weeks—between 8th April and 14th May, snow fell almost every day—the weather settled down to be steadily fine for the whole of the second half of May. We were undoubtedly lucky in this one matter over which we had no control. But it is important to stress that this does not mean that conditions were favourable for the Assault on any day during that period, for there was always the wind, and the wind was unpredictable. It chanced that the two who reached the top did so on a comparatively still day, but this had been preceded, and was doubtless followed, by others when conditions were impossible.

To these factors, then, the triumph should be attributed, it matters not in what proportion: to all who had climbed on Everest before; to our planning and other preparations; to the excellence of our equipment; to our Sherpas and ourselves; to the favour of the elements. And I would add one more asset, intangible, less easy to assess: the thoughts and prayers of all those many who watched and waited and hoped for our success. We were aware of this hidden force and we were fortified by it.

*   *   *

Was it worth while? For us who took part in the venture, it was so beyond doubt. We have shared a high endeavour; we have witnessed scenes of beauty and grandeur; we have built up a lasting comradeship among ourselves and we have seen the fruits of that comradeship ripen into achievement. We shall not forget those moments of great living upon that mountain.

The story of the ascent of Everest is one of teamwork. If there is a deeper and more lasting message behind our venture than the mere

209

ephemeral sensation of a physical feat, I believe this to be the value of comradeship and the many virtues which combine to create it. Comradeship, regardless of race or creed, is forged among high mountains, through the difficulties and dangers to which they expose those who aspire to climb them, the need to combine their efforts to attain their goal, the thrills of a great adventure shared together.

And what of others? Was it worth while for them too? I believe it may have been, if it is accepted that there is a need for adventure in the world we live in and provided, too, that it is realized that adventure can be found in many spheres, not merely upon a mountain, and not necessarily physical. Ultimately, the justification for climbing Everest, if any justification is needed, will lie in the seeking of their "Everests" by others, stimulated by this event as we were inspired by others before us. From the response to the news of our success, not only in our own country and Commonwealth but also in many other lands, it seems clear that the zest for adventure is still alive everywhere. Before, during and especially after the expedition, we received countless gifts and messages of goodwill and delight, in both prose and verse, from all over the world, from heads of Governments and humble folk alike. Very many of these messages were sent by children and young people. The ascent of Everest seems to have stirred the spirit of adventure latent in every human breast.

And there is no lack of signs that this quickening of the spirit may have results of a permanent kind. As an instance of this, I would mention that while we were in Calcutta, the Chief Minister, Sri B. C. Roy, outlined to us a project for setting up a special training school near Darjeeling, at which leading Sherpa mountaineers will introduce to boys from all walks of life the lore and craft of mountain climbing. It is proposed to do this as a memorial to our ascent of Everest, and in particular as a tribute to the Sherpas, many of whom live in Bengal. Such a scheme, analogous to the Outward Bound Schools in this country, is worthy of the highest praise.

*   *   *

What of the future? There is indeed no ground for despondency about the aftermath of Everest. Within the province of mountaineering alone, while we may perhaps have a lingering regret that this great peak no longer remains inviolate to hold out its challenge, I believe it was good and it was timely that Everest should have been climbed this summer. The attraction of Everest tended to focus too much of the resources available for promoting mountain exploration; now that its summit has been reached, it should be possible to give practical encouragement to larger numbers of enterprising explorers and mountaineers to go far and wide, in the Himalaya and elsewhere, in search of climbing and in pursuit of other interests.

Some day Everest will be climbed again. It may well be attempted without oxygen, although I do not rate the chances of success very high at present. Let us hope for the opening of the frontier dividing Nepal and Tibet to climbers from both sides of that political barrier, for the route to the top of the mountain by the North Face remains to be completed. The time may come when the prospect of traversing across the summit, climbing up by one ridge and descending by another, may no longer be a fantasy. These possibilities, and others, give scope for adventure in this one small area of the globe alone.

I also believe that we cannot avoid the challenge of other giants. Mountains scarcely lower than Everest itself are still "there", as Mallory said. They beckon us and we cannot rest until we have met their challenge too.

And there are many other opportunities for adventure, whether they be sought among the hills, in the air, upon the sea, in the bowels of the earth, or on the ocean bed; and there is always the moon to reach. There is no height, no depth, that the spirit of man, guided by a higher Spirit, cannot attain.

POSTSCRIPT
TO THIS EDITION

By Sir Edmund Hillary

IT is forty years since Tenzing Norgay Sherpa and I stood on the summit of Mount Everest and much has happened in the lives of all the expedition members since then. Certainly for me the Everest story has faded a little into the past. Like all my companions, I have had many exciting moments and challenges: driving tractors to the South Pole; raising a couple of million dollars to build Himalayan schools and medical facilities; taking jet boats up Mother Ganga from the Ocean to the Sky; and four and a half years as New Zealand High Commissioner in Delhi. But when I look back on it all there is no doubt that reaching the summit of Everest on 29th May, 1953 was a major turning-point in my life.

When we returned to Base Camp after the ascent I had no comprehension of the impact that our climb would have in the outside world. After all, I was just an unsophisticated antipodean. I expected reasonable interest from mountaineers, but what had climbing a mountain to do with the ordinary public?

As we trekked from the mountain back to Kathmandu my innocence was quickly dispelled. Every day mail runners were meeting us with masses of telegrams and newspaper cuttings indicating the immense impact the climb had universally made. When I was finally handed a letter from John Hunt addressed to "Sir Edmund Hillary" I was horrified but reluctantly forced to realize that my life, and indeed the lives of all the expedition members, had irrevocably changed.

Perhaps it was my independent New Zealand background, but fortunately I refused to take the publicity or myself particularly seriously. I had all too clear an understanding of my modest abilities, although I accepted that I was fitter than most and had a good deal of enthusiasm. In the hectic months after the climb John Hunt understandably made great efforts to emphasize the team nature of our success. I was doing the same myself, although it wasn't always easy, because I was one of the guys "who got to the top", and this seemed important to the media and public. Finally I stopped running

212

down my own contribution and became more balanced and rational in my approach. I accepted that I had made a not inconsiderable effort too.

I haven't the slightest doubt that we who were attempting Everest in 1953 were the lucky ones. We were not driven by ideas of fame and fortune (or certainly I wasn't). All we wanted to do was climb a mountain that had been a constant challenge for more than thirty years. But how things have changed! So many remarkable efforts and so many disasters. Prima donnas have come and gone; huge expeditions have moved side by side with small alpine-style efforts; the mountain has been cluttered with junk; and many of the expeditions are now outright commercial undertakings at $US 35,000 a customer. With a dozen or more expeditions together at Base Camp, the sense of freedom and challenge has long disappeared.

Why were we successful when so many other good expeditions had failed? Our climbers were competent, although not exceptional compared with the best modern standards. Our organisation was sound and our equipment adequate. Our physiologists impressed on us the importance of taking plenty of liquid and this we did, although I still lost twenty pounds from the time we established Base Camp to when we came off the mountain. The physiologists were also unsure as to whether it was humanly possible to reach the summit of Everest and survive, so we had that barrier to overcome too.

We were undoubtedly fit and strongly motivated; our oxygen equipment was erratic but effective; and we had that little bit of luck with the weather at the right time. So it was a combination of circumstances. I had the feeling that, in a sense, the mountain was waiting to be climbed—and we were the ones who were ready, willing and able to do it at the right moment.

ED HILLARY
Auckland, 1993

APPENDICES

APPENDIX I

DIARY OF THE EXPEDITION
September 1952–June 1953

Compiled by
WILFRID NOYCE

1952
Sept. 1   Wylie started work as Organizing Secretary.
Oct. 8   Hunt, Leader of Expedition, arrived in London.
Oct. 30   First Equipment Co-ordination Meeting.
Nov. 5   Selection of Party completed.
Nov. 17   First Alpine Test Co-ordination Meeting.
                 First Conference of whole Party.
                 Measuring of Party for clothing, etc.
Nov. 25   Second Alpine Test Co-ordination Meeting.
Nov. 28   Second Equipment Co-ordination Meeting.
Dec. 1–10   Visit to Paris, and Alpine Test of Equipment at Jungfraujoch
                 by Hunt, Wylie, Pugh and Gregory.
Dec. 15   Third Equipment Co-ordination Meeting.
                 Second Party Conference.

1953
1st half January
                 Packing Plan organized by Evans and working party.
2nd half January
                 Packing starts at Lusk's, Wapping.
Jan. 17–19   Oxygen frame carrying tests, at Helyg, North Wales.
Jan. 20   Final Equipment Co-ordination Meeting.
                 Trying on of clothing, etc., at Lusk's.
                 Third Party Conference.
Jan. 22   Decompression Chamber tests at Farnborough.
Jan. 25–26   Visit to Zürich by Hunt and Evans.
Feb. 5   Final Party Conference.
Feb. 12   Main party and baggage sail for India on S.S. *Stratheden*.
Feb. 20   Advance party, Evans and Gregory, fly to Kathmandu.
Feb. 28   Main party arrives Bombay.
March 8   Whole expedition and baggage assembled at Kathmandu.
March 10   First party and 150 coolies leave Kathmandu.
March 11   Second party and 200 coolies leave Kathmandu.
March 26   First party arrives at Thyangboche.
March 27   Second party arrives at Thyangboche.

March 29-April 6
         First Acclimatization period.

April 9-April 17
         Second Acclimatization period.

April 12   Icefall party reaches Base Camp (17,900 feet).

April 13   Icefall party starts on Icefall.

April 15   Hillary, Band and Lowe establish Camp II (19,400 feet).

April 17   Same party reaches ice block below Camp III site.

April 21   First half main body of stores arrives at Base from Thyangboche, including in party Morris of *The Times*.

April 22   Second half main body of stores arrives at Base from Thyangboche, party including Major Roberts with the Assault oxygen.
         Camp III established at head of Icefall (20,200 feet).
         Base Camp established on Khumbu glacier (17,900 feet).

April 24   Low Level Lift started to Camp III.

April 24-25   Reconnaissance of Western Cwm as far as Swiss Camp IV (21,200 feet).

April 26-May 1
         High Level Lift between Camps III and IV.

May 1   Camp IV established (21,200 feet) by Hunt, Bourdillon and Evans.

May 2   Preliminary Reconnaissance of Lhotse Face by Hunt, Bourdillon and Evans.

May 2–5   Rest period for Ferry teams.

May 3   Reconnaissance party to Camp V (22,000 feet).

May 4   Bourdillon and Evans, with Ward and Wylie in support, up to Camp VI (23,000 feet) on Lhotse Face Reconnaissance.

May 5   Bourdillon and Evans above Camp VI on reconnaissance.
         Ferry work starts again in Icefall and (on May 8) in Western Cwm, as far as Camp V.

May 6   Lhotse Face Reconnaissance party returns to Base.

May 10   Lowe and 4 Sherpas up to Camp V for Lhotse Face.

May 11   Lowe and Ang Nyima, based on Camp VI, start work on Lhotse Face.
         Westmacott and 3 Sherpas in support at Camp V.

May 16   Major Roberts arrives Base with oxygen, accompanied by Morris of *The Times*.

May 17   Lowe and Noyce establish Camp VII (24,000 feet). Ward up to VII, stays with Lowe and Da Tensing.

May 18   Last Low Level Lift. Advance Base established at Camp IV.

May 20   Noyce and 8 Sherpas, ascending to Camp VII, meet Lowe, Ward and Da Tensing descending.

May 21   Noyce and Annullu complete route over Geneva Spur to South Col. Wylie and 9 Sherpas reach Camp VII.

May 22	Wylie with 14 Sherpas, Hillary and Tenzing ahead, to South Col. Dump loads. 1 Sherpa does not complete climb.
May 24	First Assault party, consisting of Bourdillon, Evans, Hunt, Da Namgyal and Ang Tensing (alias Balu), reach South Col.
May 25	First Assault party stays South Col. Second Assault party reaches Camp VII.
May 26	FIRST ASSAULT. Bourdillon and Evans reach South Summit. Hunt and Da Namgyal carry loads up S.E. ridge and dump at 27,350 feet. Hillary and Tenzing (Second Assault party), supported by Gregory, Lowe, Pemba, Ang Temba and Ang Nyima, reach South Col (Camp VIII). (Also Dawa Thondup, Topkie, Ang Norbu, Annullu and Da Tensing, carrying extra loads.) Ward and Noyce up to Camp VII in support. 7 Sherpas leave South Col.
May 27	Hunt, Evans, Bourdillon and Ang Temba down to Camp VII. Second Assault party confined on South Col by very strong wind. Evans and Ward descend to Advance Base.
May 28	Wylie and 3 Sherpas up to Camp VII in support. SECOND ASSAULT. Ridge Camp (Camp IX) established at 27,900 feet by Hillary, Tenzing, Gregory, Lowe and Ang Nyima. The latter 3 return to South Col.
May 29	Hillary and Tenzing from Ridge Camp to Summit, return to South Col. Noyce and 3 Sherpas set out from Camp VII in support. Noyce and Pasang Phutar reach Col. Gregory, Pemba and Ang Nyima descend to Camp IV.
May 30	Hillary, Tenzing, Noyce, Lowe and Pasang Phutar reach Camp IV. Westmacott (who has been maintaining the route through the Icefall) and Morris (*The Times*) have come up and return with the story.
May 31	All except 5 Sahibs and a Sherpa party down to Base. Last Ferry party to Camp III to bring down loads.
June 1	All exce Wylie and Sherpa party (staying at Camp III) down to Base.
June 2	Party assembles at Base.
June 3	Party reaches Lobuje.
June 4	Party reaches Thyangboche.
June 5	Advance party (Hunt, Bourdillon and Gregory) leaves Thyangboche.
June 7	Main party leaves Thyangboche.
June 13	Advance party reaches Kathmandu.
June 20	Main party reaches Kathmandu.

APPENDIX II

PREPARATIONS FOR THE EVEREST EXPEDITION, 1953

ORGANIZATION

(Effective from 9th October, 1952)

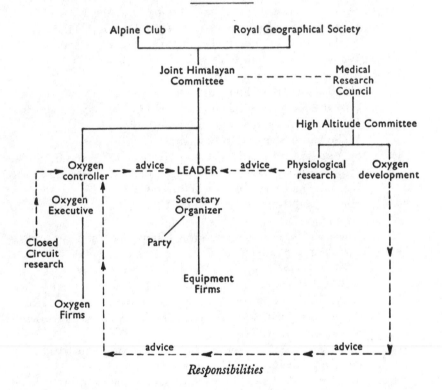

Responsibilities

Himalayan Committee
General policy
Finance
Political matters
Selection of Leader
Invitations to Members and con-
tracts

Press arrangements, publicity,
book, lectures, film, etc.
Provision of scientific advice to
Leader (through Medical Research Council)
Provision of oxygen equipment
(through Oxygen controller)

Leader
Planning
Organization of preparatory work
Selection of the party
Selection, trial and procurement of equipment, other than oxygen equipment (through the Secretary-Organizer, and, when appointed, the Equipment Officer)
Press articles

Medical Research Council
Advice to the Leader on:
  Physiology
  Diet

Hygiene
Protective clothing and equipment
Acclimatization
Advice to Oxygen controller

Oxygen Controller
Development and provision of oxygen apparatus
Advice to Leader on oxygen

Organizing Secretary
Assistance to Leader
Co-ordination
Provision of equipment other than oxygen equipment

APPENDIX III

B ELOW is reproduced the text of the Memorandum "Basis for Planning" which was drawn up in London before the Expedition's departure, and which served as a framework for the programme actually put into effect. Deviations from this original plan, dictated by conditions in the field, are explained in the footnotes. Otherwise it was carried out in its original form.

MEMORANDUM
EVEREST, 1953

BASIS FOR PLANNING

1. The ultimate aim of the Expedition, as defined by the Sponsoring Authority, is the ascent of Everest during 1953 by a member or members of the party. This aim may appear self-evident, but it is of vital importance that it should be borne constantly in mind, both during the preparatory phase and, later, in the field. All planning and preparation must lead us methodically towards the achievement of that aim.

2. The purpose of this Memorandum is to provide a basis for all who will be working on the various aspects of the planning and preparation for the Expedition. It is mainly focused on the assault. The requirements of the assault plan are basic and must be met in terms of climbers, porters, equipment and stores.

It is stressed that this is not a firm and final plan; this can only be made at a much later date in the field.

3. Planning Papers are attached as Appendices to this Memorandum as follows:

Appendix A	The Ascent (Build-up and Assault).
Appendix B	The Preparatory Period.
Appendix C[1]	The Expedition Timetable.

(Signed) JOHN HUNT

5th November, 1952,
Expedition Leader.

---

[1] Not included.

Appendix "A" to Basis for Planning

EVEREST, 1953

THE ASCENT

1. From a study of the Shipton Reconnaissance, the Swiss pre-monsoon attempt and from a general comparison of the latter with the British experience on the mountain between the wars, certain factors emerge which must influence our planning for 1953.

FACTORS

2. The absolute need for a sufficient period of comparative acclimatization before the assault.

3. The psychological effects of remaining longer on the mountain than is really necessary to the achievement of success.

4. The physiological deterioration which appears to take effect high up on the mountain.

5. The limitations on the amount of stores and equipment which can justifiably be carried high on the mountain. These limitations are set by:
   (*a*) the objective dangers of the icefall;
   (*b*) the weight which can be carried by the porters and climbers at high altitudes;
   (*c*) the number of oxygen equipments available;
   (*d*) the time problem, as it affects paragraphs 3 and 5(*a*) above.

6. The importance of a suitable and acceptable diet, together with that of ensuring the consumption of sufficient liquid during the crucial assault period.

7. The duration and period of favourable weather. This is likely to be very brief and to occur in the second half of May, or early in June.

8. The importance of exploiting this favourable period to the maximum extent. This means:
   (*a*) being positioned and ready in every sense to start the assault from the beginning of this period.
   (*b*) being so organized as to be able to continue the assault, if necessary, so long as the weather holds; in other words, to avoid the contingency of a premature retreat.

CONCLUSIONS

9. From these factors it is possible to establish certain conclusions which will form the basis of the planning. (Scientific conclusions are not dealt with under this heading.)
   (*a*) There must be an acclimatization period, which should be spent in an area other than Everest.

(b) Once the Base Camp has been established, the ascent of the mountain must be a continuous process, carefully planned so as to be completed in the minimum time consistent with success.

(c) There must be provision in the plan for a number of assaults, capable of being launched consecutively at intervals of one day, if the weather conditions allow. A maximum potential of three such assaults should be assumed.

(d) Adequate logistic support must be provided in the highest camp(s) to enable the summit party(ies) to make the most of their opportunity.

(e) The first assault party and, as far as possible, the follow-up parties, must be rested and in good condition when they start. They must, therefore, be spared the heavy work at an early stage in the build-up.

10. *The Climbing Party.*

The party must be large enough to make possible the series of assaults referred to above, and at the same time to allow for sickness and provide for supervision of the build-up behind the assault.

On the other hand, it must not be so large as to become unwieldy.

To achieve a potential of three assaults, a total of ten climbers[1] has been decided. These may be considered for planning purposes in the ratio of 6 (assault) to 4 (support). To the latter should be added the physiologist and the photographer who may be expected to take their share in the build-up.

11. *The Porter Requirement.*

The porters may be considered in three categories:

(a) Those taking part in the establishment of Advance Base (Head of S.W. Cwm).

(b) Those taking part in the establishment of the Assault Camp (South Col).

(c) Those taking part in the Assault.

To some extent, these categories will overlap, e.g. all porters will be involved to a greater or lesser degree in establishing Advance Base; certain porters required to establish the Assault Camp may take part in the Assault.

Taking into account a rough calculation of the load factors, the timetable at Appendix C and the intention to launch, if necessary, three assaults, it may be estimated that 25–30 Sherpas[2] will be required. Of these, at least 16[3] must be capable and willing to take part in the assaults and the establish-

---

[1] Tenzing was invited to join the climbing party on arrival at Kathmandu, making a total of 11.

[2] At a later stage in the London planning we increased the number of Sherpas to 34 (20 High Altitude; 14 Icefall). We actually recruited a total of 36 in addition to 2 cooks, and not counting Tenzing himself.

[3] 19 Sherpas reached the South Col. Of these, 6 did so twice.

ment of a camp on the South Col; they must, therefore, be equipped on this basis.

For planning purposes, the overall period of the ascent will be considered in phases, as follows:

12. *Phase I* (*The Build-up*).

This includes the negotiation of the icefall, and the establishment of an advance base at the head of the South-West Cwm, and of an assault camp on the South Col.

Phase II (*The Assault*).

This includes the move of the first assault party from Advance Base to the South Col and thence to the summit, followed, if necessary, by two further assaults.

13. The Expedition Timetable is set out as Appendix C.[1] From this it will be seen that Phase I should have been completed by approximately 15th May;[2] the assault should be capable of being launched at any time after this date.

14. This is considered in two stages:

Stage I.—Establishment of Advance Base (Head of the Cwm).

Stage II.—Establishment of the Assault Camp (South Col). For the purpose of this paper, a period of 10–12 days should be assumed for Stage I;[3] 4–6 days for Stage II.[4]

The Build-up—Stage I (10–12 days)

15. The problem is the move, over a period of 10–12 days, of personnel, equipment and stores from Base Camp, at 16,000 feet on the bank of the

---

[1] Not included.

[2] Casualties and the very bad weather throughout the build-up period delayed its completion until 18th May; this did not include the "carry" to the South Col, which was finished by 22nd May.

[3] At a later stage in the London planning, the period for Stage I was increased to 3 weeks. In the event we took 23 days.

[4] The time estimated for Stage II was later changed in London to 10 days. We actually took 4.

Khumbu glacier,[1] to an Advance Base at approximately 23,000 feet[2] at the head of the Western Cwm. The principal difficulty is the negotiation, and use during the build-up, of the icefall descending from the lower edge of the Cwm, over a vertical interval of over 2,000 feet.

Bearing in mind the objective danger of the icefall, its relatively low elevation and the importance of concentrating the maximum logistic backing at Advance Base for the Assault, we will assume for planning purposes that:

(a) only one camp will be established in the icefall.

(b) by the end of this first stage of the build-up, sufficient equipment and stores will have been carried forward to reduce movement between Base Camp and Advance Base to intermittent journeys only.

16. *Camps*.

These will probably be required ahead of Base Camp, during the first stage of the build-up as follows:

Camp I (foot of the Icefall)[3]	4 Meades
Camp II (in the Icefall)	4 Meades
Camp III (top of the Icefall)	4 Meades

These camps can be reduced, probably by two Meades at the end of Stage I, the spare tents being carried forward to Advance Base.

17. *Capacity of Advance Base*.

This must be capable of housing, during a peak period:

10 Climbers[4]	(of 12)
16 Porters	(of 25–30)

Of these:[5]

6 Europeans and 6 Porters will comprise the Assault Party.

2 Europeans and 6–10 Porters will be concerned with establishing the Assault Camp (South Col.)

---

[1] At the time of writing this Directive it was proposed to establish Base Camp at the Glacier lake (Lake Camp) at about 16,500 feet. Before leaving England, however, this had already been changed to the Swiss Camp I at 17,900 feet.

[2] I had originally hoped to place Advance Base at the foot of the Lhotse Face, then reckoned to be 23,000 feet, but later found to be no more than 22,000 feet. After discussion with the Swiss, however, it seemed wiser to stage our assault operations from lower down for reasons of safety and to avoid physical deterioration. Advance Base was therefore synonymous with Camp IV, 21,200 feet.

[3] See Footnote 1 above.

[4] Advance Base actually accommodated 12 climbers and 20 Sherpas at a peak period.

[5] The assault parties actually comprised 7 climbers and 5 Sherpas.

The South Col "carry" parties consisted of 2 Europeans and 14 Sherpas.

No allowance had been made in the London plan for a special party to prepare the route up the Lhotse Face.

2 Europeans will be Physiologist : Photographer, leaving a balance of
2 Europeans and 10–15 Porters, who may be assumed to be at camps between (inclusive) Base Camp and Camp III.

This requirement might be met by one 12-man Dome (or two 6-man Domes) and 7 to 8 Meades.

The Build-up—Stage II (4–6 days)

18. In order to establish the Assault Camp, it will be necessary to carry tentage, equipment and stores up the Lhotse Face, a vertical height of about 3,000 feet starting at 23,000 feet.[1] The Assault Camp must be capable of supporting at any one time, at or above the South Col, up to a total of 12 climbers and porters.[2] In order to economize on the number of oxygen equipments and cylinders, the "carry" required to complete Stage II will probably have to be done without oxygen.[3] This will entail the establishment of an intermediate camp on the Lhotse Face (Camp V);[4] its capacity should be for four climbers/porters.[5]

THE ASSAULT—(After 15th May)

19. The general concept of the assault will be the advance of the assault parties from Advance Base to the summit of Everest, spending (if necessary) one night at Camp V[6] (Lhotse Face), one night at Camp VI[7] (South Col) and (if necessary) a third night at a Camp VII[8] to be established as high as possible on the S.E. Ridge.

20. Each assault party will consist of 4 climbers—2 Europeans and 2 Sherpas. Of these, the Europeans will be the potential summit party, the bulk of the load being carried by the Sherpas.[9] Depending on the condition of the climbers in the final stages, however, it may well be that the summit party may consist of 1 European and 1 porter.

[1] See Footnote 2 on p. 226. The height of the Lhotse Face proved to be 4,000 feet from the Cwm to the Col.

[2] During the night 26th–27th May, there were 7 climbers and 4 Sherpas together on the Col.

[3] We eventually gave oxygen to the leaders of the 2 South Col ferry parties, owing to their responsibility for ensuring the success of the "carry".

[4] This was Camp VII in the event.

[5] The Lhotse Face camp (Camp VII in the actual programme) contained 19 people on the night 21st–22nd May.

[6] This was Camp VII in the event.

[7] This was Camp VIII in the event.

[8] This was Camp IX in the event.

[9] During both assaults, climbers carried loads rather heavier than the Sherpas owing to sickness in the special Sherpa team taking part in this final phase. Loads varying between 50–63 lb. were carried by the climbers up to 27,900 feet.

21. All four climbers will use oxygen from Advance Base onwards for the upward journey. In calculating the oxygen requirement, it may be assumed that oxygen will not be used for the descent below the Ridge Camp (see para. 22). Sleeping oxygen will, however, be required at the Assault Camp and at the Ridge Camp (Camp VII).[1]

22. Depending on the condition of the climbers, the success of the oxygen and the weather, it *may* be possible to reach the summit from the South Col. The first party will, however, be self-contained after leaving the Assault Camp (South Col), with a tent and equipment for the summit party (two Europeans) for one night.[2]

23. This ultimate camp will be established in any event. Should it be necessary, the summit party will remain there, the other pair returning to the Assault Camp (Camp VI).[3]

If, on the other hand, it is found possible for the summit party to continue to the top in one day from the South Col, then the other pair will set up the tent and wait to escort the summit party down to the South Col.

24. In order to make possible the "carry" of the oxygen cylinders required for the final part of the climb, in addition to the other equipment necessary for Camp VI (South Col),[4] the site will be chosen and an initial "carry" of loads will be undertaken by a party of one European and two Sherpas (to be known as the Support Party), who will have arrived at the South Col at the end of the Build-up phase. This will take place either on the same day that the first Assault Party leaves Advance Base, or on the day after (D-Day or D plus 1), or both.

This Support Party will be available to accompany the first Assault Party on its way up from the South Col should the load situation so demand.

The Support Party will descend to Advance Base as soon as this task is complete. It will use oxygen for the upward journey or journeys above the South Col.

25. The second Assault Party, composed as for the first party, will leave Advance Base one day later and will go up to Camp VI (South Col)[5] on the South Col. If the first party are not successful (or in any case), the second party will make their attempt on exactly the same basis as before, with the exception that they will be able to use the emergency camp (Camp VII [Ridge])[6] if this has been set up by the first party.

26. A third Assault Party will leave Advance Base for the South Col one day

---

[1] Sleeping oxygen was also used at the Lhotse Face camp (Camp VII in the event. Ridge Camp was Camp IX).

[2] The first assault was launched on this basis.

[3] This was Camp VIII in the event.

[4] This was Camp VIII in the event.

[5] This was Camp VIII in the event.

[6] This was Camp IX in the event.

after the second Assault Party[1] and will make an attempt on the summit if neither of the preceding parties have succeeded (or in any case).

27. In the eventual Plan, which will be made on the Mountain itself, the timing of the assaults (in terms of the vertical distances to be covered in one day) will depend primarily on the actual assistance given by oxygen.

This paper is NOT the eventual Plan and the actual value to be derived from the oxygen is not proven. While taking due account of the need for economy and of the potential value of oxygen as an "Altitude reducer", we must, therefore, lay down the basis for preparatory planning on an "un–favourable case".

28. In order to enable calculations to be made on an "unfavourable case" basis, it has been assumed that:
 (a) Three assaults are necessary, e.g. only the last is successful.
 (b) Two of the three Assault Parties will spend a night at Camp V[2] (Lhotse Face) on the upward journey, the third going straight up to the South Col from Advance Base.
 (c) Two of the three Assault Parties will spend a night at Camp VII[3] (Ridge Camp), the third going straight for the summit from the South Col.

29. From the tentative schedule at Annex[4] to Appendix A, it will be seen that:
 (a) There may be up to 12 climbers/porters[5] at the Assault Camp at any one time.
 (b) 15 separate oxygen equipments will be required, 4 for each Assault Party and 3 for the Support Party.[6]
 (c) Oxygen cylinders will be required for movement as follows:

DAY	CLIMBERS
D	7
D plus 1	11
D plus 2	8
D plus 3	12
D plus 4	4

[1] A possible third Assault was held over until the result of the first two attempts was known.
[2] This was Camp VII in the event.
[3] This was Camp IX in the event.
[4] Not included.
[5] See Footnote 5, p. 226.
[6] 12 "Assault" frames were taken, the balance being made up from our Utility frames.

DAY	CLIMBERS
D plus 5	4
Total	46 man/sets[*]

Appendix "B" to Basis for Planning

EVEREST, 1953

THE PREPARATORY PERIOD

Introduction

1. This period includes both the march-out to Khumbu (in principle the month of March), and the acclimatization period (in principle the month of April) preceding the actual operations on Everest itself.

The object of this paper is to provide a forecast of the activities of the party during these two months, as a basis for provisioning, the recruiting of porters/carriers and the ordering of equipment.

2. It is assumed that the march-out will require a period of three weeks from Kathmandu[†] and that up to four weeks will be devoted to acclimatizing[‡] in the Khumbu district, making a total of seven weeks in all.

These four weeks may have to be curtailed should the weather and/or the conditions on Everest demand an advancement of the planned date for initiating operations on the mountain. It is unlikely that it will be possible to prolong the period of acclimatization prior to starting the build-up.

The March-out

3. We must bear in mind that, as an expensive sponsored expedition of national importance, we cannot indulge in the same liberties as a private party. It is of particular importance that all possible steps should be taken during the march-out to ensure that the health and the strength of the party are preserved.

---

[*] Each "set" could hold 1, 2 or 3 "Assault" Light Alloy oxygen bottles, each weighing about 10½ lb. At a flow rate of 4 litres a minute one bottle could be expected to last approximately 3 hours. Thus, for a full day's climbing, 2 bottles would normally be carried in a "set", making a requirement of 92 Light Alloy bottles. We actually took with us 60 "Assault" or Light Alloy bottles, plus 100 "Utility" bottles (nearly twice the capacity of the Assault bottles and almost twice as heavy). These were used for training experiments and also in the Assault for sleeping, and supporting climbers.

[†] The march-out lasted 17 days.

[‡] Three weeks was spent on acclimatizing and getting fit.

4. To this end:

(a) The medical officer is requested before the party leaves Kathmandu to draw up and issue essential hygiene rules to be observed by everyone, and to assist by advice during the march itself.

(b) The diet of the party will be basically Expedition rations, supplemented from local resources, as approved by the Medical Officer. A Sherpa cook will be engaged from Kathmandu onwards.[1]

For provisioning purposes a 75 per cent ration scale should be allowed for during the march-out.

(c) Camp sites will be chosen away from villages; local houses will not be used during this period.

5. It is also important that expedition boots and other equipment provided expressly for the ascent of Everest should not become worn out during the approach march.

Members of the Expedition are therefore requested to provide themselves with light clothing and footwear for the march. Shorts and "rubbers" or "Chapplis" are recommended.

The Acclimatization Period

6. The main objectives to be attained in this period will be:

(a) to continue and improve the acclimatization of members from the condition reached on arrival in Khumbu.

(b) to familiarize everyone with the expedition equipment and rations, including the use of the oxygen equipment.

(c) to enable everyone to get to know each other "on the rope".

(d) to explore country in the general vicinity of Everest, but NOT the mountain itself.

7. As regards 6(a) and 6(d) it is important that we do not allow ourselves to be diverted from our main objective by undertaking ambitious climbing projects during this period. We must constantly bear in mind that this is simply a period of preparation for our real goal.

8. As regards 6(b), the oxygen officer is requested to instruct, arrange for trials to be made, and supervise practice in the use of oxygen equipments.

9. As regards 6(c), it is proposed to divide the period into two spells of, say, 8–10 days, with a break of 3–4 days in the middle.[2]

The party will divide into 3–4 small caravans each of 3–4 Europeans and 4–5 High Altitude porters: each party will carry out its own programme and

---

[1] Two cooks were engaged.

[2] Acclimatization parties were of 6–8 days' duration. The rest period between each was of 2–3 days' duration.

all will reassemble at a base camp for rest and discussions at the end of the first spell.

The parties will then be reconstituted and move out again for the second acclimatization spell.

10. As regards 6(*d*), particular importance is attached to the timing of our operations on Everest. Partly for psychological reasons and partly because of the probable physical conditions obtaining on the mountain itself until late April, it is desirable to direct our activities in other areas.

11. In principle, expedition rations will be eaten throughout the acclimatization period; it is hoped, however, that local fresh food (including meat on hoof) will be available at Base Camp.

The Porters

12. It is planned to recruit 25–30 porters, making an eventual total number on the mountain of about 40 (12 Europeans: 28 Sherpas).[1]

Of these 28 Sherpas, it is anticipated that about 16 will be required for high-altitude climbing (at and above Advance Base), the remainder being needed for the build-up as far as the top of the Icefall.

In calculating high-altitude rations, equipment and clothing, therefore, these 16 must be fully provided for. The balance of 12–14 porters will require equipment, clothing and rations suitable for operations up to the top of the icefall.

13. The 16 high-altitude porters must clearly all be men with previous expedition experience. They will be required throughout the preparatory period, in particular during the acclimatization period in the Khumbu district.

The remaining 12–14 may be recruited later and locally;[2] they should join the Expedition before the main operations start on the mountain itself.

---

[1] The largest number on the mountain at any one time was 14 climbers and 38 Sherpas.

[2] 19 were recruited later locally. Since equipment had not been brought for 5 of these, 5 local men were found who were willing to make use of clothing and equipment from earlier expeditions.

APPENDIX IV

NOTES ON CERTAIN ITEMS OF EQUIPMENT
By CHARLES WYLIE

BOOTS

(a) High Altitude Boots

AFTER the Cho Oyu Expedition it was felt that there was a real need for a special high altitude boot, especially on Everest. Pugh had established that in terms of physical effort, one pound's weight on the feet was equivalent to five pounds on the shoulders. We aimed to cut down weight at the expense of durability; boots to be worn only above, say, 20,000 feet did not need to be so durable as they would only have to last a few weeks. They must, however, be strong enough for the attachment of crampons and for kicking steps in frozen snow. At the same time, we wanted them to be very much warmer than normal boots, as cases of frostbite in the high Himalaya have been only too frequent. It was also important that they should not freeze; wet boots will inevitably freeze up, and so they had to be waterproof.

After trying out in the Alps several possible answers to this problem, including the Army Mukluk, and special all-rubber boots, we decided to take boots of a revolutionary design made specially for us by The British Boot, Shoe and Allied Trade Research Association, of Kettering. The design and production of these boots are described here in some detail, as an illustration of the care and thought given to all our equipment by British Industry and of the value of scientific principles boldly applied with confidence based on research knowledge.

The uppers were made on the vapour-barrier principle, i.e. the insulating material—which has to be kept dry to maintain its efficiency—was enclosed in a waterproof envelope designed to exclude wet snow from the outside and perspiration from the inside. To protect the boots further in wet snow, a thin outer cover of rubber-coated stockinette was fixed to the outside edge of the sole; this cover could be removed if it was found to be unnecessary above a certain height.

The production of thirty-three pairs of these boots in five weeks provided Mr Bradley, their conscientious designer, with many problems. Thirty firms of his Association were concerned in their manufacture or in providing materials. Special lasts had to be made for the Sherpas from typical diagrams and foot measurements sent by the Himalayan Club in Darjeeling. Some

233

Sherpas taking size 6 boots had wider feet than Hillary's size 12! The boots had to be tested at each stage of their construction and finally in the cold chamber at Farnborough, where they were found to be satisfactory at −40°C.

In practice, the boots were very popular, and were used constantly from Camp III to the Summit, i.e. for a much longer period than that for which they had been designed. The thin outer covers proved too weak over this period, and developed tears and holes through which snow entered and wet the boot. The Swiss system of a detachable gaiter, as worn by Tenzing (see cover photograph), would be better. The boots also fitted too loosely for safe climbing on steep or difficult ground.

(b) General Climbing Boots

The arguments in favour of special high altitude boots applied as well, though to a lesser extent, to our normal climbing boots. Even at 20,000 feet there is a risk of frostbite, and a light boot helps to prevent fatigue at any height. These boots would, however, have to last some time, although the period could be limited to some three months. Mr Robert Lawrie, one of our foremost climbing-boot makers, tackled this problem with great energy and enthusiasm and produced boots weighing only 3 lb. 12 oz. a pair, lined with opossum fur between two layers of leather and with a woollen felt insole and a very thin rubber sole. This thin vibram sole proved rather too thin and started coming away at the toes. However, Noyce, who was given a course in boot repair by Mr Lawrie before the expedition sailed, saved the situation with some really professional repair work.

Both the High Altitude and General Climbing boots were designed with a low opening, to allow the foot to slip into frozen boots more easily, and lacing through "D" rings rather than holes, for ease when lacing with frozen fingers. Both these features were advantageous.

In spite of all the designers' efforts, both types of boots got wet on occasions and froze during the night, unless kept inside one's sleeping-bag. Nevertheless, we enjoyed the advantage of light boots throughout the expedition, and there were no cases of frozen feet.

TENTS

Our different varieties of tents have already been described in Chapter IV. They are discussed more fully in the following paragraphs.

When planning, we had considered the possibility of using a smaller version of our standard two-man Meade tents for the higher camps, to save weight. We decided, however, that the benefit of the saving in weight was more than counteracted by the additional discomfort of a cramped tent. On the mountain we were always glad of our roomy tents and never grudged the extra weight. This was so much the case that a standard Meade was eventually used at Camp IX, in spite of the fact that we had brought three different types of lightweight tent for this highest camp.

The Meade design, which has not altered basically since the expeditions of the 1920s, again proved to be the best as well as the simplest of the many types we used.

Piano-wire stiffeners were fitted to the ends of the tent entrance sleeves, making entry and exit very much easier. In normal weather the sleeves could be closed with a twist of this wire, rather than by tapes.

Tents destined for all camps above Advance Base were provided with detachable nylon inners for extra warmth. These inners weighed very little and when tested had been found to give an extra four degrees of warmth. They were seldom used below Advance Base, however, and tended to become separated from their parent tent.

A heavier twelve-man Dome tent was taken, designed by Colonel Croft as an arctic warfare tent for the Army. We also took a lighter, pyramid-shaped tent, similar to the Dome, with certain modifications. These larger Domes were always in use, the one as a mess-cum-sleeping tent for us, the other for the Sherpas. Both eventually were put up at Advance Base. In small camps a Pyramid tent was generally used as a cookhouse and community centre by the Sherpas. These could, if necessary, hold five men; one was taken to the South Col.

We also took with us a number of waterproof sheets or tarpaulins 10 by 15 feet, weighing only 8 lb. each. These were very useful throughout the expedition, but particularly on the march, either as roofing for the cookhouse, or as supplementary tentage, or to protect stores from snow or rain.

WINDPROOF CLOTH

The selection of cloth for our windproof clothing, and for our tents, was greatly simplified for us by the help and advice of the Ministry of Supply research experts at the Royal Aircraft Establishment at Farnborough. They were interested in windproof clothing for the Services, and had at their disposal means to test the various qualities of any cloth.

Obviously the degree of windproofness was of first importance, but the cloth also had to be as light as possible, snag-proof, and fairly waterproof. We eventually chose a first-class cloth which was shown, in wind-tunnel tests, to be completely windproof in winds of 100 m.p.h. It weighed only 4¾ oz. per square yard and was as tear-resistant as many other heavier cloths. Proofed with Mystolen, the tents could be made quite waterproof and the clothing at least shower-proof. It was of a cotton warp and nylon weft, and made by John Southworth & Sons Ltd., of Manchester.

We used a single thickness of cloth both for our windproofs and tents, and were very satisfied with its performance.

WIRELESS

The wireless plan was drawn up with the help of Brigadier Smijth-Windham, wireless officer of the 1933 and 1936 Expeditions, and the work placed in the hands of Brigadier Moppett, a Director of Pye Telecommunications, Cambridge. We are most indebted to this firm for their gift of equipment provided so speedily for us.

The plan required "walkie-talkie" sets for communication between camps on the mountain up to two miles apart and a short-wave receiver for special meteorological bulletins and general entertainment. A transmitting set for contact with the outside world was not taken because of the extra weight; moreover, it could not contribute to the only object of the expedition, which was to reach the Summit. In addition, it would have required a wireless officer to be added to our already large party. This decision also meant that all our radio equipment could be operated by dry batteries.

The equipment had to be robust, light, compact, requiring the minimum of maintenance and able to withstand rain and snow and temperatures from −40 to 100° F. Climbers must be able to set up the equipment with gloved hands and operate it while lying in their sleeping-bags. To meet this specification, eight "walkie-talkie" sets were adapted by Pye from their "Walkie-phone", PTC122, a Very High Frequency set with crystal control on both transmission and reception, with a fixed frequency of 72 megacycles. They had flexible tape aerials, and weighed 5 lb. each. Dry batteries, supplied by Vidor Ltd., were carried in a "waistcoat" which could be worn underneath the climber's down clothing or stuffed inside his sleeping-bag and kept warm by body heat, to prevent loss of efficiency at very low temperatures. The high-tension batteries gave 41 hours' use at −10° C. An external aerial on a folding duralumin tripod was constructed so that sets could be used remotely from inside a small tent.

The range of these sets depends greatly upon the topography of the intervening ground, because V.H.F. waves do not travel around large obstacles. There is, however, little interference and the sets are easy to operate. They gave very good service from camp to camp, particularly in a net between Camps I, II and III during the build-up phase, even though these camps were not in visual contact. It was not necessary to use them on the move. They were used up to Camp VII (24,000 feet); a set was also taken to the South Col but was unfortunately damaged in transit.

The short-wave receivers were the normal Pye export model, PE70B, with loudspeaker and dry batteries, specially boxed in a strong wood case. Its 15-foot rod aerial fitted on to the same tripods as the "walkie-talkie" sets.

These receivers were used at Base Camp and Advance Base—positions which suffered from the screening effect of the encircling high mountains. Even so, excellent reception was obtained from All-India Radio, who from 1st May broadcast special weather forecasts prepared by Dr Mall of the India Meteorological Department. The B.B.C. also re-broadcast these bulletins for our benefit, occasionally including very welcome personal or goodwill messages. During the long cold evenings Ceylon Commercial proved a popular entertainment programme, boosting our morale with such exhortations as, "When you're feeling low, use ——'s stomach powder".

COOKERS

From observations made on the Cho Oyu Expedition, Pugh told us that we would each require at least eight pints of liquid per day on Everest. It followed that a cooker of maximum efficiency was essential.

The most effective and economical source of heat is a paraffin burner and the Primus stove with a high altitude burner was the obvious choice. To conserve the heat and at the same time economize on fuel, a shield in sections completely surrounding the cooking-pans was designed for us by Mr C. R. Cooke.

The shield directed heat to the base and sides of the pans. A lid, which could also be used as a frying-pan, fitted over the top of the shield. An extra-large spirit cup was fitted to ensure the burner was sufficiently heated to vaporize the paraffin before it reached the jet.

Even hard wind-packed snow is four times as bulky as the water it contains, so two extra-large pans were fitted, of a capacity of 4 and 3½ pints in our large stoves, and 2½ and 2 pints in our smaller ones.

An ordinary burner is unreliable above 15,000 feet, so a silent type of self-pricking burner was selected after tests in the Decompression Chamber at Farnborough, which proved it to be satisfactory at 40,000 feet. Since cooking must often be done in a totally enclosed tent, the burners were also tested for the presence of poisonous carbon monoxide gas and found to be entirely safe. These burners were also self-cleaning; the jet could be cleaned by simply turning a knob. By turning the knob the other way, the jet could be closed against leakage of fuel.

Four small and eighteen large cookers were taken, holding 1 and 2 pints of fuel, and weighing 3½ and 4½ lb. respectively. In addition, two double-burner cooking ranges were taken for Base and Advance Base Camp.

In spite of the usual robust treatment, both from the Sherpas and from us, the cookers on the whole worked well. This was largely due to good maintenance by Ed Hillary. In particular, Hillary and Tenzing were able to provide themselves with sufficient drink at Camp IX at 27,900 feet before their climb to the Summit.

In the hope that they might prove to be the answer to cooking at the highest camp, we also took six Butane gas cookers. Although they had the great advantage of simplicity—to light them one merely lit a match and turned a tap—they lacked the heating power of a Primus and did not work well at extreme altitudes. However, each container was also supplied with a mantle and could be used for lighting. In this rôle they gave us excellent service in the long evenings in the big Dome tent.

BRIDGING EQUIPMENT

The need for some means of bridging wide crevasses had been recognized by Shipton as a result of his reconnaissance expedition in 1951. Something light, portable and strong was required, long enough to bridge a gap of 25 feet if necessary. The Swiss had used ropes, but we aimed at something easier for the constant stream of laden porters.

The problem was put to Lyte Ladders Ltd., of Newport. They first produced a bridge made rigid by bracing underneath. Although the rigidity was an advantage, the bracing would have been difficult to assemble with cold hands, and added to the weight. Eventually one of the Company's standard heavy-duty parallel builder's aluminium alloy ladders was chosen. The sag was considerable over a 25-foot gap, but it held the manager, the works foreman and myself together, without signs of collapse, so simplicity won the day.

The ladder was made up into five 6-foot sections, 14 inches wide, and each section was fitted with extruding sleeves to enable sections to be joined together. Four screws secured each junction. The whole ladder weighed only 57½lb.

The largest gap bridged by us was a crevasse at the entrance to the Cwm; it was about 16 feet wide and so needed three sections of our bridge. Over this distance sagging was negligible. The crevasse was slowly closing and the ends of the ladder, which were frozen into the surface of the glacier, had often to be chipped free to prevent the ladder buckling.

APPENDIX V

OXYGEN EQUIPMENT
By T. D. BOURDILLON

THREE principal types of apparatus were used: Open-Circuit, Closed-Circuit and Sleeping Sets. All three depended on high-pressure gas cylinders for oxygen storage, and both climbing sets used similar carrying frames.

THE OXYGEN CYLINDERS

Two different cylinders were used. One, which was formed from drawn dural tube, weighed when charged, and with a light-alloy reducing valve, $11\frac{1}{2}$ lb. This weight varied slightly from cylinder to cylinder. It held 800 litres of oxygen at a pressure of 3,300 p.s.i. and was used with a light-alloy reducing valve mounted directly on one end.

The other was the wire-wound R.A.F. Mark VD steel cylinder. Charged to 3,300 p.s.i. and with a brass reducing valve this weighed 21 lb. and held 1,400 litres of oxygen. Some of these cylinders were fitted with a stop valve and connected by a copper pipe to a reducing valve; with others the reducing valve was mounted on the cylinder.

THE CARRYING FRAME

Two types of frame were used. One, made of welded aluminium tube, was designed to carry up to three dural cylinders. The other, of welded aluminium alloy, carried either one dural or one R.A.F. cylinder. Both frames were supported on a horizontal webbing band resting low on the back and kept in place by two shoulder straps. They were designed to carry the load high and close to the back.

THE OPEN-CIRCUIT SET

With this set the climber inhaled air enriched by added oxygen, and expired to atmosphere.

The set is illustrated in figs. 1 and 2 overleaf.

Oxygen at a nominal pressure of 50 p.s.i. was led from the cylinder and reducing valve through a flexible pipe to an R.A.F. Mark VI dual-outlet manifold (shown cut away in fig. 2). This manifold contained two metering apertures, so that the climber had a choice of two flow rates. Three different manifolds gave flow rates of 2 or 4, $2\frac{1}{2}$ or 5, and 3 or 6 litres a minute.

A modified R.A.F. Mark IV Economizer delivered oxygen during

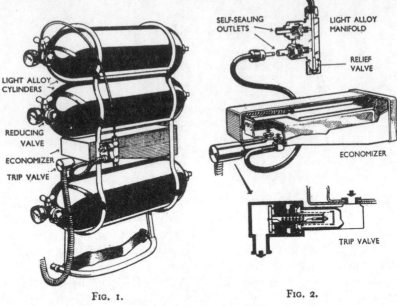

FIG. 1.   FIG. 2.

THE OPEN-CIRCUIT APPARATUS

inspiration only, thus avoiding unnecessary waste during expiration. The uniform flow of oxygen from the manifold passed into a spring-loaded reservoir bag in the economizer. At the start of inspiration a trip valve in the economizer was opened by slight suction from the mask, permitting the bag to empty into the mask. The economizer and trip valve are shown in fig. 2.

An R.A.F. "H" mask was used, fitted with a third inlet valve and a protective rubber snout. The warm, expired gases passed over the inlet valves.

The weights of the Open-Circuit set with the lightened economizer were:

with one R.A.F. cylinder	28 lb.
with one dural cylinder	18 lb.
with two dural cylinders	29½lb.
with three dural cylinders	41 lb.

THE CLOSED-CIRCUIT SET

In this set there was no opening to the outside air. The climber inhaled a high concentration of oxygen directly from a breathing bag. He exhaled through a soda lime canister which absorbed the expired carbon dioxide and allowed the exhaled oxygen to return to the breathing bag. Direction of flow was ensured by two non-return valves. The oxygen absorbed from the circuit

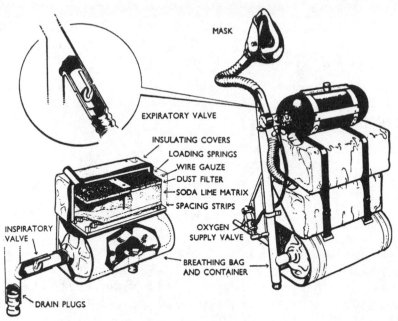

MASK

EXPIRATORY VALVE

INSULATING COVERS
LOADING SPRINGS
WIRE GAUZE
DUST FILTER
SODA LIME MATRIX
SPACING STRIPS

INSPIRATORY
VALVE

OXYGEN
SUPPLY VALVE

BREATHING BAG
AND CONTAINER

DRAIN PLUGS

FIG 3.—CLOSED-CIRCUIT APPARATUS

by the climber was replaced from a high-pressure cylinder through a reducing valve and a manually controlled supply-valve. The apparatus is illustrated in fig. 3 and more fully described elsewhere (*Alpine Journal, 59, No. 288*).

Since high ventilation rates and intolerance of resistance to breathing were expected, special efforts were made to reduce the resistance to gas flow as far as possible. Thus all tubing was of 1⅛ in. or 1¼ in. bore. The figures realized were very satisfactory: about 2.2 cm. water gauge for expiration and 0.8 cm. for inspiration at a rate of 200 litres/minute and at approximately sea-level pressure.

Great care was also taken to ensure maximum efficiency of use of the soda lime. To this end machine-filled replaceable canisters were used and the soda lime was held under a spring pressure of 60 lb., to prevent the granules from shifting in transit.

THE SLEEPING SET

A cylinder, reducing valve and outlet manifold (as used in the Open-Circuit climbing set) supplied 2 litres of oxygen per minute to a "T"-piece. This divided the oxygen equally between two light face masks and economizing bladders of a type used by the British Overseas Airways Corporation but modified to allow a higher ventilation rate. The low-pressure part of the apparatus weighed only a few ounces.

QUANTITIES OF APPARATUS

Although the quantities were kept to an absolute minimum and in fact proved barely adequate, a considerable amount of apparatus was involved. It included:

60 light-alloy cylinders
100 R.A.F. cylinders
80 soda lime canisters
8 Closed-Circuit sets
12 Open-Circuit sets
12 training and carrying sets.

The acclimatization period spent at intermediate heights was of great value. It enabled all the party to gain experience of the apparatus under comparatively easy conditions. A number of defects were revealed, which would have been more serious had they first been discovered on Everest.

During the acclimatization period, and later above Camp VII, Open-Circuit apparatus was used successfully on several occasions by Sherpas. However, it was difficult to train Sherpas in the use of oxygen apparatus: their lack of previous experience with mechanical equipment threw a heavy responsibility on the Europeans in mixed parties. The preparation of apparatus and the supervision of its use were a severe burden on and above the South Col.

It was expected that their natural acclimatization would enable Sherpas wearing climbing sets to carry above the South Col without having used sleeping sets during the previous night. Only enough sleeping oxygen was carried to the South Col for the Assault parties and for the Europeans intended to lead the carrying parties. The markedly superior performance of Europeans carrying above the South Col was probably mainly because no Sherpa other than Tenzing used sleeping oxygen on the Col.

The great benefits incurred from the use of sleeping oxygen at and above 21,500 feet were one of the most striking features of the expedition. When using it one slept better, was noticeably warmer and woke conspicuously more rested and refreshed.

The behaviour of the climbing apparatus depended on altitude.

Below 22,000 feet it was found with both types of set that the increase in performance given by the oxygen was less marked than the great reduction in effort and fatigue. In a cold wind the heat generated in the Closed-Circuit was an advantage, but in the warm still weather common in the Western Cwm it was decidedly uncomfortable. At this height there appeared to be little difference between the performances given by the two sets.

COMPARATIVE CLIMBING RATES BETWEEN 25,800 FEET AND 27,300 FEET

Party	Type of oxygen apparatus	Rate of climb ft./hour	Gross load lb.	Snow conditions
Lambert and Tenzing, 1952	no apparatus while climbing	233	—	step cutting and kicking in unbroken snow
Gregory, Lowe and Ang Nyima	Open-Circuit at 4 l/m	430	40	
First Assault party, 1953	Closed-Circuit	933	52	
Hunt and Da Namgyal	Open-Circuit at 4 l/m	494	50	steps already made
Second Assault party, 1953	Open-Circuit at 4 l/m	621	40	

Between 22,000 feet and 26,000 feet, no strictly comparable runs were made, partly because the route between these altitudes varied greatly in difficulty from day to day, and partly because of the shortage of oxygen cylinders. What evidence there is suggests a major increase of performance with both sets, and more with the Closed-Circuit than the Open. Some fresh troubles occurred at these altitudes. The outlet manifolds of two Open-Circuit sets developed leaks (possibly due to low-temperature hardening of their rubber seals), and the breathing valves in the Closed-Circuit froze up immediately after the canisters had been changed. This freezing was due to the insertion of a fresh cold canister into a set that was already in use and therefore moist. It is unfortunate that this problem did not arise until the first Assault had begun, and the simple methods of dealing with it described elsewhere (*Alpine Journal, 59, No. 288*) were not used in the first Assault.

On the South Col the first Assault party was considerably delayed by damage to one Closed-Circuit set. It was found that the oxygen supply-valve had been forced past its stop and the valve damaged in a mistaken, but well-meant attempt to effect greater economy when resting.

Above 26,000 feet the heat generated in the Closed-Circuit and the fact that with it one inhaled moist gas were major advantages. Ice formed in the Open-Circuit masks on three occasions, and one Closed-Circuit set developed a fault giving a reduced performance and a high ventilation rate. This fault occurred at about 28,100 feet in difficult conditions and was not diagnosed: it may have been due to an air leak.

Times are available for five parties climbing over the same route between the South Col and the Swiss 1952 Camp, on the South-East ridge.

The first three ascents in this table show clearly the great increase in performance given by oxygen apparatus and the very marked superiority of the Closed-Circuit over the Open. The last two ascents are not strictly comparable, since they were using steps already made; as might be expected they show climbing rates higher than that of the other Open-Circuit party, but still markedly lower than that for the Closed-Circuit.

The results of this expedition suggest that the best combination of oxygen apparatus for very high altitude climbing is an Open-Circuit sleeping set giving a comparatively low concentration of oxygen and a Closed-Circuit climbing set. It seems desirable to use the sleeping set from about 21,000 feet and the climbing set from the same or a slightly greater altitude. The use of a suitable peroxide offers the possibility of a very light climbing set if apparatus can be developed in which the rate of reaction is satisfactorily controlled. All apparatus should be as simple as possible, and in particular if compressed gas storage is used there should be a reducing valve and pressure gauge mounted permanently in each cylinder or sphere.

A very large number of people and organizations contributed to the development and production of oxygen apparatus for this expedition; a reference to this has been made in Appendix IX.

APPENDIX VI

DIET

By GRIFFITH PUGH and GEORGE BAND

HIMALAYAN rations usually consist of a combination of bulk stores taken out from England or obtained in India, and foodstuffs purchased locally in the Himalayas. Rice, potatoes, tsampa, dahl, ghi,[1] eggs, chicken and meat are the chief foods available locally; fresh fruit and vegetables are seldom, if ever, obtainable.

The earlier Everest expeditions took with them a great variety of bulk stores, which the party soon grew tired of on the mountain. Later expeditions have come to depend increasingly on local food supplies, limiting their bulk stores to essential items not procurable locally, such as sugar, jam, biscuits and butter.

There was evidence on the Reconnaissance of 1951 and on the Cho Oyu Expedition of 1952 that some members of the party deteriorated physically owing to inability to tolerate the strange and bulky diet, and it was considered that the general fitness of the 1953 Everest party would be improved by providing a diet conforming as closely as possible with European diet. This could be done by making more use of tinned or vacuum-packed foods.

Instead of bulk stores, the items for each day were packed together in man-day units or multiples thereof—a system which is now widely used by armed forces operating in small groups in the field. The advantages of this system on a Himalayan expedition are as follows: the sorting and making up of loads and the distribution of rations is greatly simplified; shortages of essential items due to over-consumption or pilfering are avoided; there is less chance of contamination of food by flies and in handling. These advantages are gained at the expense of additional weight and cost; and it is obvious that the proportion of the various items in the daily ration should be correct. In the latter respect the nutritional survey done on Cho Oyu was of great assistance. The organization of the packing of these rations was undertaken by the Army and many of the items were made available from Army stores. The expedition has to thank Lieut.-Colonel Kingsmill and his department at the War Office for their valuable help in this respect.

The composition of the various types of ration is presented in the table at the end of this appendix. For purposes of rationing the present expedition was divided into three phases: (1) the approach and return marches; (2) the acclimatization and "build-up" periods; and (3) the period spent above

---

[1] Tsampa = flour made from roasted barley; dahl = lentils; ghi = clarified butter.

245

22,000 feet, including the Assault. The "Compo" boxes containing 14 men's rations for one day, and the beverage boxes containing 14 men's rations for two days were intended for phases 1 and 2.[1] The biscuits for consumption with these rations were taken separately in standard army boxes, and it was intended that the rations should be supplemented with rice, potatoes and eggs purchased locally. In phase 2 it was anticipated that the party would be getting tired of "Compo" rations and it was planned to open some of the luxury boxes to increase variety at this stage, and to bring up a certain amount of fresh meat on the hoof. In the Western Cwm and on the Lhotse Face it was thought probable that a changeover would have to be made to Assault rations in order to save weight.

Rations for phase 3 were planned in accordance with the following considerations. Past experiences showed that above a certain altitude, depending on their state of acclimatization, climbers' appetites show marked deterioration. On Cho Oyu in 1952 the calorie value of the food eaten between 19,000 and 22,000 feet was of the order of 3,200 Calories compared with 4,200 Calories on the approach march. Above 24,000 feet on Everest in 1933 the calorie intake was calculated to be about 1,500 Calories. At high altitude a large proportion of the total calorie intake consists of sugar taken in tea, lemonade and other beverages. Some men become intolerant of fatty foods; some hanker after special foods which may not be available. High up on Everest in 1933 Shipton had a craving for a dozen eggs; Smythe wanted Frankfurters and Sauerkraut; in 1924 Somervell's favourite diet was strawberry jam and condensed milk; on Cho Oyu Hillary wanted pineapple cubes and Secord wanted tinned salmon. In general, men prefer to eat nothing rather than put up with something that is distasteful to them, and if they do not eat they deteriorate all the more rapidly. The weight and bulk of the rations that can be carried high on a mountain is necessarily restricted, and the basic items and their packings must be as light as possible. It is desirable to exclude bulky items and those containing a high percentage of water, e.g. bread and potatoes, although some concession to food idiosyncrasies may have to be made.

The plan evolved for the 1953 expedition was to pack the Assault rations in units consisting of one man's rations for one day. Considerable economy of weight and bulk was achieved by vacuum packing. Each separate item as well as the composite twenty-four-hour unit was put up in an air-tight plastic bag and sealed under a vacuum. The Assault ration was planned on a liberal scale to allow of individual selection of items and quantities. It was intended that Assault parties should open their rations before the Assault, reject such items as they felt they would not require, and substitute items selected from the luxury boxes, according to their own preferences. The composition of the

[1] Party of 13 plus Sherpa Tenzing.

luxury boxes was decided in England by the climbers themselves, each of whom was asked to choose certain foods which he felt he would like to eat at great altitude.

A detailed analysis of records of this year's experience is not available at the time of writing. However, all except one of the party approved in principle of taking packed rations as opposed to bulk. Most of the men wanted more local food, especially more fresh meat and less tinned meat. This proposal should be accepted with caution, as local supplies are not always adequate. It was agreed that packed rations for the Assault should include only basic items acceptable to all (the exact specification of these will not be easy!) and more use should be made of bulk stores, such as those contained in luxury boxes. It was found that the party desired normal food up to 22,000 feet, probably because they were better acclimatized than on Cho Oyu and other post-war expeditions. The "Compo" ration was eaten up to Advance Base Camp. In the Western Cwm there was a strong demand for potatoes and fresh meat. Potatoes were sent up, in spite of their weight, as well as a limited supply of mutton.

At high altitude the cooking of fresh meat, rice and potatoes is extremely slow and expensive of fuel (at 21,000 feet water boils at 185° F. compared with 212° F. at sea-level). The problem has been solved by the use of pressure cookers, which have now come to be regarded as an essential item on Himalayan expeditions, although there was considerable resistance to their use at first. The Sherpa cooks, this year, thought so highly of them that they were even prepared to improvise pressure cookers of their own. Such a cooker consisted of a biscuit tin with the lid forced on and a small hole stoppered with a stick acting as a safety valve.

The Assault rations were eaten on the Lhotse Face and above. They were repacked at Base Camp. Both pemmican and Grape-nuts, which were acceptable the previous year on Cho Oyu, were rejected. Statements obtained from the climbers on returning from the Assault show that between half and one modified high altitude ration was eaten per man per day. The items from bulk such as sardines, fruit juice and tinned fruit were much appreciated, as also were certain items of food, such as Vita-Weat, honey and cheese left behind by the Swiss on the South Col and discovered intact. The Sherpas in the Western Cwm and above received one Assault ration between two men per day plus three-quarters of a pound of tsampa. This amount of tsampa proved insufficient and had to be increased to one and a quarter pounds per man per day.

By the time the party came down the Icefall for the last time "Compo" rations were finished, and the march back to Kathmandu was done on

Assault rations plus local food. It was then that we came to appreciate the value of the "Compo" rations by contrast with the Assault rations. The party insisted on having as much meat and chicken as possible on the march back, but it was not always possible to obtain sufficient quantity. Local chickens are small and tough, but nevertheless acceptable if pressure cooked. The party wanted a chicken each for supper every night, but usually there were only five between a party of nine men. Apart from chickens, two small sheep were eaten. As is usual after Himalayan expeditions, the party continued to have enormous appetites for several weeks after getting back to Kathmandu.

TABLE OF RATION SCALES

1. "COMPO" BOX. 14 man-days. Gross weight 42 lb. Suppliers: Army. Each case was marked on top and side with day of week.

Menu 1. Monday

Breakfast and March, Bottom layer

Oatmeal Bis.	1 × 12	oz. tin
Bacon	5 × 15	oz. tin
Butter	2 × 15	oz. tin
Jam	2 × 9	oz. tin
Marmalade	2 × 9	oz. tin
Cheese	2 × 8	oz. tin
Choc./Sweets	3 × 12½	oz. tin
Salt/Matches	4 oz. Salt	1 Box Matches

Main Meal, Top layer

P. Meat	8 × 12	oz. tin
Carrots	3 × 10	oz. tin
R. Cake	4 × 10	oz. tin

Menu 2. Tuesday

Breakfast and March, Bottom layer

Oatmeal Bis.	1 × 12	oz. tin
Sausages	5 × 15	oz. tin
Butter	2 × 15	oz. tin
Jam	2 × 9	oz. tin
Marmalade	2 × 9	oz. tin
Cheese	2 × 8	oz. tin
Choc./Sweets	3 × 12½	oz. tin
Salt/Matches	4 oz. Salt	1 Box Matches

Main Meal, Top layer

Steak and Kidney	8 × 16	oz. tin
Baked Beans	3 × 16	oz. tin
R. Cake	4 × 10	oz. tin

Menu 3. Wednesday

Breakfast and March, Bottom layer

Oatmeal Bis.	1 × 12	oz. tin
Bacon	5 × 15	oz. tin
Butter	2 × 15	oz. tin
Jam	2 × 9	oz. tin
Marmalade	2 × 9	oz. tin
Cheese	2 × 8	oz. tin
Choc./Sweets	3 × 12½	oz. tin
Salt/Matches	4 oz. Salt	1 Box Matches

Main Meal, Top layer

Pork Lunch. Meat	8 × 16	oz. tin
Carrots	3 × 16	oz. tin
Td. Fruit	4 × 16	oz. tin

Menu 4. Thursday

Breakfast and March, Bottom layer

Oatmeal Bis.	1 × 12	oz. tin
Bacon	5 × 15	oz. tin
Butter	2 × 15	oz. tin
Jam	2 × 9	oz. tin
Marmalade	2 × 9	oz. tin
Cheese	2 × 8	oz. tin
Choc./Sweets	3 × 12½	oz. tin
Salt/Matches	4 oz. Salt	1 Box Matches

Main Meal, Top layer

Stewed Steak	8 × 16	oz. tin
Peas	3 × 10	oz. tin
R. Cake	4 × 10	oz. tin

On top of tins:

2 × 2½ oz. packets Soup powder
2 Fibre Cloths
1 packet containing Toilet paper and Can-opener

Choc./Sweets tin contained 10 oz. chocolate and 2½ oz. boiled sweets

Menu 5. Friday

Breakfast and March, Bottom layer

Oatmeal Bis.	1 × 12	oz. tin
Bacon	5 × 15	oz. tin
Butter	2 × 15	oz. tin
Jam	2 × 9	oz. tin
Marmalade	2 × 9	oz. tin
Cheese	2 × 8	oz. tin
Choc./Sweets	3 × 12½	oz. tin
Salt/Matches	4 oz. Salt	1 Box Matches

Main Meal, Top layer

Salmon	16 × 8	oz. tin
Peas	3 × 10	oz. tin
Td. Fruit	4 × 16	oz. tin

Menu 6. Saturday

Breakfast and March, Bottom layer

Oatmeal Bis.	1 × 12	oz. tin
Sausages	5 × 15	oz. tin
Butter	2 × 15	oz. tin
Jam	2 × 9	oz. tin
Marmalade	2 × 9	oz. tin
Cheese	2 × 8	oz. tin
Choc./Sweets	3 × 12½	oz. tin
Salt/Matches	4 oz. Salt	1 Box Matches

Main Meal, Top layer

Pork Lunch. Meat	8 × 16	oz. tin
Diced Mixed Vegetables	3 × 10	oz. tin
R. Cake	4 × 10	oz. tin

Menu 7. Sunday

Breakfast and March, Bottom layer

Oatmeal Bis.	1 × 12	oz. tin
Bacon	5 × 15	oz. tin
Butter	2 × 15	oz. tin
Jam	2 × 9	oz. tin
Marmalade	2 × 9	oz. tin
Cheese	2 × 8	oz. tin
Choc./Sweets	3 × 12½	oz. tin
Salt/Matches	4 oz. Salt	1 Box Matches

Main Meal, Top layer

Stewed Steak	8 × 16	oz. tin
Peas	3 × 10	oz. tin
R. Cake	4 × 10	oz. tin

TABLE OF RATION SCALES—continued

2. BEVERAGE BOXES:
   28 man-days   Number of cases 46
   Gross weight 32 lb.   Suppliers: Wilts United Dairies

Each box contained two trays, each tray representing one day's beverages for 14 men. All packets were vacuum packed.

Composition: Each tray contained:

Sugar	4 × 19½ oz. packets
Tea	2 × 10 oz. packets
Milk Powder	4 × 8 oz. packets
One-minute Quaker Oats	1 × 10 oz. packets
Stoned Dates	2 × 8 oz. packets
Seedless Raisins	1 × 16 oz. packets
* Coffee or Cocoa	2 × 13 oz. packets

* In each Beverage Box one tray contained cocoa, the other coffee.

3. BISCUIT BOX: Number of cases 11
   Gross weight per case 33¾ lb.   Suppliers: Army

Each case contained six tin boxes each containing fifteen 6-oz. packets of plain service biscuits.

4. ASSAULT RATION BOXES:

8 × 2½ lb. units, each containing one man's ration for one day. Vacuum packed in a plastic-covered tinfoil pouch.

Gross weight per box 30 lb. Suppliers: Wilts United Dairies.

Composition:

Grape-nuts	3 oz.	
Rolled Oats	1 oz.	
Milk Powder	3 oz.	
Sugar	2 × 7 oz.	All vacuum packed
Jam	2 oz.	
Plain Biscuits	3 oz. packet	
Sweet Biscuits	3 oz. packet	
Chocolate	2 oz.	
or Mint Bar	2 oz.	1 Bar
or Fru-Bix	2 oz.	
or Banana		
Boiled Sweets	2 oz. vacuum packed	
Pemmican (low fat)	2½ oz.	
Salt	5½ grm. in dispenser	
Cheese	1 oz. portion	
Coffee or Cocoa	1 oz. vacuum packed	
Lemonade or Orangeade Powder	1 oz. vacuum packed	
Fibre Cloth	1 piece	
Toilet Paper	5 sheets	
Tea	1½ oz.	

Modified assault ration as used on the Assault

Seventy rations were repacked at Base Camp. Each modified unit consisted of two men's ration for one day packed in the tinfoil pouch.

Composition:

Rolled Oats	2 × 1 oz. packets
Milk Powder	1 × 3 oz. packet
Sugar	4 × 7 oz. packets
Jam	1 × 2 oz. packet
Sweet Biscuits	2 × 3 oz. packets
Mint Bar or Banana Bar	2 × 2 oz.
Cheese	2 × 1 oz. packets
Boiled Sweets	1 × 2 oz. packet
Salt	2 × 5½ oz. grm. dispenser
Cocoa	1 × 1 oz. packet
Tea	1 × 1½ oz. packet
Soup	1 × 2¼ oz. packet
Lemonade Powder	2 × 1 oz. packets.
Gross weight 4 lb.	

5. LUXURY BOXES:

Gross weight 35 lb. Number of Boxes 5. Suppliers: Andrew Lusk.

Total contents:

Assorted Soups	165 packets
Nescafé	30 × 4 oz. tins
Canned Pears	5 × 16 oz. tins
Canned Apricots	5 × 16 oz. tins
Canned Pineapple	5 × 20 oz. tins
Sardines	29 × ¼ club tins
Glucose Tablets	6 cartons
"Sun" Chutney	4 bottles
"Green Label" Chutney	4 bottles
Marmite	8 × 4 oz. jars
Lait (Mont Blanc)	24 tubes
Self-heating Soups	12 tins
Onion Flakes	2 × 1 lb. tins
Ovosport Bars	50 packets
Tomato Juice	2 × 16 oz. tins
Orange Juice	3 × 16 oz. tins
Mustard	1 × ½ lb. tin
White Pepper	1 × ½ lb. tin
Mixed Herbs	1 tin
"Klim" Milk Powder	1 lb. tin
Ham	1 × 9 lb. tin
Rum	1 bottle
Brandy	1 bottle
Cheddar Cheese	1 × 12½ lb.
Saucisson	22 lb.

6. MISCELLANEOUS:

Sugar for Sherpas:	Gross weight: 210 lb.	Suppliers: Tate & Lyle.
Chocolate:	Gross weight: 100 lb.	Suppliers: Rowntrees.
Tea:	Gross weight: 100 lb.	Suppliers: Pollitt.
Scone Mix:	Gross weight: 93 lb.	Suppliers: Ready Mix.

7. COMPOUND VITAMIN CAPSULES (Suppliers: Lederle)

Vitamin A	5,000 I.U.
Vitamin D	500 I.U.
Thiamin Hcl.	3·0 mg.
Riboflavin	2·0 mg.
Pyridoxine Hcl.	0·2 mg.
Ascorbic acid	75·0 mg.
Niacinamide	20·0 mg.
Ca Pantothinate	1·0 mg.
Folic acid	1·0 mg.
Vitamin B12	1·0 γ

Each member of the party was issued with 100 compound vitamin capsules at the start of the Expedition.

APPENDIX VII

PHYSIOLOGY AND MEDICINE
By Griffith Pugh *and* Michael Ward

AS long ago as 1924, climbers on Mount Everest showed that after nine weeks spent at intermediate altitudes men could climb to 28,000 feet and sleep two or three nights above 27,000 feet. Unacclimatized men, exposed to these altitudes, rapidly lose consciousness and die, as was first shown by the early balloonists in the 1870s. When men in a decompression chamber at sea-level are exposed to reduced barometric pressure simulating conditions at high altitude, they become unconscious within ten minutes at a pressure equivalent to 25,000 feet, and within three minutes at a pressure equivalent to 27,000 feet.

The greatest altitude at which men are known to live permanently is 17,500 feet. There is a Mining Settlement at Aconquilcha in the Andes situated at this altitude. It is said that the miners there preferred to climb 1,500 feet a day to their work in the mines rather than occupy a camp built for them by the Mining Company at 19,000 feet.

Climbers on Everest found that their performance continued to improve up to 23,000 feet, but above that altitude severe and rapid deterioration took place, marked by progressive weakness, lethargy, non-recovery from fatigue and muscular wasting. Slow physical deterioration occurs at altitudes between 21,000 feet and 23,000 feet but is masked by the process of acclimatization, so that headaches and other altitude symptoms clear up and for a time performance improves. Eventually, however, there is loss of appetite, wasting of body tissues and a decline in energy and capacity for work. The following table gives the longest periods which mountaineers on Everest have spent at various altitudes above 20,000 feet.

20,000 feet to 21,000 feet	Four–five weeks	Various expeditions
23,000 feet	Eleven days	Odell, 1924
22,000 feet to 24,600 feet	Eleven days	Lowe, 1953
25,700 feet	Five nights	Birnie, 1933
27,400 feet	Three nights	Smythe, 1933.

The physical strain of going above 26,000 feet is such that few, if any, are capable of more than one such ascent in an expedition, and complete recovery from such an experience takes many weeks.

One of the remarkable things about acclimatization to high altitude is the great variation between individuals in their capacity to ascend to altitudes above 20,000 feet. Some men do not seem to be able to go above 21,000 feet and probably only exceptional men can go above 27,000 feet without supplementary oxygen. There is also wide variation in performance in any one individual from day to day, and climbers are described as either "going well" or "going badly".

There is, at present, no means of selecting men who will do well high up other than trial on the mountain. The reaction to simulated altitudes in a decompression chamber shows no correlation with subsequent performance on the mountain. Every expedition has noted, however, that tolerance of high altitude increases with each visit to the Himalayas and that the advantage gained from previous experience of high altitudes persists over an interval of many years.

There has been much discussion about the most favourable age for Himalayan mountaineering. The majority of successful Himalayan climbers have been between twenty-five and forty years of age. It seems likely that the great powers of endurance necessary for this type of work are built up gradually over many years.

The technique of acclimatizing as rapidly as possible requires further study. The expeditions to Everest by the Northern route had imposed on them a six weeks' period at 13,000 feet to 17,000 feet during their approach march through Tibet. Even so, members of the first two expeditions suffered from altitude sickness on the mountain. The 1933 expedition, profiting by their experience, spent several days at each camp above Base Camp to allow time for acclimatization to develop. As a result of the extra fourteen days on the mountain, they reached the higher camps in better condition than the previous parties had done. The 1933 expedition emphasized the importance of limiting the time spent above 23,000 feet to a minimum on account of high-altitude deterioration.

The Southern approach to the Himalayas through Nepal allows parties to reach high altitude after a three weeks' approach march at altitudes around 6,000 feet with passes at 10,000 feet to 12,000 feet. It has been usual for post-war expeditions to spend but a week in going from 12,000 feet to 19,000 feet. Symptoms of mountain sickness (headaches, vomiting, disturbance of respiration) have been common between 15,000 feet and 17,000 feet but have passed off in a few days. Physical performance, however, has been poor by comparison with performance later in the expedition. Men who have gone down to lower altitude to rest, whether on account of sickness or to fetch stores, have noticed a marked improvement in their general condition on going high again, and have clearly benefited by the rest at lower altitude. After a rest at 16,000 to 17,000 feet some climbers suffer from lassitude and shortness of breath on the climb back to 20,000 feet but the effect is transient.

Certain experienced Himalayan climbers hold the view that at the beginning of an expedition not more than a few days should be spent between 12,000 feet and 14,000 feet, a longer period being of little assistance in securing acclimatization above 18,000 feet. In support of this view is the fact that Sherpas residing at Namche (about 12,000 feet) often complain of headaches and shortness of breath in crossing the Nangpa La at 19,000 feet. Physiological observations made on Cho Oyu, however, suggest that if men go straight to 18,000 feet and above, and stay there, they deteriorate physically during the first two weeks.

In view of the great variation between individuals in their reaction to altitude it is impossible to lay down hard-and-fast rules about the best procedure in order to acclimatize most rapidly. A wise principle seems to be that camps in the early stages of an expedition should be placed at altitudes such that all members of the party are able to eat and sleep well. During the day they may climb without harm as high as they can. After the acclimatization period, when the party has established camps at higher altitude in preparation for their final assault, experience has shown that men who become exhausted from over-exertion, or who become ill from some other cause, should be sent down to rest at lower altitude. Unless this is done, they may not recover quickly enough to be effective when they are needed later on.

This plan of going down to lower altitude for rests was adopted with great success on the present expedition. The height reached by parties on their first period of acclimatization was about 20,000 feet, with two or more nights spent between 17,000 feet and 18,000 feet. After five days' absence they returned to Thyangboche (under 13,000 feet) for three days' rest before going up again to 20,000 feet. There was a further period of rest at Thyangboche before going to Base Camp (nearly 18,000 feet). Altogether, three weeks were allotted to preliminary acclimatization before serious work on the Icefall began. After the "Build-up" period of transporting stores to the head of the Cwm, the party went down in groups for three days' rest at Lobuje (16,500 feet). Although all members of the expedition lost weight they remained fit, so that there was always sufficient man-power to maintain the pace of preparations for the Assault. The observation that repeated visits to the Himalayas increased tolerance of high altitude was again confirmed. Apart from Tenzing, the five climbers who went highest had all been on Cho Oyu the previous year. This does not prove that others in the party could not have gone as high as some of these if they had had the opportunity, but it is possibly significant that the only men who did not go well at high altitude were the two "first timers". They recovered, however, with rest at a lower altitude, and played an important rôle later on.

Physiological Changes at High Altitude The adaptation of the body to a low atmospheric pressure has interested physiologists for over eighty years.

The first discovered and best known adaptive change is an increase in the number and concentration of the red cells of the blood which contain the oxygen-carrying pigment, haemoglobin. This was discovered by Viault in

1871. There is reason to suppose that this effect is not as important as was once thought, among other reasons because some men with relatively low haemoglobin levels have good physical performance at high altitude.

Of much greater importance is the increase in volume of air breathed per minute (ventilation rate). In this way the decreased density of the air is compensated by passing more air through the lungs per minute. The increased ventilation is regulated by stimulation of receptor organs situated along the aorta and carotid arteries which are sensitive to a fall in the oxygen tension of the arterial blood. The respiratory centre in the brain, which controls the movements of breathing, responds normally under sea-level conditions not to the oxygen tension of the blood, which is constant except during extreme physical exertion, but to the direct effect of carbon-dioxide tension of the arterial blood. At high altitude the increased ventilation causes a fall in the carbon-dioxide pressure in the lungs which is reflected in a corresponding fall in the tension of carbon-dioxide in the arterial blood. Thus, at high altitude, the respiratory centre in the brain lacks its normal stimulus and is responding to stimuli reaching it from peripheral receptor organs sensitive to oxygen tension. This change in the regulation of breathing is not easily accomplished, and at first there is "hunting", like that occurring in any mechanical self-regulating device which is not functioning with sufficient sensitivity. This shows itself in the periodic, or so-called Cheyne-Stokes, breathing which is commonly noticed at high altitude and which may be very unpleasant. It is not yet known for certain whether the sensitivity of the respiratory centre eventually becomes adjusted to the low arterial carbon-dioxide tension at high altitude, or whether the peripheral stimulus of oxygen lack continues to be the chief stimulus to respiration at high altitude. In the first few days after going to high altitude before ventilation and other compensatory changes in the body have become established, the tissues suffer from oxygen lack; and the effect of this on the brain is responsible for the symptoms of mountain sickness, which are weakness, nausea, vomiting, loss of appetite, sleeplessness, headache. Other adaptive changes taking place in the body are the following:

(a) Increase in the output of the heart at rest; this has been shown to pass off after a few days at an altitude of 14,000 feet, but experiments on animals suggest that it persists above 20,000 feet.

(b) The disturbance of the acid-alkali balance of the blood due to lowering of CO^2 tension is compensated by excretion of alkaline urine.

(c) Increase in the myohaemoglobin content of the muscles. Myohaemoglobin is an oxygen-carrying pigment similar to haemoglobin. This effect has been demonstrated in animals but not as yet in man.

All these changes tend to maintain as closely as possible to sea-level value the oxygen tension in the tissues upon which the chemical processes of metabolism depend. Probably other, as yet unknown, changes occur in the tissues themselves, which permit them to function normally at reduced oxygen tension. The combined action of all these changes results in a remarkable degree of compensation, so that up to 20,000 feet or 21,000 feet a man can feel perfectly fit and well and engage in moderately hard physical work. Compensation is, however, incomplete: both the maximum rate of climbing, and the number of hours of climbing that can be done in a day, are decreased at high altitude, being about half their sea-level value at 21,000 feet even in acclimatized men. Above 21,000 feet there is loss of weight and muscular wasting, leading eventually to a decline in physical performance, increasing disinclination for exercise and loss of appetite. Animals kept in an atmosphere corresponding to an altitude of 20,000 feet show degenerative changes in the liver and other organs, and it is probable that similar changes occur in man. Thus although a measure of compensation occurs which renders a man going to high altitude more efficient and comfortable as he becomes acclimatized, at the same time there are degenerative changes which ultimately force him to go down.

COLD

Protection against cold is one of the chief problems at very high altitude. In addition to low air temperatures, heat loss from lungs in warming and humidifying the inspired air is greatly increased, owing to the considerable rise in the breathing rate both at rest and at work. It was anticipated that temperatures of minus 40 degrees C. might be encountered high up on Everest. This prediction was made in the light of balloon data from Indian Hill Stations in 1933, although no temperature records were available for altitudes greater than 24,000 feet on Everest. It seems likely, however, that the weather just before the monsoon is exceptionally warm: otherwise former parties, with the equipment then available, would have suffered more severely than they did from cold.

A survey of equipment problems was made in 1952 on the Cho Oyu expedition, and it was clear that many improvements, based on scientific developments in cold-weather protective clothing used by the Allied Services in the war and afterwards, could be made use of. The protective clothing was designed to be adequate for temperatures down to minus 40 degrees C. and weighed, including boots and gloves, 17 lb. compared with 23 lb. for the equivalent Arctic equipment, though giving comparable protection. Sleeping-bags and air mattresses were designed to secure the maximum physical comfort at night, the need for which was stressed by Norton as long ago as 1924—toughness, if it implies neglecting to take measures to reduce fatigue and strain, has no place in Himalayan planning.

APPENDIX VII

FLUID REQUIREMENTS

Knowledge of the fluid intake of climbers at high altitude is important. Unless the fluid requirement of the body is met, a considerable water deficiency may build up over the course of a few days, causing lassitude and weakness over and above that due to the effect of altitude. It seems likely that this happened to the Swiss party on the South Col of Everest in May 1952, when over a period of three days their water intake was less than a pint per man per day.

Since all water on high mountains has to be obtained by melting snow or ice, an adequate water supply depends on the provision of reliable stores and sufficient fuel. Estimates of the daily fluid intake of men on Cho Oyu in 1952, and on the present expedition based on the number of mugfuls of soup, lemonade or tea drunk per day yield a figure of 5 to 7 pints per day, to which must be added about half a pint for the fluid content of cooked food.

At this level of fluid consumption, evidence was obtained that the output of urine was normal, which means that the fluid intake was adequate. Nor was there any evidence on the Assault that fluid intake was inadequate.

The large fluid intake of men at high altitude is explained by the high rate of water loss from the lungs due to the dryness of the air and the increase in the rate and depth of breathing. Loss of fluid in the form of sweat may also be considerable in men climbing on glaciers during the heat of the day. The heating effect of the sun's radiation in the Himalayas is intense: on Cho Oyu, for example, in May 1952 sun temperatures of 156 degrees F. were recorded at 19,000 feet.

The question has been asked whether salt deficiency may play a part in high-altitude deterioration. It is well known to dwellers in hot climates that profuse and long-continued sweating may lead to a state of weakness and exhaustion due to salt deficiency, if the salt lost in sweating is not balanced by a sufficient intake of salt in the food. The large fluid intake of climbers at great altitude has suggested the possibility that sweating may be sufficiently profuse to cause a drain on the salt reserve of the body. It seems unlikely, however, that such a condition can arise in climbers since their large fluid requirement is explained by loss of moisture from the lungs which contains no salt, rather than by sweating. Direct measurements made on the present expedition suggest that between 2½ and 3½ pints of fluid per day are lost in this way. This accounts for half the daily fluid intake and is three or four times the corresponding value at sea-level in a temperate climate.

OXYGEN

Whereas it is certainly true that knowledge of man's power of acclimatization to extreme altitude has been largely contributed by climbers on Everest, the futile controversy over the ethics of using oxygen, and the failure to

257

accept the findings of pioneers in its application, handicapped for thirty years the introduction of a method which promises to revolutionize high-altitude mountaineering. Apart from the question of whether mountains over 27,000 feet can be successfully climbed without its use, oxygen undoubtedly reduces the mountaineering hazards and greatly increases subjective appreciation of the surroundings, which, after all, is one of the chief reasons for climbing.

Oxygen apparatus was taken on all the past Everest expeditions except the 1921 reconnaissance. Until the Swiss expedition last year, the only serious attempts to use it were those of Finch in 1922 and Lloyd in 1938. Finch used an open-circuit apparatus weighing 25 lb. and supplying 2.25 litres of oxygen per minute. He wore the apparatus constantly while climbing between 21,000 feet and 27,000 feet and slept with it on the night before his final climb to 27,300 feet. He claimed subjective benefit from its use, and stated that his climbing power was improved compared with that of the porters. Odell's experience of oxygen in 1924 did much to increase the then existing prejudice of mountaineers against the use of oxygen. He failed to derive significant benefit from his apparatus in climbing between 21,000 feet and 23,000 feet, and later on between 25,000 feet and 27,000 feet. The rate of oxygen flow used was, however, only 1 litre per minute except during the last minute or two at 27,000 feet, when it was increased to 2 litres per minute. In 1938 both Lloyd and Warren used open-circuit oxygen. The apparatus weighed 25 lb. and gave a flow of 2.25 litres of oxygen per minute. Lloyd used it up to 27,000 feet and claimed subjective benefit and increased climbing power on easy ground, although there was less improvement on difficult stretches. Shipton, however, was not convinced that Lloyd's performance was significantly different from that of his companion Tilman. A closed-circuit apparatus was also tried, but was abandoned on account of the sensation of suffocation which developed after a short period of use. The conclusions drawn from experience in the use of oxygen on Everest up to 1952 were that although subjective benefit might be obtained, the weight of the oxygen apparatus counterbalanced whatever favourable effect the oxygen might have on performance.

Experiments carried out at 20,000 feet on Menlung La during the 1952 expedition to Cho Oyu provided certain basic information on which the oxygen equipment for this year's expedition was planned. The principal findings were as follows:

1. The more oxygen one breathed the greater the subjective benefit.
2. The weight of the apparatus to a large extent offset the increased physical performance.
3. A flow rate of 4 litres per minute was the minimum required to achieve satisfactory effects.
4. There was great reduction in pulmonary ventilation.

5. There was great relief in the feeling of heaviness and fatigue in the legs during exercise. In view of this it seemed likely that endurance would be improved although this was not tested at the time.

Bourdillon, who superintended the oxygen sets and acted as one of the subjects in these experiments, returned home convinced that closed-circuit oxygen which would permit the climber to breathe an atmosphere of pure oxygen was the answer to the oxygen problem.

The Medical Research Council High-Altitude Committee, under the chairmanship of Sir Bryan Matthews, which was appointed to advise on all matters connected with oxygen equipment decided, however, that first priority should be given to open-circuit apparatus on the grounds that this would satisfy the physiological requirement, while being simple, easy to operate and unlikely to break down. It was felt that although closed-circuit apparatus was desirable, not only because it gave oxygen at sea-level pressure but also because it would reduce the loss of heat and moisture from the lungs, it might not be possible to produce a sufficiently reliable set in the time available. Nevertheless, it was recommended that the development of closed-circuit apparatus should be undertaken for trial purposes. The scale and description of the equipment taken on Everest in 1953 is described in Appendix V as well as details of its use.

The physiological effects of supplementary oxygen fully confirmed the predictions based on the 1952 work. Performance was somewhat better than had been anticipated. There was some improvement in the rate of climbing at high altitude; but the principal effect was increase in the amount of work that could be done in a day without serious fatigue. Oxygen during sleep permitted recovery from fatigue and greatly reduced high-altitude deterioration. The climbers also reported great improvement in their subjective state, so that they were able to appreciate their surroundings, and climbing once more became a pleasure. Hillary, on the final stretch above the South summit, was able to do mental arithmetic and calculate accurately the flow rate of oxygen necessary to ensure that the supply did not run out. He removed his oxygen mask on the summit of Everest and spent ten minutes taking photographs without supplementary oxygen, thus showing that man does not immediately become unconscious when deprived of his oxygen supply at 29,000 feet. The possibility of this happening had always been a source of anxiety, although there was evidence from Finch and Lloyd's experience that the risk was not too great to accept. Another effect of oxygen was that the sense of well-being due to oxygen persisted for an hour or more after the oxygen was discontinued.

MEDICINE

The pre-war Everest expeditions paid careful attention to hygiene during the march across Tibet, but in spite of this they suffered a good deal from respiratory and bowel infections, both during the march and on the mountain. The Tibetan plateau is a notoriously windy and dust-ridden place and this was thought to account for the high incidence of these conditions. On the mountain colds and sore throats were troublesome. They were attributed to the rapid breathing of cold dry air and the resulting breakdown of the defences of the upper respiratory tract. Somervell in 1924 described how a portion of the epithelial lining of his throat sloughed off and nearly choked him on the upper slopes of the mountain.

Since the war expeditions have had the advantages of antibiotics, and have tended to neglect the rules of hygiene. On the present expedition, because of the high incidence of sickness on Cho Oyu the previous year, a careful plan of hygiene was adopted and followed where possible. The chief measures were as follows:

1. No camping in or near villages, or sleeping in local houses.
2. Protection of food and utensils from flies.
3. Boiling of all drinking water, and, failing this, the use of water-sterilizing tablets.
4. Supervision of Sherpa cooks to ensure cleanliness in the preparation of food.
5. The use of bellows for the inflation of air mattresses.

Paludrine was issued to Sahibs, Sherpas and coolies. The risk of malaria is, however, small before the monsoon. Although mosquitoes were few, D.M.P. anti-mosquito cream was valuable against other insects. Anti-insect powder proved an essential item of equipment since lice, fleas and bed-bugs were encountered.

The following were outstanding features of the expedition from the medical point of view. The inevitable minor bowel and respiratory complaints associated with the coming together in one party of Sherpas and Europeans from many different places were over before the middle of May. Diarrhoea and sore throats were controlled by antibiotics. Only two out of eleven climbers were unwell during the preparation of the route on the Lhotse Face and the Assault period. Above Advance Base (Camp IV, 21,200 feet) most people had irritative coughs which disappeared very quickly on going down. Severe sore throats were not experienced, as in the case of former expeditions; this was due, possibly, to the use of oxygen. The party was remarkably fit at all stages of the expedition, especially after the long period in the Western Cwm and above. The profound exhaustion and deterioration found in previous parties was not seen—those who had been very high were tired but recovered quickly. Members of the Alpine Club meeting the party on its return to England were impressed by their healthy appearance in comparison with that of previous Everest parties.

PHYSIOLOGICAL STUDIES

A programme of physiological work was carried out on the present expedition in continuation of studies carried out on Cho Oyu in 1952. This work was made possible by the generosity of the Royal Society and the Medical Research Council. The effects of high altitude on respiration, on the haemoglobin content of the blood and on nutrition were studied, as well as the effect of supplementary oxygen on men asleep and while climbing. The results of this work, as well as a detailed account of the medical aspects of the expedition, will be published in scientific journals.

APPENDIX VIII

EVEREST, 1953

ASSAULT LOAD TABLES

(as prepared at Lake Camp on 16th April and revised after decision on the Plan, 8th May)

Item	Lhotse Face (Camp VII)				South Col (Camp VIII)				Ridge (Camp IX)				Notes
	Two Open-Circuits		Closed-Circuit/Open-Circuit		Two Open-Circuits		Closed-Circuit/Open-Circuit		Two Open-Circuits		Closed-Circuit/Open-Circuit		
	No.	Weight lb.	No.	Weight lb.	No.	Weight lb.	No.	Weight lb.	No.	Weight lb.	No.	Weight lb.	
COOKERS (a)	2	15	2	15	2	15	2	15	1	5	1 (b)	5	(a) & (b)
FUEL	4 qt.	10	4 qt.	10	4 qt.	10	4 qt.	10	2 qt.	5	1 qt.	3	—
RATIONS (in lb. per 24 hrs.) for carrying parties	14 × 24	28	15 × 24	30	8 × 48	32	7 × 24	14	—		—		—
RATIONS for First Assault (c)	10 × 24	20	2 × 24	4	4 × 48	16	2 × 48	8	2 × 24	4	—		(c)
RATIONS for Second Assault (c)	4 × 24	8	8 × 24	16	2 × 48	8	2 × 48	8	2 × 24	4	2 × 24	4	(c)
ASSAULT OXYGEN CYLINDERS (d)	7	77	2	22	16	176	16	176	8	88	4	44	(d)
SLEEPING OXYGEN CYLINDERS	—	—	4	80	2	40	3	60	2	40	1	20	—

Closed-Circuit Oxygen Canisters	—	—	2	18	—	—	4	36	—	—	—	—	—
Tents Meade	3 (*e*)	45	2	30	2	30	1	15	1	15	1	15	(*e*)
Tents Pyramid	—	—	—	—	1	25	1	25	—	—	—	—	—
Tents Light	—	—	—	—	—	—	1	6	—	—	—	—	—
Sleeping-bags	—	—	—	—	—	—	—	—	2 (*f*) (half)	10	2 (half)	10	(*f*)
Air Mattresses	—	—	—	—	—	—	—	—	2 (*f*)	6	2	6	(*f*)
Wireless Sets	1	14	1	14	1	14	1	14	—	—	—	—	—
Miscellaneous	—	15	—	15	—	15	—	15	—	10	—	5	—
TOTAL	—	232	—	254	—	381	—	402	—	187	—	112	Grand Total
No. of Sherpas (*g*)	@ 30 lb. = 7		@ 30 lb. = 8		@ 30 lb. = 12		@ 30 lb. = 13		@ 25 lb. = 7		@ 25 lb. = 4		(*g*)

Notes:

(*a*) Large cookers used except at Camp IX, weight 7½ lb.
Small cookers used at Camp IX, weight 5 lb.
(*b*) One cooker left at Camp VI during Reconnaissance 3rd–5th May.
(*c*) Rations for First and Second Assaults include percentage for bad weather.
(*d*) Includes Assault Oxygen for leaders of South Col parties and for whole of Camp IX carry.
(*e*) One Meade tent already carried to Camp VI during Reconnaissance 3rd–5th May.
(*f*) Sleeping-bags and air mattresses for all going as far as South Col (Camp VIII) inclusive have *not* been taken into account.

Grand Total

For Two Open-Circuits 800 lb.
For Closed-Circuit/Open-Circuit 768 lb.
(*g*) This assumes that Sahibs will carry only own kit, plus sleeping-bags and air mattresses.

APPENDIX IX

ACKNOWLEDGMENTS OF ASSISTANCE IN LAUNCHING THE EXPEDITION

IN addition to those mentioned in the text of this book, we desire to express our particular gratitude to the following, who gave us exceptional assistance in various ways:

A. INDIVIDUALS

Officials of H.M. Customs and Excise
Mr Simpson of the Board of Trade
Mr Anderson of the Ministry of Supply
Wing Commander Roxburgh, Institute of Aviation Medicine
Mr Kenchington, Royal Aircraft Establishment, Farnborough
Dr Renbourne, Royal Aircraft Establishment, Farnborough
Mr London, Royal Aircraft Establishment, Farnborough
Sir Harold Himsworth, Secretary of the Medical Research Council
Dr Edholm of the Medical Research Council
Mr Winfield of the Physiological Department, Cambridge
Brigadier Smijth-Windham of Supreme Headquarters Allied Powers in Europe
Lt. Col. Finch of the War Office
Lt. Col. Kingsmill of the War Office
Major d'Avigdor of the War Office
Group Captain Wiseman-Clarke of the Air Ministry
Squadron Leader Gall of the Air Ministry
Squadron Officer Ravenhill of the Air Ministry
Dr R. B. Bourdillon of the Electro-Medical Research Unit, Stoke Mandeville
Mr Grosvenor of the Admiralty Experimental Diving Unit, H.M.S. *Vernon*, Portsmouth
The Council and Staff of the Royal Geographical Society
Mr Blakeney, Assistant Secretary, The Alpine Club
Dr Raymond Greene, Member of the 1933 Everest Expedition
Brigadier Moppett of Pye Telecommunications Ltd.
Mr Lawrie, Alpine Equipment Specialist
Commander Harris of the Medical Research Council
Mr Barrett of Siebe Gorman & Co. Ltd.
Mr Green, Chief Designer, Reynolds Tube Co., Birmingham
Mr Taunton of Wilts United Dairies Ltd.
Captain Forrest and Ship's Company, S.S. *Stratheden*

Mr Mann, David Harcourt Ltd., Birmingham
Mr Timings, David Harcourt Ltd., Birmingham
Mr Widgery of Normalair
Nurse Wainwright of the Quarry Hill Nursing Home, Shrewsbury

The Commander-in-Chief and Officers, Indian Army
The Commander-in-Chief and Officers, Indian Air Force
Major General Williams, Chief Engineer Indian Army, and All Ranks of the
    Indian Engineers working on the new road to the Valley of Nepal
The Commander and Officers of the Indian Military Mission to Nepal
The Commander-in-Chief and Officers, Nepalese Army
Major General Commanding and Officers, Brigade of Gurkhas
The Staff of Mackinnon and Mackenzie's, Bombay
Dr Mull of the Observatory, Alipore
The Dun School, Dehra Dun
Mr Hotz, Hotel Cecil, Delhi
Mr Leyden, Himalayan Club, Bombay
The Postmaster and Staff, Kathmandu Indian Sub-Post Office

B. FIRMS AND OTHER BODIES

(a) General Equipment

Agfa Ltd.	Photographic material
Bill, W., Ltd.	Shetland pullovers
Black, Thomas, & Sons Ltd.	Kitchen and feeding equipment
Braemar Knitwear Ltd.	Cashmere pullovers and woollen underwear
British Boot, Shoe & Allied Trades Research Association	High Altitude boots
British Nylon Spinners	Windproof cloth
British Ropes Ltd.	Climbing rope
Carreras Ltd.	Cigarettes
Condrup Ltd.	Primus stoves, shields for pressure cookers
Courtaulds Ltd.	Rayon string vests
Cow, P.B., & Co. Ltd.	Air mattresses, rubberized cloth for breathing-bags
D.E.O.M., Société, France	Butane gas cookers
Dunlop Rubber Co. Ltd.	Micro-cellular boot soles, tent floors
Edgington, Benjamin, Ltd.	Tents, tarpaulins, sleeping-bags, marker flags
Fair Deal Supplies	Nylon shirts
Flint, Howard, Ltd.	Windproof clothing, mitts

Frankenstein & Sons Ltd.	Double-layer air mattresses
Herts Pharmaceuticals	Adhesive tape
Howard's Bedding, Canada	Sleeping-bags
I.C.I. (Plastics Division)	Polythene bags
Ilford Ltd.	Photographic materials
Indian Aluminium Co., India	Hurricane lamps
Indian Army	2-inch mortar bombs
Imperial Tobacco (Ogden Branch)	Tobacco
Jaeger Ltd.	Woollen mitts
Kenyon, Wm., & Sons Ltd.	Climbing rope
Kodak Ltd.	Photographic material
Lawrie, Robert, Ltd.	Mountaineering equipment
Lillywhites Ltd.	Goggles
Lloyd, Richard, Ltd.	Tobacco
Lyte Ladders Ltd.	Sectional ladder
Meteorological Office	Altimeters, anemometer
Mitchell, Stephen, & Son	Tobacco
Morland Ltd.	Camp boots
Paul Laboratories, Canada	Snow cream
Pautry et Cie., France	Aluminium containers, utensils and snow shovels
Perret, E. W., Ltd.	Flags
Platers & Stampers Ltd.	Pressure cookers
Player, John, & Sons	Tobacco and cigarettes
Pye Telecommunications Ltd.	Radio equipment
Rolex Watch Co. Ltd.	Watches
Royal Geographical Society	Aneroids, compasses, photo theodolite
Simond, France	Ice-axes, crampons, pitons and snow cream
Smiths Clocks Ltd.	Alarm clocks, watches
Smith, W. H., & Son	Stationery
Southworth, John, & Sons Ltd.	Windproof cloth
Spatz, Switzerland	Down mitts
Time-Life Magazine, U.S.A.	Contax cameras, Biogon lenses
Unilever Ltd.	Soap, lipsalve
Vidor Ltd.	Batteries, torches
War Office	12-man tent, 2-inch mortar
West & Partners	Photostat copies of maps
Wills, W. D. & H. O.	Cigarettes
Wico-Zelt, Switzerland	2-man tent
Yorkshire Ramblers Club	Rope ladder

APPENDIX IX

(b) Rations and Ration Packing

Bird, Alfred, Ltd.	Grape-nuts and coffee
Bonded Fibre Fabrics Ltd.	Fabric for ration boxes
Bovril Ltd.	Pemmican
Compagnie Générale du Lait, France	Condensed milk tubes
Costa, G., & Co.	Soups
Crawfords Biscuits	Biscuits
Duche & Knight Ltd.	Waterproof adhesive for packaging
Glaxo Laboratories	Milk powder
Heinz, J. H., & Co. Ltd.	Self-heating soups
Huntley & Palmer Ltd.	Canned rich cake
Indian Army	Rum
Knorr-Swiss, Switzerland	Soups
Mapletons Nut Food	Nut bars, fruit bars
Nestlés Ltd.	Nescafé and soups
Oxo Ltd.	Oxo cubes
Pollitt, John, & Co.	Tea
Quaker Oats Ltd.	Porridge oats
Ready Mixes Co.	Scone-mix
Robinson, E. S. & A., Ltd.	Material for vacuum packing
Romney, George, Ltd.	Kendal mint cake
Rowntree Ltd.	Chocolate
Simpkin, A. L., & Co. Ltd.	Glucose tablets
Société d'Alimentation de Provence, France	Saucissons
Tate & Lyle Ltd.	Sugar
Thompson & Norris	Fibreboard cases
Three Cooks Ltd.	Soups
Typhoo Tea	Tea
Unilever Ltd.	Soups
Wander, A., Ltd.	Ovosport blocks
Wilts United Dairies Ltd.	Vacuum packing of Assault rations and beverage boxes

(c) Oxygen Equipment

Admiralty (H.M.S. *Vernon*)	Dural cylinders
Air Ministry Gas Factory, Cardington	Oxygen
Barnet Instruments Ltd.	Pressure gauges
B.O.A.C.	Oxygen equipment

267

British Oxygen Co. Ltd.	Oxygen
Chemical Defence Experimental Establishment, The	Help with oxygen apparatus
Dunlop Rubber Co. Ltd.	Breathing tubes and special respiratory apparatus
Electro-Medical Research Unit	Closed-Circuit apparatus
Gatehouse & Sons	Webbing for carrying frames
Harcourt, David, Ltd.	Special pressure gauges
Johnson & Johnson	Filter material for soda lime canisters
Ministry of Supply	Service equipment
Normalair Ltd.	Main contractors for Assault sets; manufacture of lightweight economizers, light-alloy carrying frames and adaptors for Swiss Dräger cylinders; modification of dual outlets; assembly and testing of complete equipment
Reynolds Tube Co.	Manufacture of Dural Cylinders for Assault sets; light-alloy tubing for carrying frames
Rocket Propulsion Department, Royal Aircraft Establishment	Development of oxygen equipment
Rolls Razors	Dry shavers
Siebe Gorman & Co., Ltd.	Main contractors for training sets, manufacture of utility carrying frames, supply of light-alloy regulators, manifold plugs; machining of Base Plugs for Assault cylinders; assembly and testing of complete equipment
Sutcliffe, Speakman & Co.	Soda lime
Veedip Ltd.	Masks

(d) *Medical Supplies*

Allen & Hanbury Ltd.	Cooper, McDougal & Roberton
Boots Ltd.	Department of Army Health and Hygiene
British Drug Houses	
Burroughs Wellcome & Co.	Duff, D. F., Esq., F.R.C.S. (loan of stretcher)
Christian, P., Switzerland	
Ciba Laboratories Ltd.	Duncan Flockhart & Co. Ltd.

Geigy Laboratories
I.C.I. (Pharmaceuticals) Ltd.

Lederle Laboratories

C. FINANCIAL ASSISTANCE

Donations from Individuals

Mrs Carlile
Mrs D. Chapman
Mr J. O. M. Clark
Mr G. Holtby-Walker
Dr J. W. A. Hunter
Mrs M. E. Leadbeater
Mr Charles Lehmann
Mr Lipscomb
Mr R. W. Lloyd
Sir E. R. Peacock
Staff, Savoy Hotel, Blackpool

Firms and Societies

Bird, Alfred, & Son Ltd.
Christie, Manson & Woods Ltd.
Dunlop Rubber Co. Ltd.
Imperial Chemical Industries Ltd.
Mowlem, John, & Co. Ltd.
Nestlé & Co. Ltd.
Oxo Ltd.
Reckitt & Colman Ltd.
Rowntree & Co. Ltd.
Royal Society of Medicine
Tomatin Distillers & Co. Ltd.
Unilever Ltd.
Western Heritable Investment Co.

Banks

Barclays Bank Ltd.
Coutts & Co.
District Bank Ltd.
Glyn Mills & Co.
Hambros Bank Ltd.
Lloyds Bank Ltd.
Martins Bank Ltd.
Mercantile Bank of India Ltd.
Midland Bank Ltd.
National Bank of India Ltd.
National Provincial Bank Ltd.
Westminster Bank Ltd.
Williams Deacon's Bank Ltd.

Insurance Companies

Alliance Assurance Co.
Atlas Assurance Co. Ltd.
Commercial Union Assurance Co.
Lambert Brothers (Insurance) Ltd.
Lloyd's
London Assurance Co.
London Lancashire Insurance Co. Ltd.
North British & Mercantile Insurance Co. Ltd.
Phoenix Assurance Co. Ltd.
Royal Exchange Assurance
Royal Insurance Co. Ltd.
Sun Insurance Co.

APPENDIX X

THE MOUNT EVEREST FOUNDATION

The 1953 British Expedition to Mount Everest of which this memorable book tells the story was not only a landmark in international mountaineering achievement – the first ascent of the highest mountain in the world. The expedition's success and its profits gave birth to a charity, the main purpose of which has been to support mountaineering endeavour and scientific advancement in mountain regions. This charity, the Mount Everest Foundation, is the daughter of that 1953 expedition, founded and run by elected representatives of the Alpine Club and the Royal Geographical Society.

During the last forty years the MEF has supported nearly one thousand expeditions with grants which total almost £500,000. The majority of the grants are awarded to small expeditions, with an emphasis on innovation – unclimbed peaks, new routes and mountain exploration in remote areas in the Great Ranges. The first ascents of Kangchenjunga, Nuptse, Annapurna South Face, the Ogre and Spantik were made by MEF-supported teams, as were alpine-style climbs on Jannu, Broad Peak, Menlungtse, Dhaulagiri, and Everest itself. Scientific expeditions to Mulu (Sarawak), the Karakoram (the RGS International Karakoram Project), and to the Kun Lun (the British Mount Kongur Expedition) have also been awarded substantial grants. The Foundation promotes the protection of the mountains, their peoples and culture, and requires teams to follow a strict environmental policy.

These projects, and many many more, have been helped by the initial generosity of the 1953 Everest expedition and subsequent donations which have kept the MEF alive, while the Foundation's Finance Committee has over the years sought to protect and enhance its capital. The value of the Foundation to British mountaineering has been immeasurable. We trust it will continue to provide financial help and expertise for expeditions into the 21st century.

CHARLES CLARKE
Chairman: MEF Committee of Management 1990–92

The MEF is a company limited by Guarantee (543894) and a registered charity (208206)
Registered Address: c/o Royal Geographical Society, 1 Kensington Gore, London SW7 2AR
Patron: H.R.H. The Duke of Edinburgh, K.G., K.T.

GLOSSARY

arête	a narrow ridge.
belay	to secure the climber to a projection with the rope; the projection itself.
Bergschrund	a large crevasse separating the upper slopes of a glacier from the steeper slopes of ice or rock above.
chang	a beer brewed from rice.
chimney	a narrow vertical gully in rock or ice.
col	depression in a mountain chain, a pass.
cornice	overhanging mass of snow or ice along a ridge, shaped like the curling crest of a wave and generally formed by the prevailing wind.
couloir	gully or furrow in a mountainside.
crampon	metal frame with spikes, fitting the sole of the boot, for use on hard snow or ice; to move wearing such spikes.
crevasse	a fissure in a glacier, often of great depth.
cwm	an enclosed valley on the flank of a hill.
icefall	a frozen cascade of ice, often on a gigantic scale, created when a glacier passes over a change of angle or direction in the slope of the ground beneath.
monsoon	a wind in South Asia which blows from the S.W. in summer, the wet monsoon, and from the N.E. in winter, the dry monsoon.
moraine	accumulation of stones and débris brought down by the glacier.
pitch	a stretch of difficult ice or rock between ledges.
piton	metal spike with a ring or hole in the head, which can be driven into rock or ice and which is used in conjunction with a snap-link (or Karabiner or Mousqueton) to secure the rope passing between two climbers.
rakshi	a spirit distilled in Nepal from rice.
rope	links members of a party for safety; a party may be referred to as "a rope".
sangar	low wall serving as a windbreak.
scree	slope of small loose stones.
sérac	tower or pinnacle of ice.
Sherpas	hillmen of Tibetan stock from Eastern Nepal.
Sherpanis	Sherpa women.
snap-link	large metal spring-loaded clip which can be fixed to the rope or piton.
snow-bridge	a layer of snow bridging a crevasse.

spur a rib of rock running down from a main ridge or arête.

step a vertical or steep rise on a glacier or mountain slope.

"Tiger" proficiency badge awarded by Himalayan Club to Sherpas on the Club's rolls.

traverse to cross a mountain slope horizontally or diagonally; such a crossing.

tsampa flour of roasted and ground barley: staple food of Sherpas.

yeti an unidentified creature believed to dwell in the Himalayan mountains, which has been nicknamed the "Abominable Snowman".

INDEX

INDEX